Fantastic Paper Holiday Decorations

Teddy Cameron Long

A Sterling/Tamos Book
Sterling Publishing Co., Inc. New York

A Sterling/Tamos Book

Sterling Publishing Company, Inc.
387 Park Avenue South, New York, NY 10016

TAMOS Books Inc.
300 Wales Avenue, Winnipeg, MB, Canada R2M 2S9

10 9 8 7 6 5 4 3 2 1

Distributed in Canada by Sterling Publishing Co., Inc.
c/o Canadian Manda Group, P.O. Box 920, Station U
Toronto, Ontario, Canada M8Z 5P9
Distributed in Great Britain and Europe by Cassell PLC
Villiers House, 41/47 Strand, London WC2N 5JE, England
Distributed in Australia by Capricorn Link (Australia) Pty Ltd.
P.O. Box 6651, Baulkham Hills, Business Centre, NSW 2153, Australia

Projects and Illustrations Teddy Cameron Long
Photos by Walter Kaiser, KKS Commercial Photography
Design A.O. Osen

Library of Congress Cataloging-in-Publication Data
Long, Teddy Cameron.
Fantastic paper holiday decorations/Teddy Cameron Long
p. cm.
"A Sterling/Tamos book."
Includes index.
ISBN 1-895569-18-4
1. Paper work. 2. Holiday decorations. I. Title.
TT870.L66 1994 93-39110
745.594'1--dc20 CIP

Canadian Cataloging-in-Publication Data
Long, Teddy Cameron
Fantastic paper holiday decorations
Includes index.
ISBN 1-895569-18-4
1. Paper work. 2. Holiday decorations. I. Title.
TT870.L66 1994 745.594'1 C93-098168-5

Printed in Hong Kong

ISBN 1-895569-18-4

Table of Contents

Introduction

Homemade and handcrafted holiday decorations can turn a celebration into something special. Add your creative touch to paper, glue, paint, and some sparkle and you'll produce spectacular results. Adorning a door, mantel, window, table top, tree, or used as gifts, your fabulous made-by-hand creation will surprise and delight. Make a spooky spider web for your door with a spider door knob or a dangling skeleton mobile to welcome little trick-or-treaters on Halloween or make a fishing for apples game. Tape cute ducks in the rain on your window for Easter or a colorful turkey for harvest time. You might want to make your own cards for Valentine's Day or papier-mâché heart boxes for lovely gift heart necklace, earrings, hair clips, or rings. Even Christmas can present lots of surprises that you make yourself. From angels, teddy bears, reindeer, elves, garlands, and catstair candy canes to hang on the tree, to paper bows for boxes, table centerpieces, candleholders, Christmas door wrap, an advent calendar, and much more. Whatever the occasion, you'll find great decorating ideas in this book.

Choose from over 100 holiday crafts. Each is easy to make, mostly from materials you have in your own home. Each project has complete instructions with detailed diagrams to guide you every step of the way. Color photographs of the projects provide suggestions for finishing. This book provides useful and delightful holiday decorating ideas that can be made at home by children and adults or undertaken as individual or group projects at schools, community centers, or day-care establishments. Choose projects that decorate people or rooms—from fantastic jewelry to spectacular window and door displays. You'll find a great selection and any of these lovely and unusual crafts will help put you in the holiday mood.

Valentine's Day

Window Decorations Bouquet of Roses

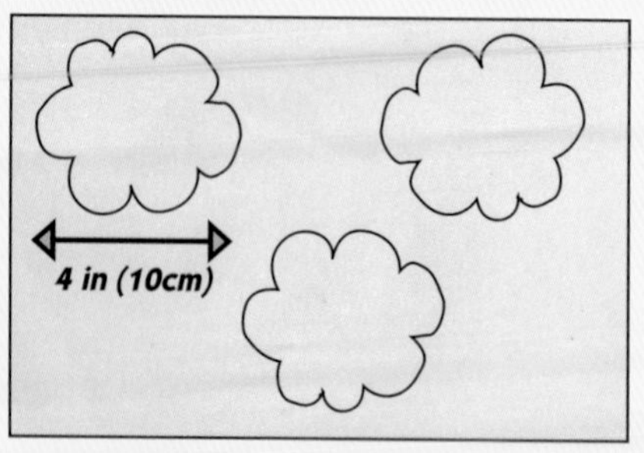

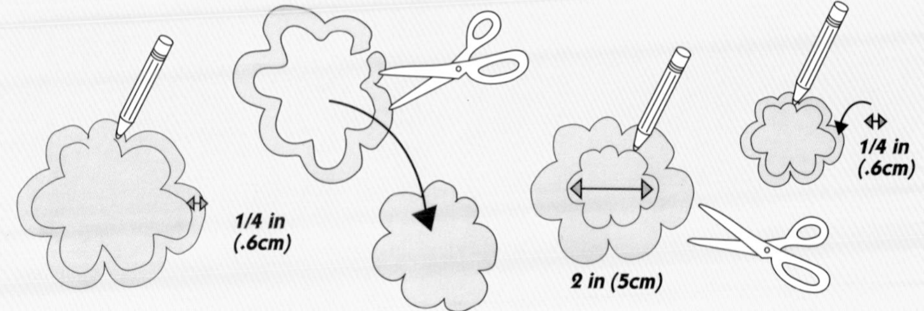

1 Draw 3 roses on red construction paper in the dimensions shown.
2 Cut out. Draw a line 1/4 in (.6cm) around inside edge of each rose, as shown.
3 Carefully cut off this border, as shown. Set aside.
4 On the cut-out center piece, draw another rose about 2 in (5cm) in diameter.
5 Cut out. Draw a 1/4 in (.6cm) border around this cut-out rose and carefully cut off the outline as before and set aside. In the small centers remaining draw rosebud shapes.

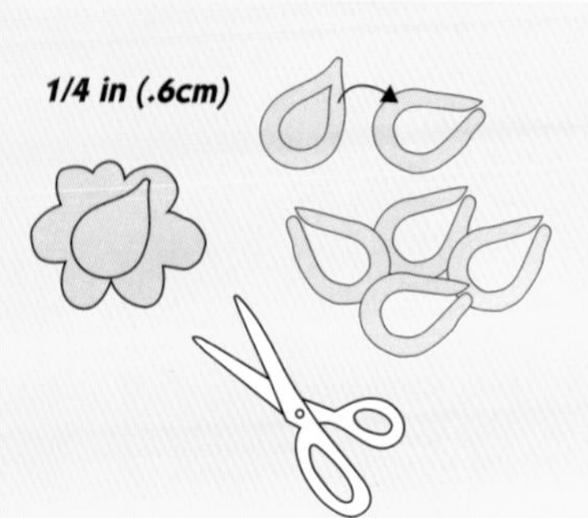

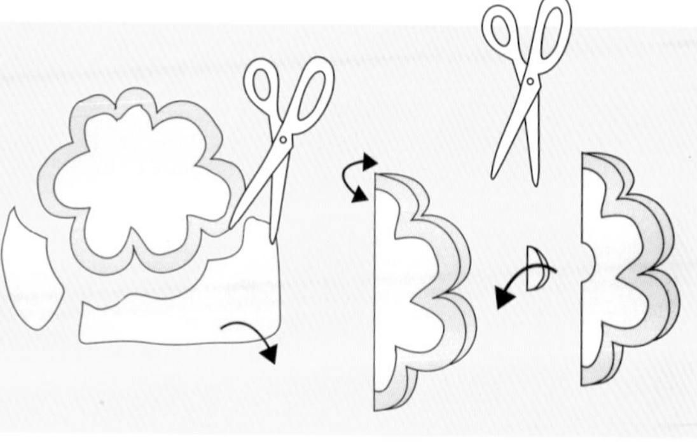

6 Use paper scraps to make additional rosebud shapes. Total needed is 6. Cut out. Draw a 1/4 in (.6cm) border inside rosebud shapes and cut out.
7 Spread glue stick gently over the construction paper outlines and place them, glue side down with cut ends joined, on red tissue paper.
8 Cut out around outline of shapes.
9 Fold each rose in half.
10 Cut out a half circle from the center of the fold, as shown. Unfold.

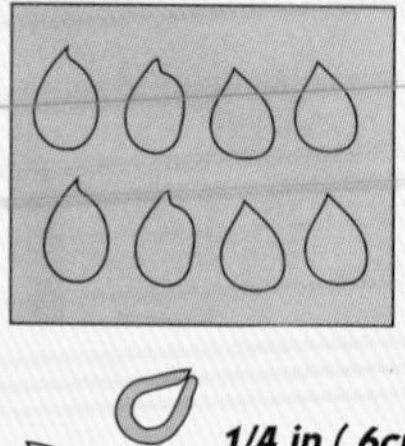

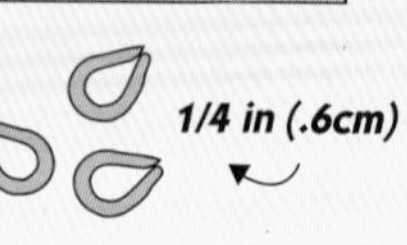

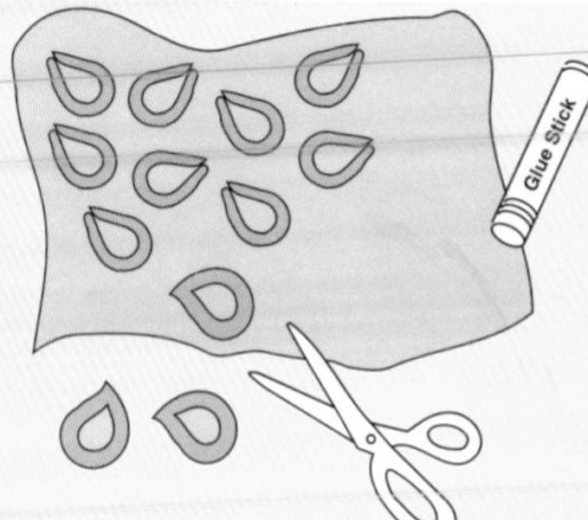

11 Cut out a yellow tissue circle slightly larger than the cut out circle in the rose. Glue the yellow tissue circle over the hole.
12 Draw and cut out many leaf shapes from green construction paper. Draw 1/4 in (.6cm) around inside and cut out.
13 Spread glue stick over the green outlines and place them on green tissue paper. Cut out.
14 Glue the roses, buds, and leaves together in a bunch. Glue a ribbon loop at the top and hang roses in front of a window.

Doily Heart

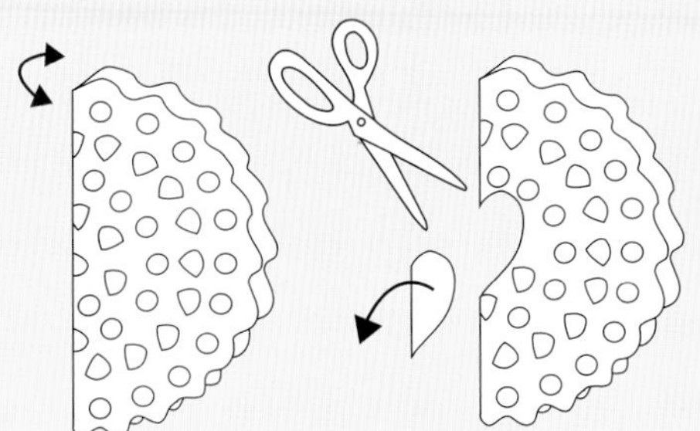

1 Fold a purchased paper doily in half.
2 Draw half a heart shape along the fold, as shown. Cut out.
3 Unfold the doily.

4 On purple construction paper draw and cut out a heart that is large enough to cover the hole. Draw and cut out the center of the purple heart, leaving the paper outline.

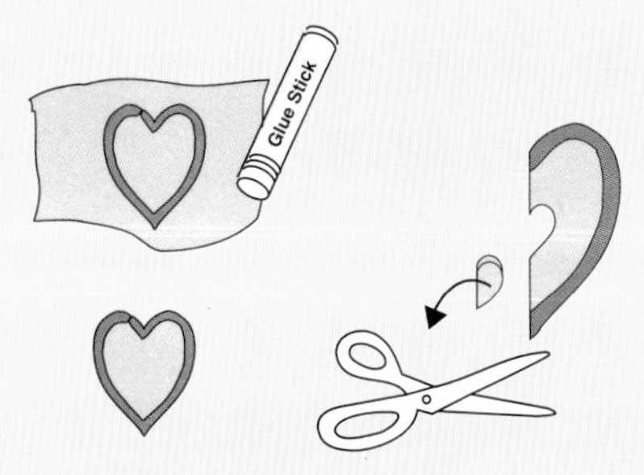

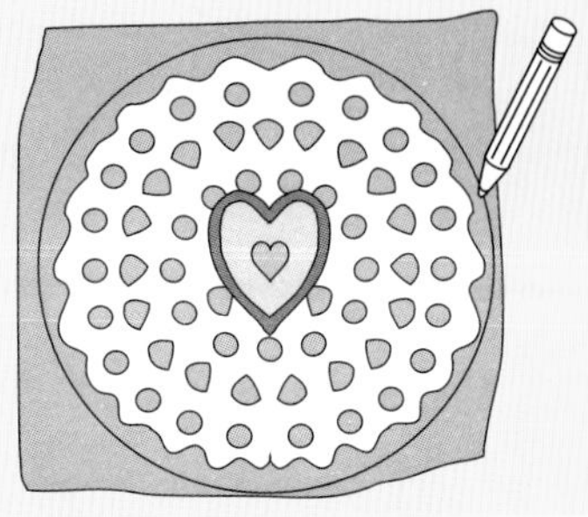

5 Glue the outline onto pink tissue paper. Cut out around heart shape.
6 Fold the heart in half. Cut out a small half heart shape, as shown.

7 Draw and cut out a red tissue heart, large enough to cover the hole in the pink tissue. Glue the red tissue heart over the hole.
8 Glue this purple, pink, and red heart over the hole in the center of the doily.
9 Place the doily on purple tissue. Trace around the doily, and cut out the tissue circle.

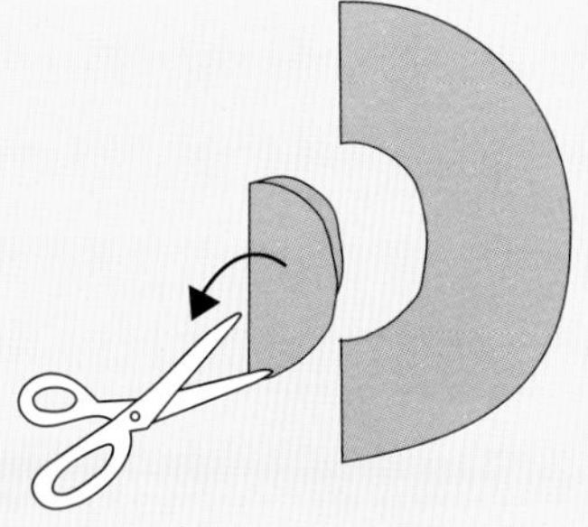

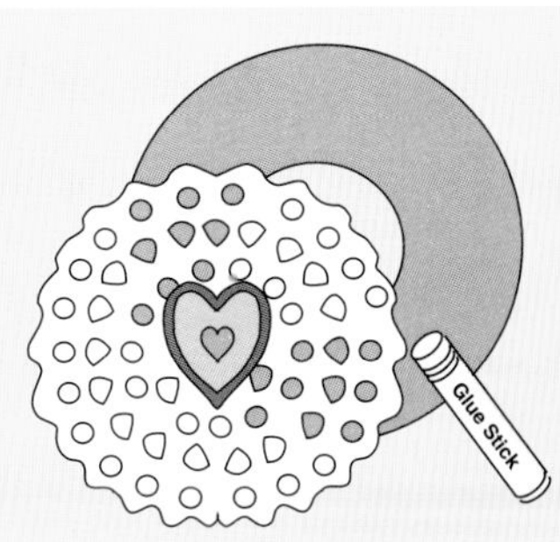

10 Fold the tissue circle in half and cut out a half circle from the center. Cut the circle large enough so the heart in the center of the doily will not have purple tissue behind it.
11 Glue the purple tissue circle to the back of the doily. Tape the doily in the window.

Papier-Mâché Heart Box & Paper Roses

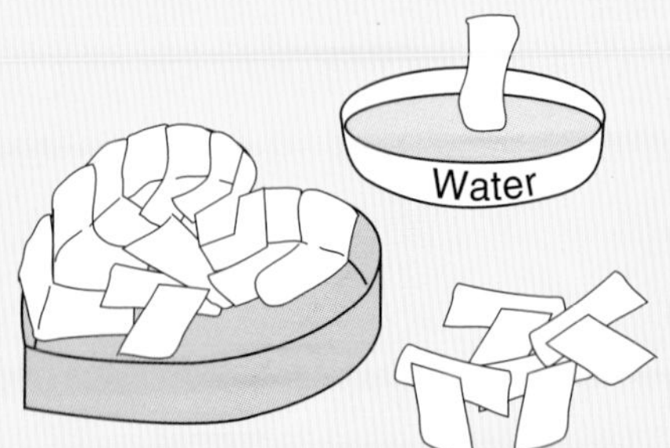

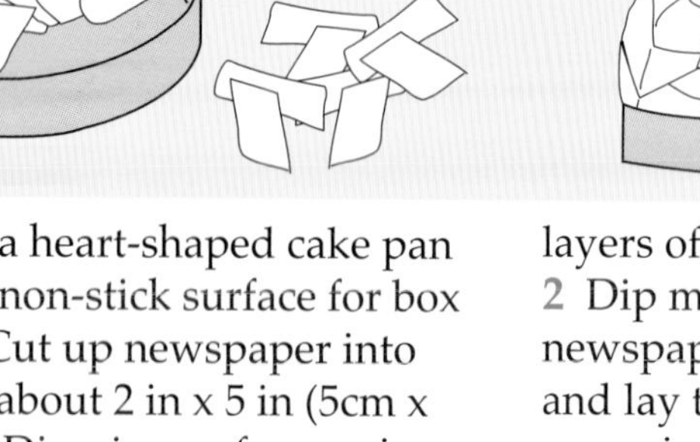

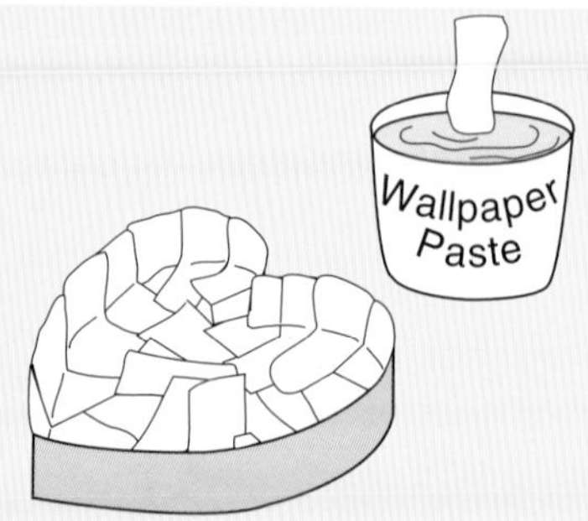

1 Use a heart-shaped cake pan with a non-stick surface for box form. Cut up newspaper into pieces about 2 in x 5 in (5cm x 12cm). Dip pieces of paper in water and lay them inside the cake pan. Cover the entire bottom and up the sides with 2 layers of wet newspaper pieces.

2 Dip more pieces of newspaper into wallpaper paste and lay them on top of the wet paper in the pan. Cover the bottom and sides of the pan with 4 to 5 layers of newspaper pieces with paste.

3 Turn the pan over. Cover the top and sides of the pan with 2 layers of newspaper pieces dipped in water, as before. Again, cover the wet newspaper with 4 to 5 layers of newspaper pieces dipped in wallpaper paste.

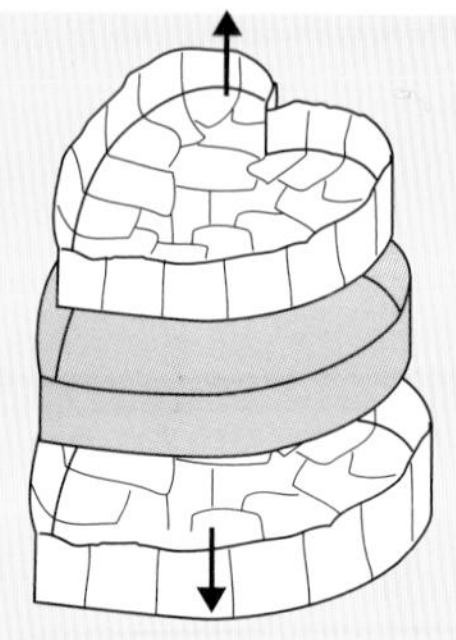

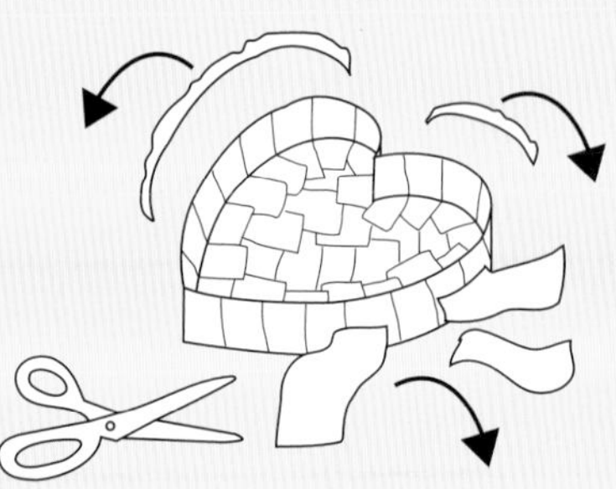

4 Set aside to dry. When hard, remove the 2 hearts from inside and outside the pan.

5 Trim the edges with scissors. Peel off loose paper from surface.

6 The heart made inside the pan is the bottom of the box. The heart made outside the pan is slightly larger and will be the lid.

7 Paint and shellac.

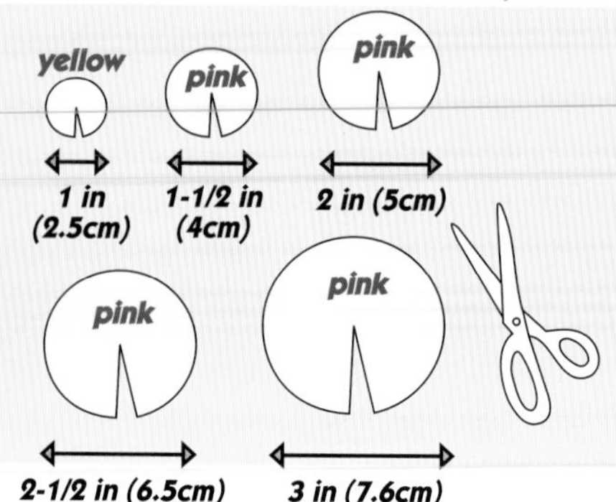

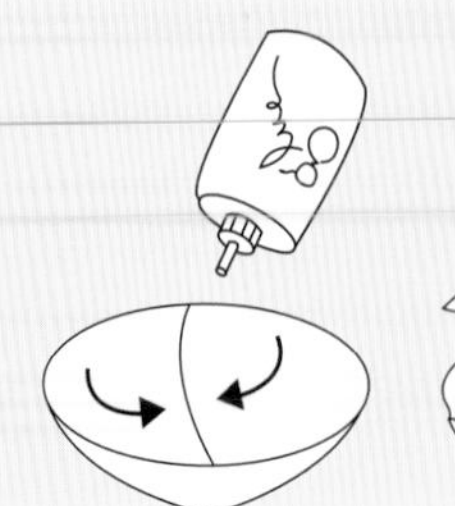

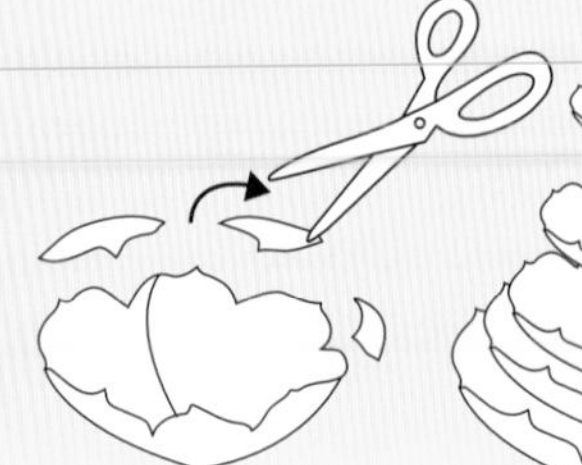

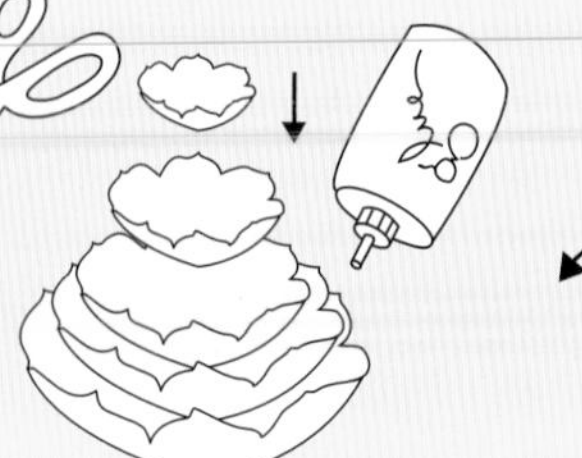

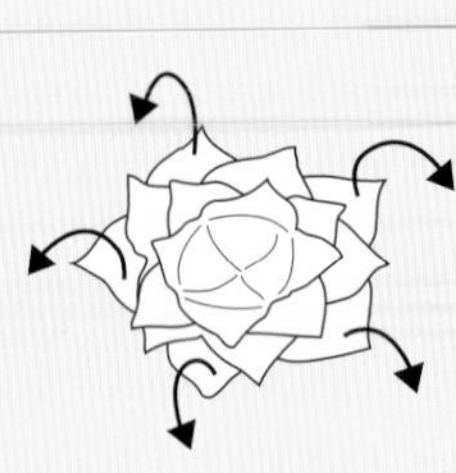

1 To make paper roses, cut one circle from yellow construction paper and 4 circles from pink construction paper in the dimensions shown. Make a cut from the edge to the center of each circle, as shown.

2 Overlap the cut edges and glue, forming a cup shape from each circle.

3 Cut the open edge of the cups into petal shapes, as shown.

4 Glue the petals one inside the other, from largest to smallest, yellow cup on top.

5 Bend each petal slightly back. Glue on top of heart box.

Paper Heart Box

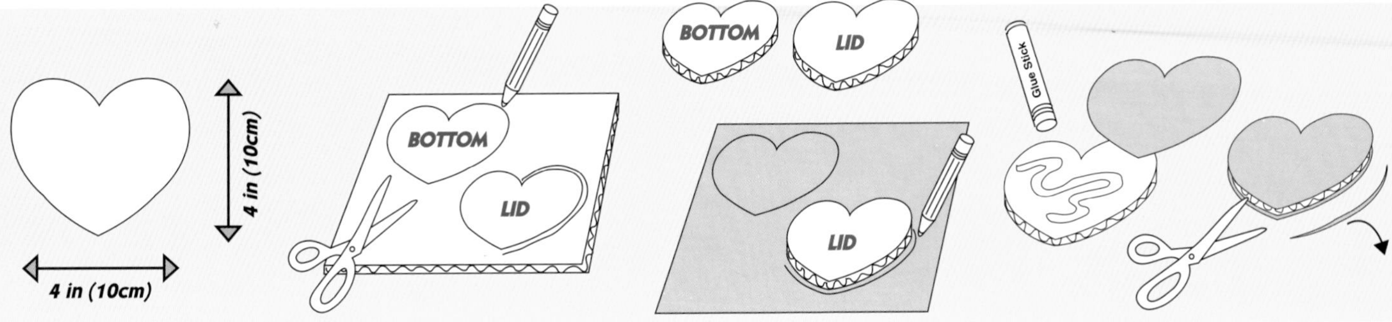

1 Make a paper heart pattern in the dimensions shown.
2 Trace around the pattern on smooth cardboard. Trace a second heart and draw it slightly larger for the lid. Cut out both cardboard hearts.
3 Lay the lid heart on red construction paper and trace around it. Turn it over and trace a second heart.
4 Cut out both paper hearts. Spread the cardboard heart with the glue stick and attach a paper heart to each side.
5 Trim the edges of paper with scissors if necessary.

Cover the remaining cardboard heart (the bottom) in the same manner.

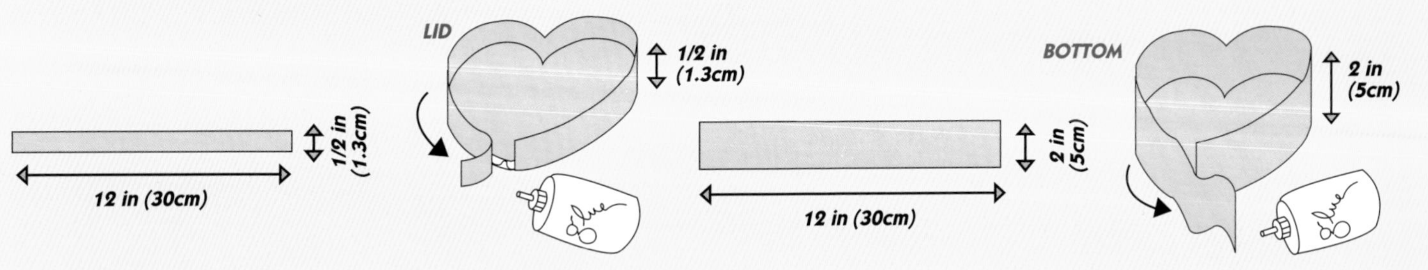

6 To make the sides of the lid, cut a strip of red construction paper, as shown. Spread glue around edge of lid and press on the strip, keeping bottom of strip at work surface.
7 Strip edge will extend up to form lid. Trim excess paper.
8 To make the sides of the bottom, cut another strip of red paper, as shown. Glue to the edge of the cardboard heart, as for lid. Strip edge will extend up to make depth of box.
9 Fit lid over bottom. Decorate with glue and glitter to hide seams.

Crazy Pendant

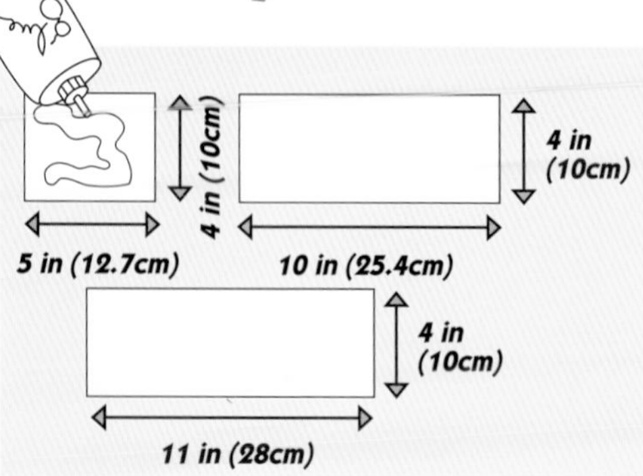

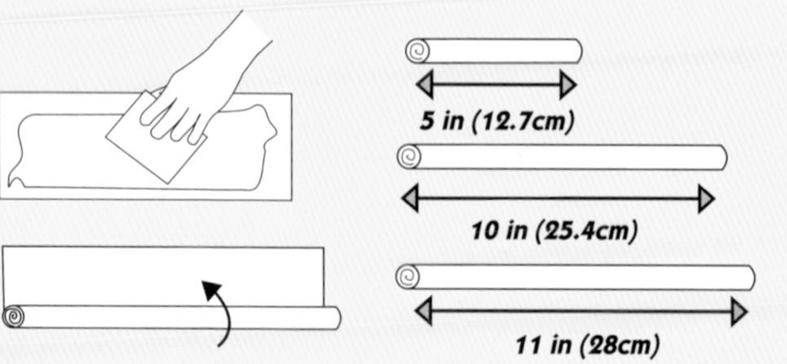

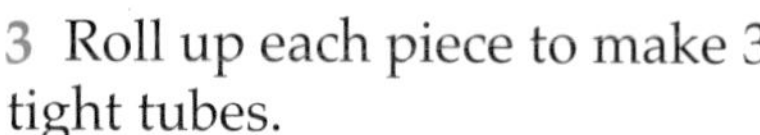

1 Cut 3 pieces of newspaper in the dimensions shown.
2 Spread each piece of paper with glue.

3 Roll up each piece to make 3 tight tubes.

4 Twist tubes into thin ropes.

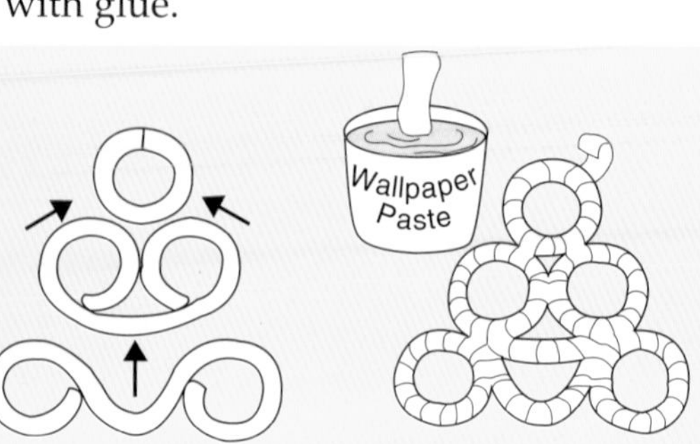

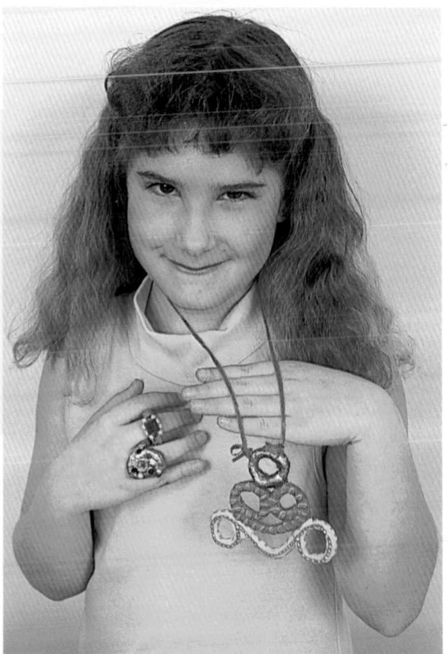

5 Bend tubes into curls and glue together, as shown.
6 Cover curled tubes with small pieces of newspaper dipped in wallpaper paste. Allow to dry. Paint and shellac.
7 Tie a ribbon to the pendant to make a necklace.

Rings

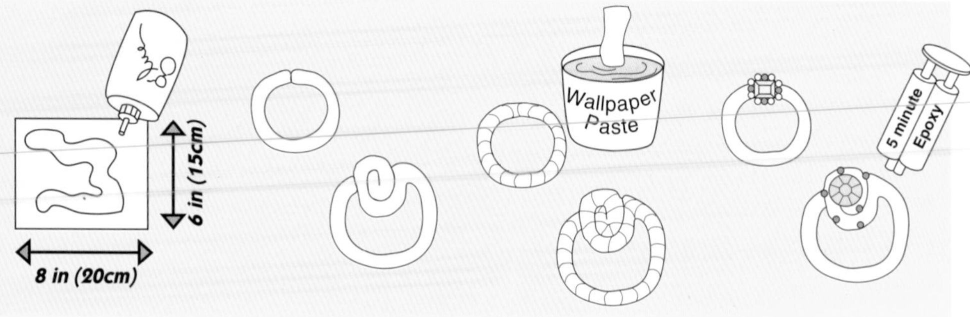

1 Cut a piece of newspaper, as indicated. Drizzle with glue.
2 Make into thin rope, as above.
3 Bend paper rope into rings. Cut off excess paper to fit your finger, or roll up the extra length into curls at top of ring, as shown. Tape in place.
4 Wrap rings with small pieces of newspaper dipped in wallpaper paste. When dry, paint and shellac.
5 Attach rhinestones to the rings with 5-minute epoxy.

Stenciled Valentine Cards & Envelopes

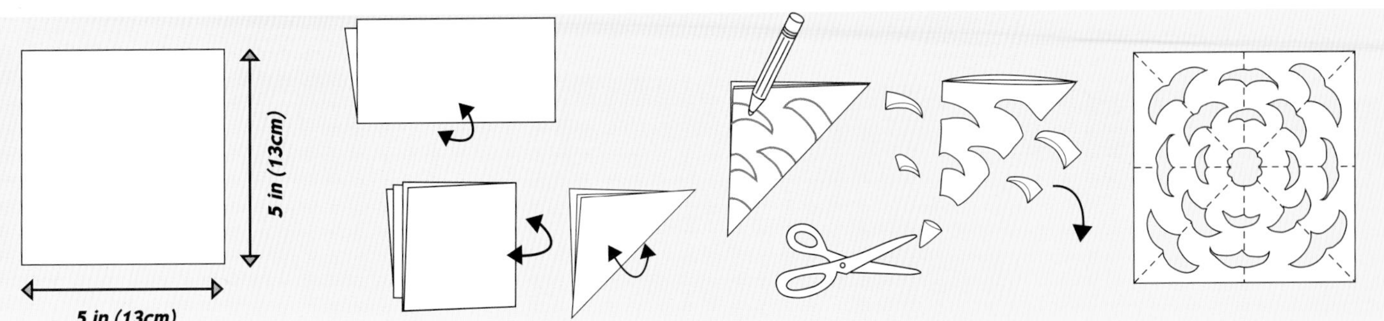

1 To make stencil, cut a square from stiff paper, as indicated.
2 Fold in half.
3 Fold in half again, short ends together.
4 Make a fold diagonally from the folded corner, bottom right to the free corners at top left, as shown.
5 Draw notches from both folded sides, as shown, and a quarter circle at the folded corner.
6 Cut out these notches.
7 Unfold the flower stencil.

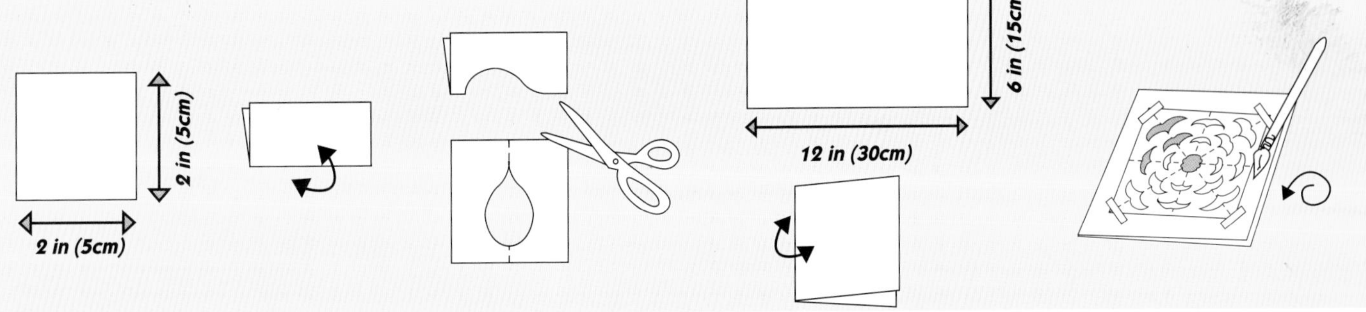

8 To make a leaf stencil, fold a square piece of stiff paper in half, as shown.
9 Cut out a half tear-drop shape from the folded side, as shown. Unfold to reveal leaf stencil.
10 For card, cut a piece of stiff paper 6 in x 12 in (15cm x 30cm). Fold in half, short ends together.
11 Place the flower stencil in the center of the card. Hold in place with small pieces of tape. Apply paint to the holes in the stencil. A stiff brush works best. Use a small amount of paint on brush, removing excess paint on a paper towel. Apply paint by rubbing brush in small circles.

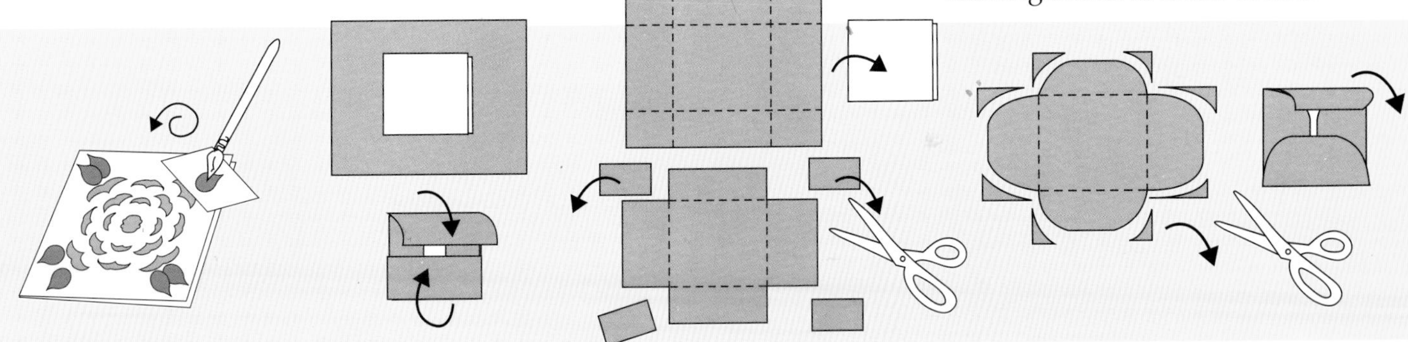

12 When paint is dry, remove the stencil. Use the leaf stencil to add leaves around the rose in the same way, if desired.
13 For envelope, set the stenciled card in the middle of a sheet of construction paper. Fold excess paper around the card, as shown.
14 Unfold, remove card, and cut out the corner squares and discard, as shown.
15 Round corners, as shown. Fold sides over and glue 3 of the sides in place. Leave top open.

Heart-Shaped Banner

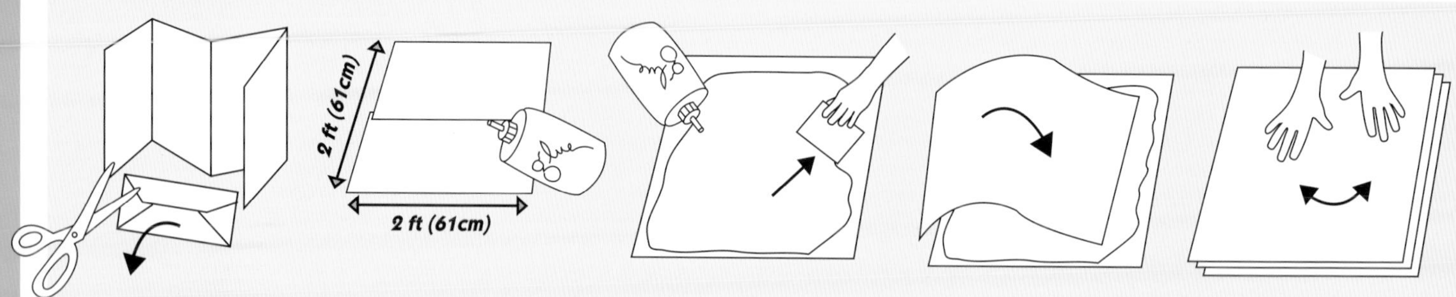

1 Cut open 2 brown paper bags, cut out bottoms, and lay bags flat.
2 Glue the 2 bags together along the long side to make one large sheet. Trim to make sheet 2 ft (61cm) square. Repeat to make 2 more square sheets.
3 Drizzle glue all over one sheet. Spread the glue with a scrap of cardboard or wood.
4 Lay a second flat sheet on top of the glue and smooth in place.
5 Spread with glue in the same way and add the third flat sheet, smoothing in place to make a triple thickness sheet.

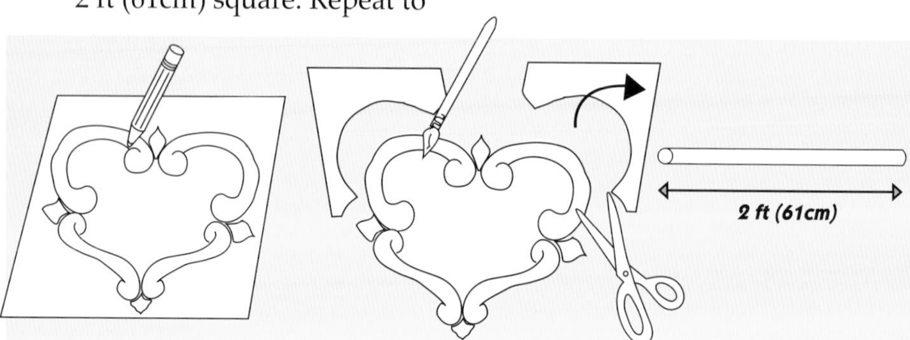

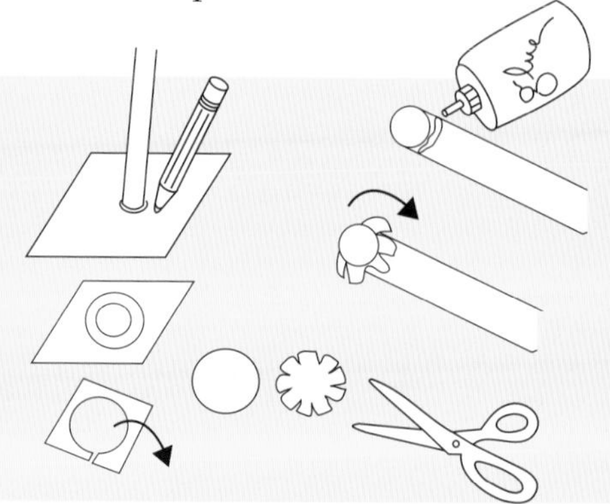

6 Draw a heart shape on the sheet. Add scrolls around the edges, if desired.
7 Cut out. Paint pink and gold, see photograph.
8 Cut a cardboard wrapping paper tube 2 ft (61cm) in length.
9 Place end of tube on a piece of brown paper. Trace around it.
10 Draw around the first circle to make a larger circle. Cut out larger circle. Make cuts around the circle up to the smaller circle, as shown.
11 Spread glue around the end of the tube, place the paper circle over the open end and press the cut tabs down on the glue. Cover the other end of the tube in the same way. Paint and shellac.

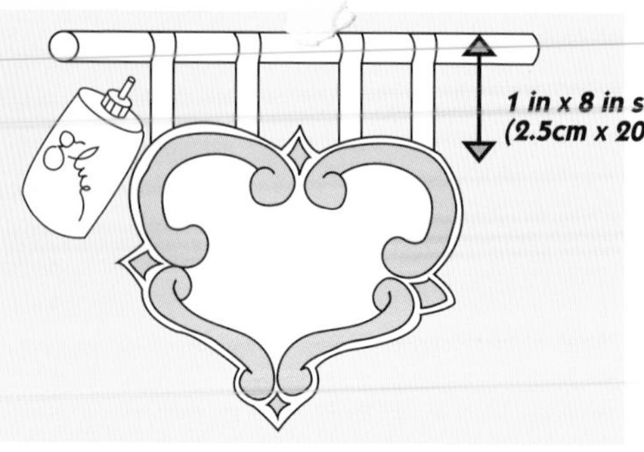

12 Cut strips of white or gold paper, as indicated. Glue one end of each strip to top of heart, and the other end of strip to the cardboard tube. Hang tube from ceiling with strong string. Make as many of the following hearts as needed, one for each guest at your party.

Paper Heart with Doily

1 Draw a heart on colored construction paper. Place heart on top of another piece of colored construction paper.
2 Cut out heart shape, cutting through both pieces of paper to make 2 identical heart shapes.
3 Spread glue around bottom edge of one heart, leaving top unglued.
4 Place second heart on top of first, gluing the 2 hearts together along bottom edge to form a pocket.
5 Glue a heart-shaped paper doily in a contrasting color on top of the paper hearts.
6 Cut a strip of paper from a scrap of colored construction paper, as indicated. Glue the ends of the strip inside the heart pocket for a handle.

Cinnamon Heart Bundles

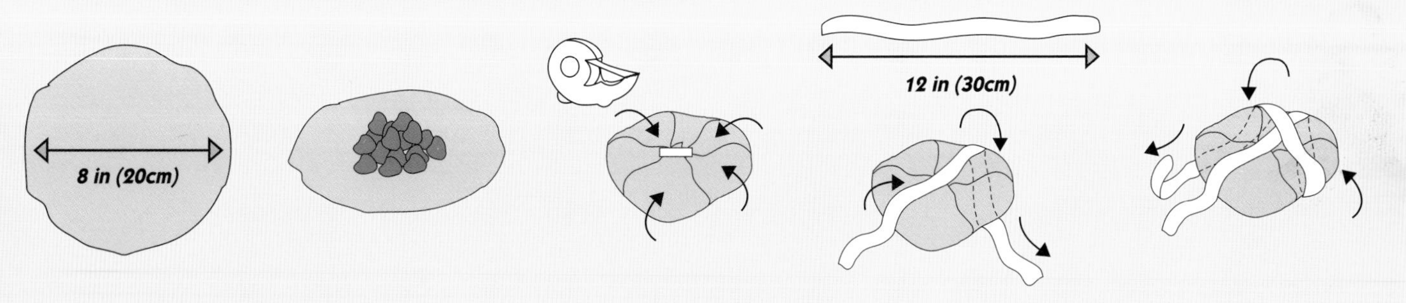

1 Cut a circle of colored tissue paper, as shown.
2 Place 1/4 cup cinnamon hearts in the center.
3 Fold the sides of the circle over the cinnamon hearts and tape, making a small packet.
4 Cut a piece of ribbon , as shown. Wrap the ribbon around the packet starting at one side, wrapping over the top and under the packet, coming out on the opposite side, as shown.
5 Wrap the ribbon back over the top, underneath, and out on the other side where you started.

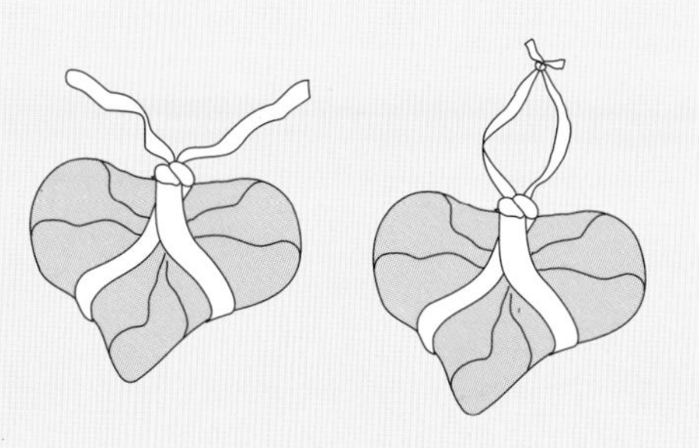

6 Pull the ribbon snugly and tie the 2 loose ends together at the top, shaping the packet into a heart.
7 Tie the loose ends in a loop and trim. Staple or glue to the heart banner, see photograph.

See p14 for Woven Heart instructions.

Woven Hearts

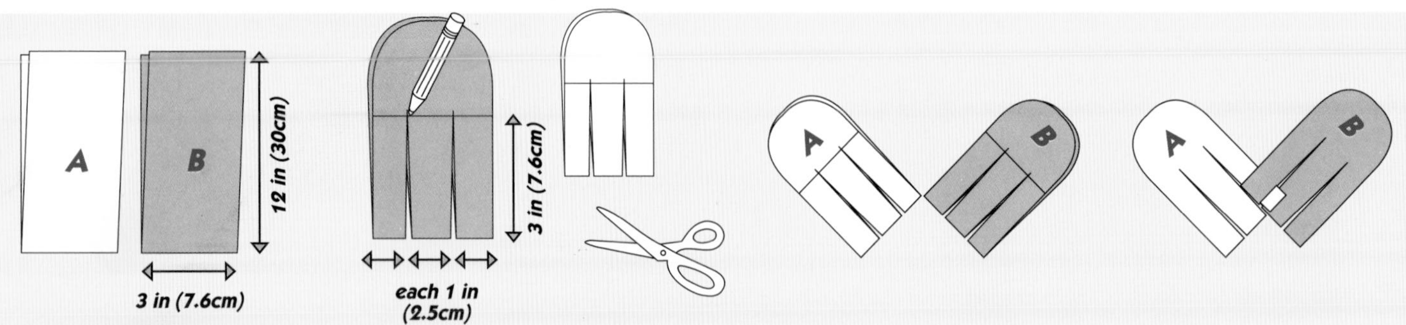

1 Cut 2 pieces of paper, each a contrasting color, as indicated. Fold each in half, short ends together.
2 Place folded end at the bottom and draw a line across the paper above the folded edge, as shown, making a square. Draw 2 lines dividing the square into 3, as shown. Draw an arch across the top of the paper. Cut off top leaving a rounded edge, as shown. Cut along the 2 pencil lines from the folded edge up. Repeat with the contrasting paper.
3 Place the 2 prepared pieces of paper in a "V," folded corners together.
4 Slide the first flap of color A between the 2 layers of the first flap of color B, as shown.

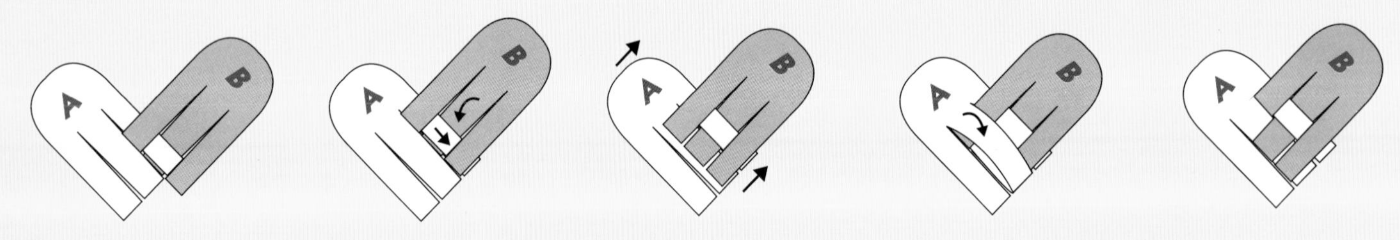

5 Slide the center flap of color B through the first flap of color A.
6 Then slide the first flap of color A through the last flap of color B.
7 Slide color A piece farther up color B, then begin again with the center flap of color A.
8 This time, slide the first flap of color B between the layers of the center flap of color A.
9 Slide the center flap of color A through the center flap of color B.

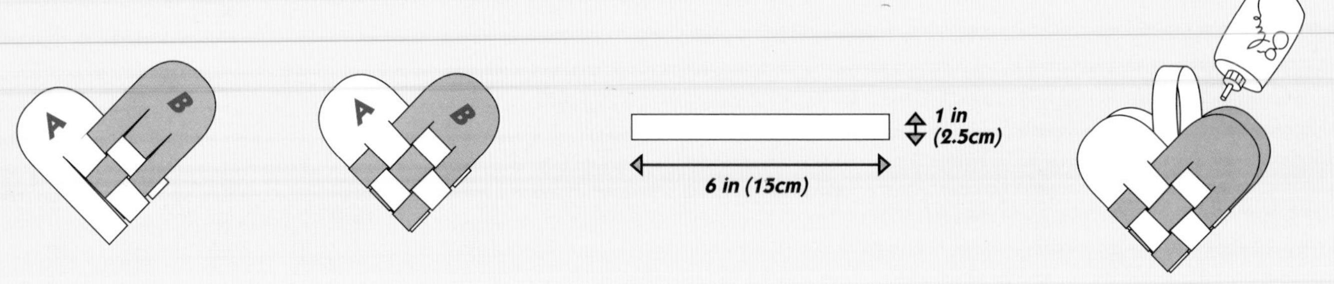

10 Then slide the last flap of color B through the center flap of color A.
11 Weave the final flap of color A through color B the same way. This will complete the checkerboard effect. The heart will open from the top like a pocket.
12 To make a handle, cut a strip of paper following dimensions shown.
13 Glue one end on each side of the pocket. Heart may be filled with treats for a Valentine gift. Staple or glue to the heart banner, see photograph p12.

Converted Fruit Basket

1 Use an empty peach or blueberry cardboard fruit basket. Draw a large heart at each end of the basket and small hearts along the sides, as shown.
2 Cut away the extra cardboard around the top of the hearts.
3 Cover the seams on the outside of the basket with pieces of paper dipped in wallpaper paste. When dry, paint and decorate. Shellac.

Rope Heart Necklace

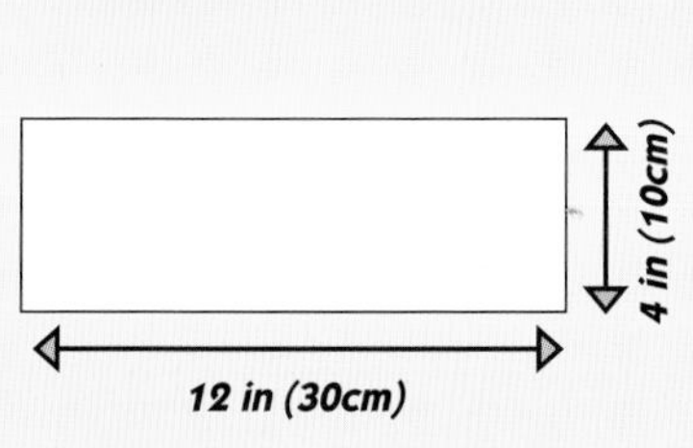

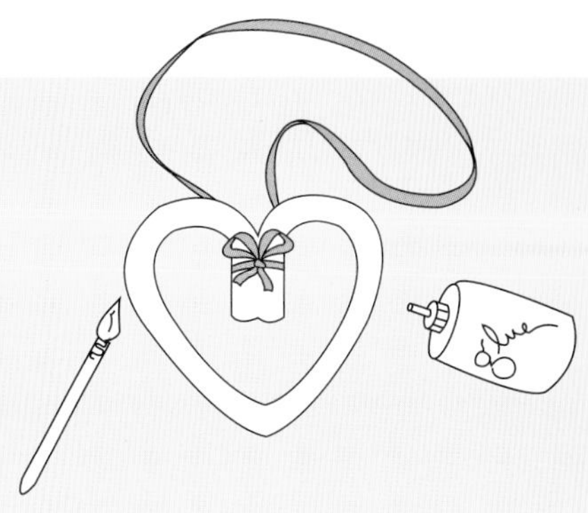

1 Cut a piece of newspaper as indicated.
2 Spread with glue and make a thin rope, see p10 *Crazy Pendant.*
3 Shape into a heart, as shown.
4 Cover the heart with pieces of newspaper dipped in wallpaper paste. Set aside to dry. When dry, paint and shellac.
5 Tie a ribbon on the heart to make a necklace.

Papier-Mâché Pulp Pendant

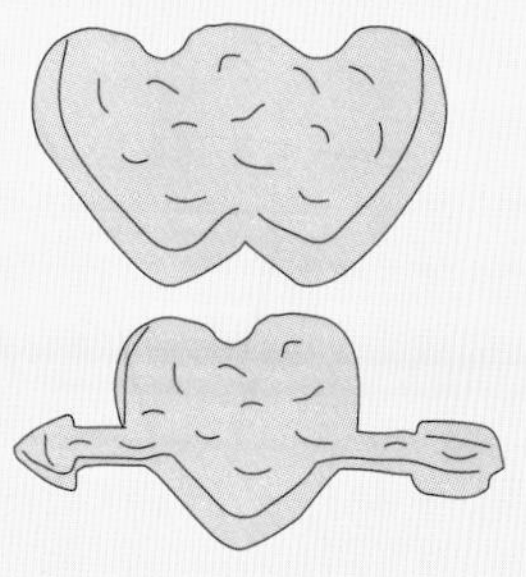

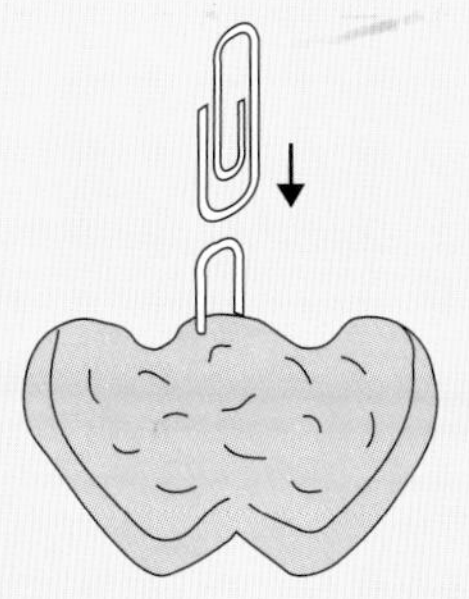

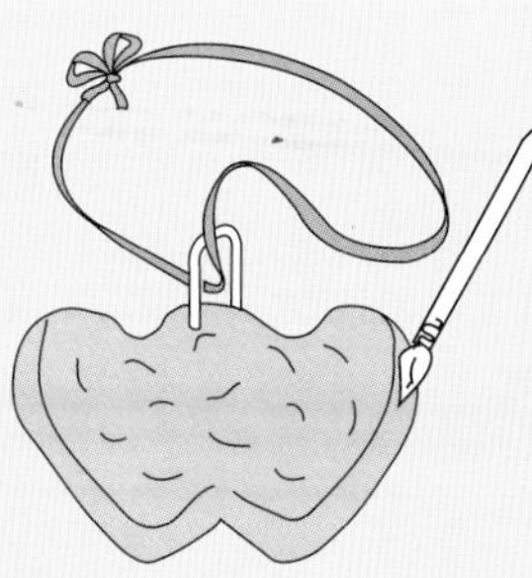

1 Make papier-mâché pulp, see p36. Mold pulp into a double heart shape or heart with arrow, as shown.
2 Embed a paper clip at the top while the pulp is still wet. Set paper clip in pulp so that one loop extends out of the pulp.
3 When pulp is dry, paint and shellac.
4 String a ribbon through the metal loop and tie around neck.

Braided Heart Wreath

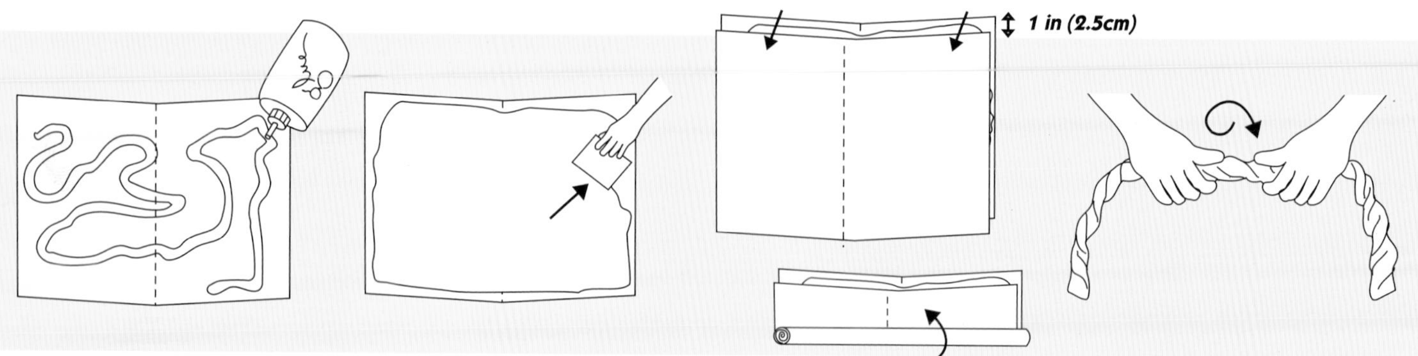

1 Cover a work surface with plastic or paper. Lay a full size sheet of newspaper flat and drizzle white glue all over it.

2 With a scrap piece of cardboard, spread glue to cover the entire sheet.

3 Lay another full size sheet of newspaper on top of the glue, 1 in (2.5cm) lower than the sheet below it, as shown.

4 Starting from the bottom, roll the 2 sheets together into a tube. The uncovered edge with glue will hold the roll together.

5 Twist the paper tube into a rope. Set aside. Make 8 more double-thickness newspaper ropes in the same way.

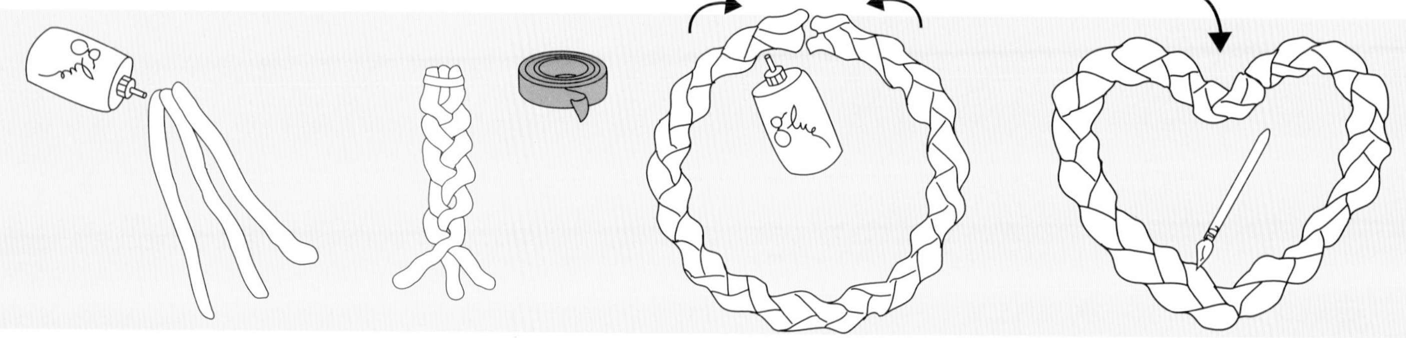

6 Lay 3 ropes side by side on the work surface and glue them together at one end.

7 Tape to hold them together, then braid. At end of braid, glue and tape another rope to each strand of the braid and continue to braid them together. Add the last 3 ropes in the same way and finish braiding.

8 Bring the 2 ends of the braid together and glue to form a wreath. Form wreath into a heart shape while still flexible.

9 When dry, remove tape. Paint and shellac. Tie a ribbon around top to hang wreath.

Valentine Pig Popcorn Bowl

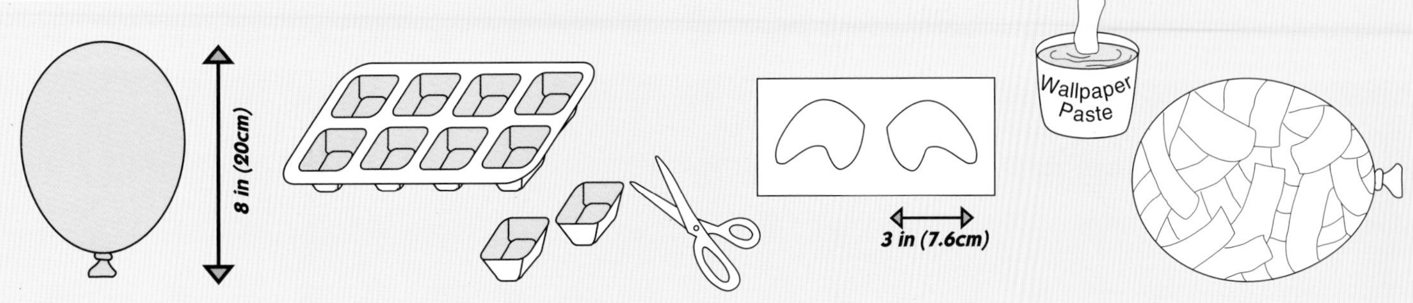

1 Blow up a round balloon to about 8 in (20cm) in diameter and tie. Set aside.

2 From an egg carton, cut out 5 separate cups.

3 From thin cardboard (cereal box), cut out 2 pig ears, as shown.

4 Cover the balloon with strips of newspaper dipped in wallpaper paste. Cover with 5 to 6 layers of paper strips.

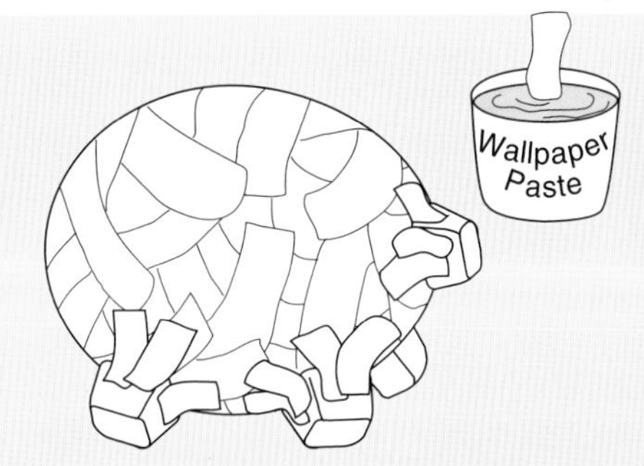

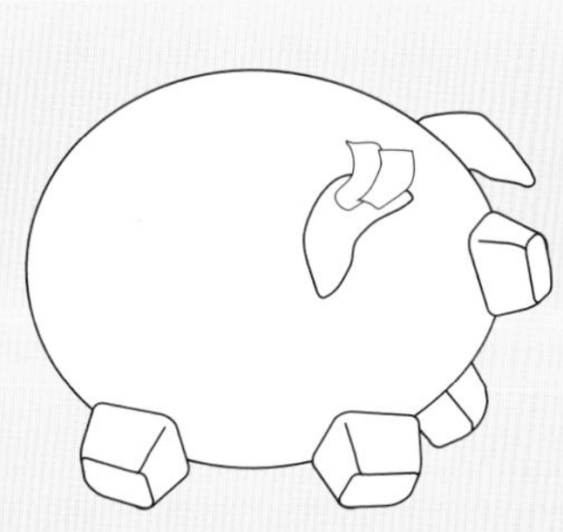

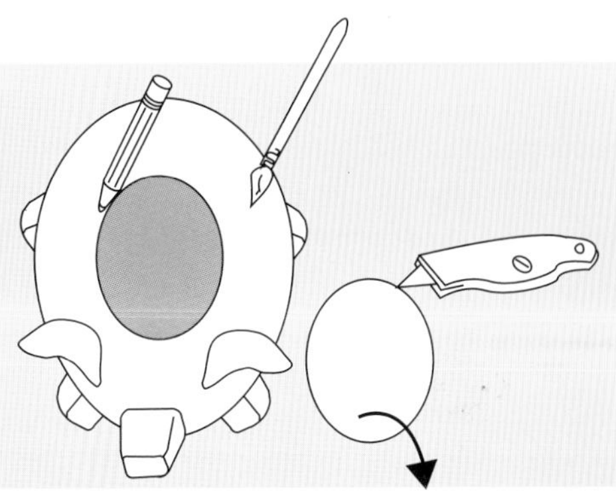

5 Attach 4 of the egg carton cups to the underside of the balloon with more newspaper strips and paste. These are the pig's feet. Attach the last egg carton cup to the front of the balloon in the same way for a snout.

6 Attach the pig's ears with more newspaper strips and paste. Set aside to dry.

7 When dry, draw an oval shape on the pig's back. With a sharp knife, very carefully cut out the oval shape. Remove the balloon. Paint and shellac. Add red sticker hearts, if desired. Fill "bowl" with dry popcorn.

Valentine Candle Centerpiece

1 Find an empty can large enough to hold a large candle.
2 Trace around the can on smooth heavy cardboard and cut out the circle.

3 Fill the can with gravel or rice and place the cardboard circle over the open end.
4 Tape in place.

5 In the corner of a square of paper draw a heart, as shown, to make a pattern. Cut out.

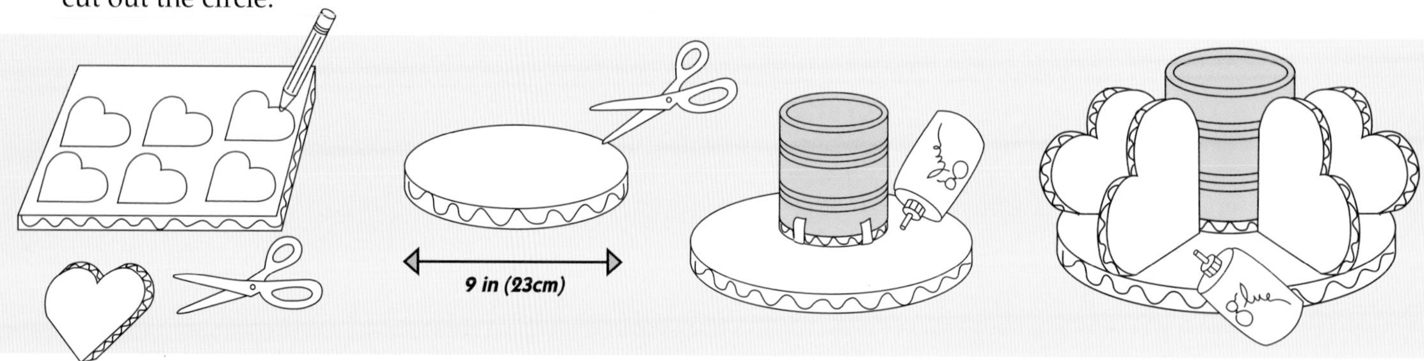

6 Place the paper heart on a piece of heavy cardboard and trace around it. Repeat to make 6 hearts. Cut out all the hearts.

7 Draw another circle on cardboard, as shown, and cut out.
8 Glue the can in the center of the circle, cardboard side down.

9 Glue the cardboard hearts around the can, as shown.

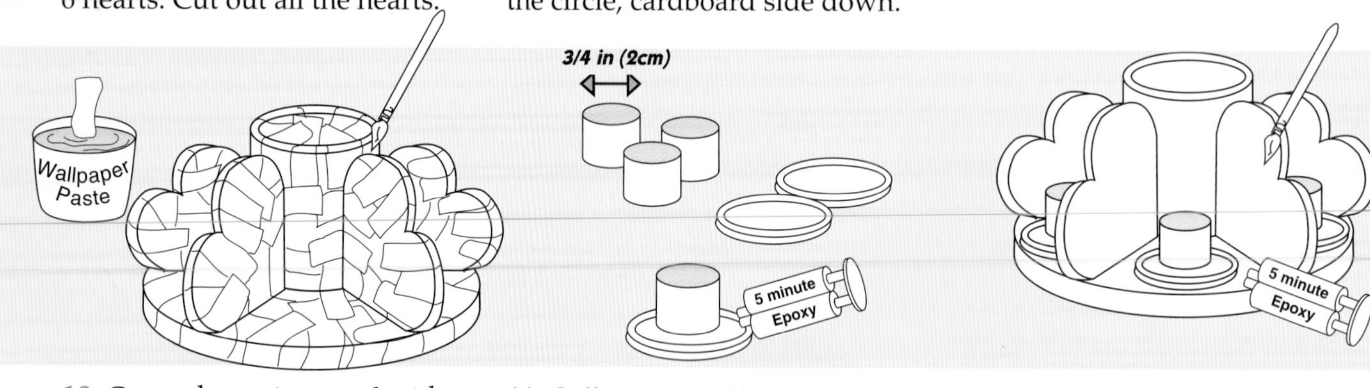

10 Cover the entire stand with strips of newspaper dipped in wallpaper paste. When dry, paint and shellac.

11 Collect 6 metal lids, and 6—3/4 in (2cm) copper caps (available from the plumbing section of a hardware store) to make fire-resistant candle holders.

12 With 5-minute epoxy, attach one copper cap in the middle of each lid. Then epoxy each lid on the cardboard circle between each heart. Paint the metal parts with metallic paint. When dry add candles. *Light candles only when adults are present.*

Valentine Place Mats

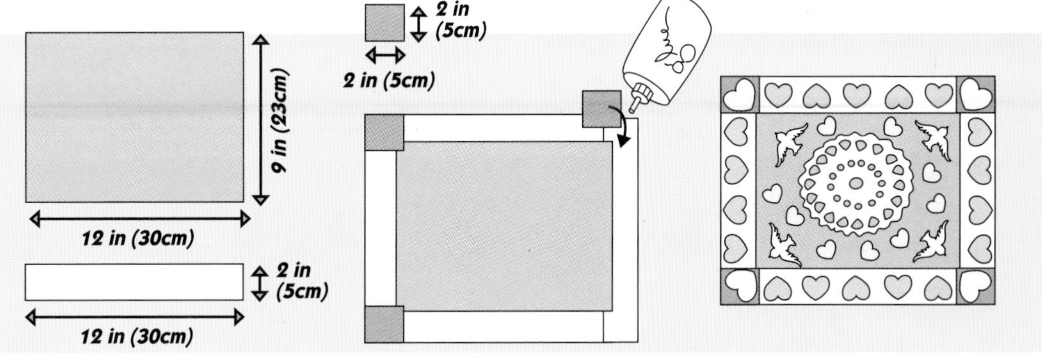

1 Follow Halloween Place Mat instructions, p47.

2 Apply Valentine hearts, doves, and doily, as shown.

Valentine Place Cards

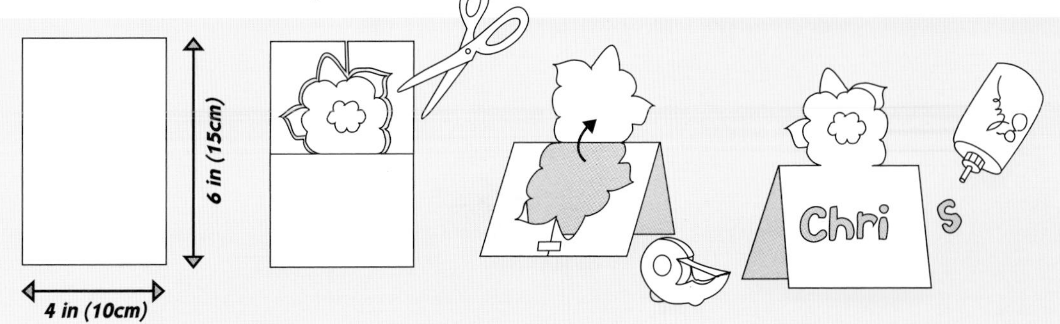

1 Follow Halloween Place Card instructions, p47.

2 Write names on bottom half, or draw and cut out letters to glue on the place card.

For Catstair Garland, see p67.

Easter

Marie

Egg Window Hanging

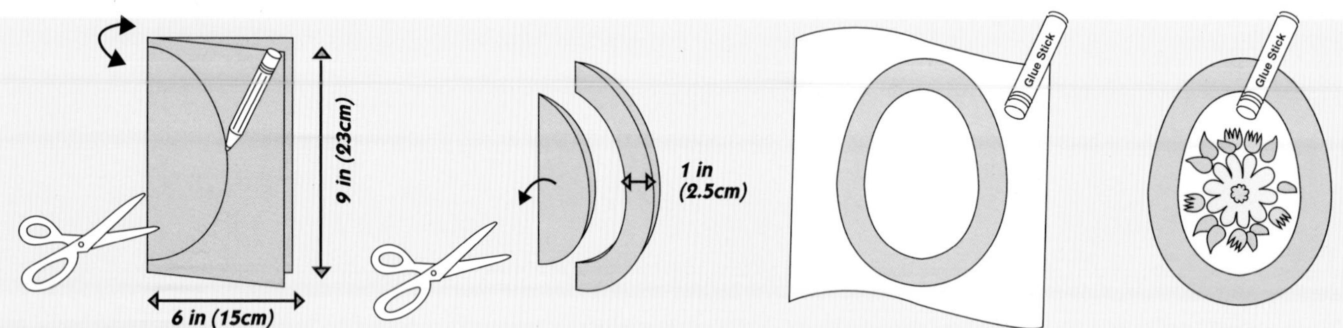

1 Fold a 9 in x 12 in (23cm x 30cm) piece of purple construction paper in half. Draw half an egg shape around the fold, as shown. Cut out.

2 Draw a 1 in (2.5cm) border inside the cut edge. Cut out the center. Unfold the border piece.
3 Spread glue stick on border and press it on white tissue paper. Cut out around egg.

4 Draw and cut out a flower 2-1/2 in (6.3cm) in diameter from pink tissue paper.
5 Spread glue stick on flower and place in center of egg.

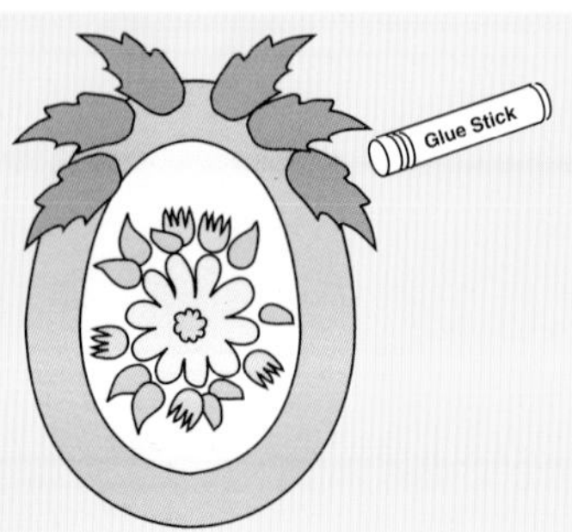

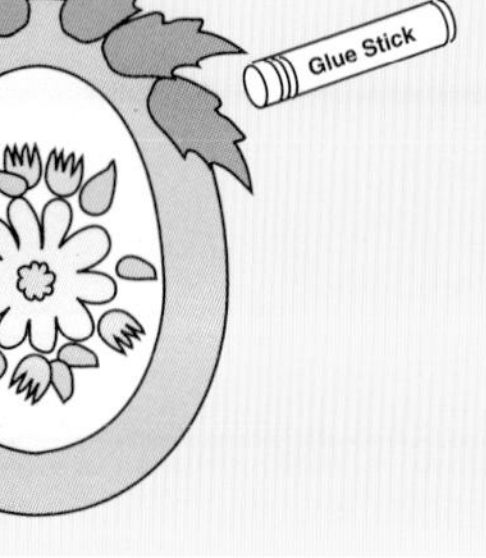

6 Draw and cut out small flowers and leaves from assorted colors of tissue and glue around the center flower.
7 Draw leaves on green construction paper and cut out.

8 Glue to top of egg.
9 Make a bow from 1 in (2.5cm) strips of colored tissue paper, see p66.
10 Glue to top of egg, as shown. Tape egg in window.

Ducks in the Rain Window Hanging

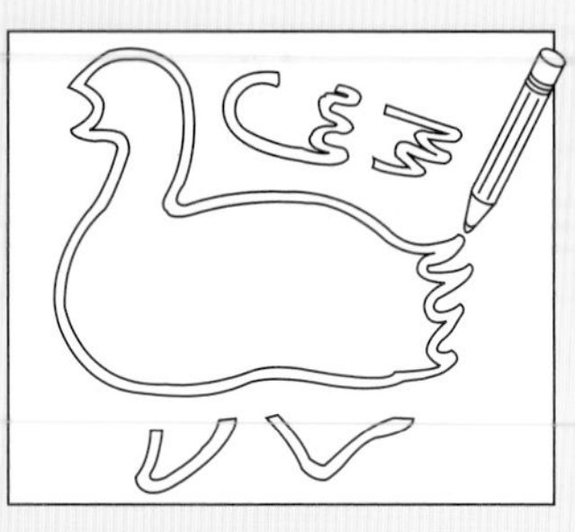

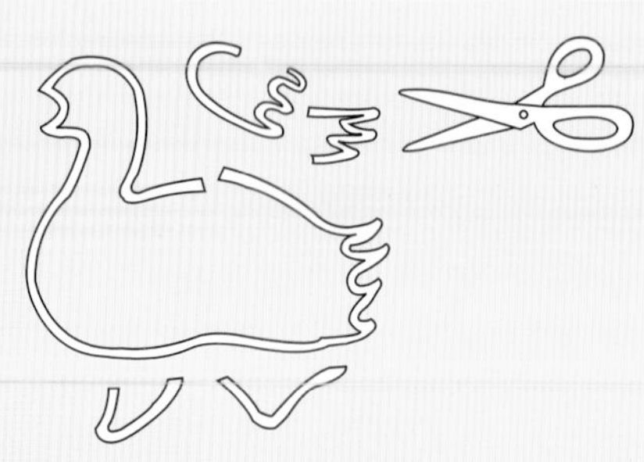

1 Draw a mother duck body shape, wing shapes, and legs with a border on white construction paper, see pattern p92.
2 Cut out the border for each part in one continuous piece.

3 Glue body, wing, and leg outlines onto white tissue paper, as shown. Cut out.

4 Draw the beak and 2 lower leg parts with borders on orange construction paper, see pattern p92.

5 Cut out as before.
6 Glue to orange tissue paper and cut out.
7 Glue beak and legs to body.

8 Cut out a green eye from construction paper and glue to head.

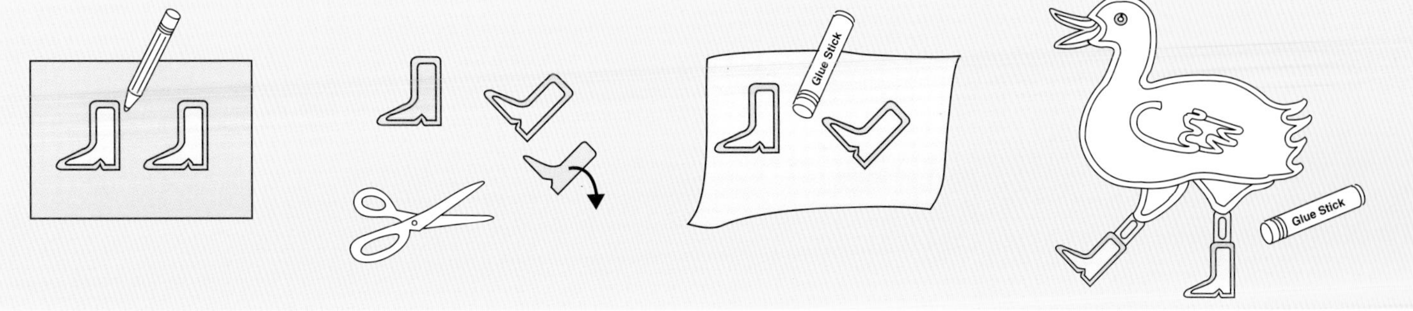

9 Draw 2 boots with borders on pink construction paper, see pattern p92. Cut out.
10 Draw and cut off the outline, and glue to pink tissue paper.
11 Cut out and glue to the orange legs.
12 Use the photo as a guide for color and make 4 ducklings, boots, and raindrops using the same technique as for mother duck, see pattern, p92.

Topiary Tree

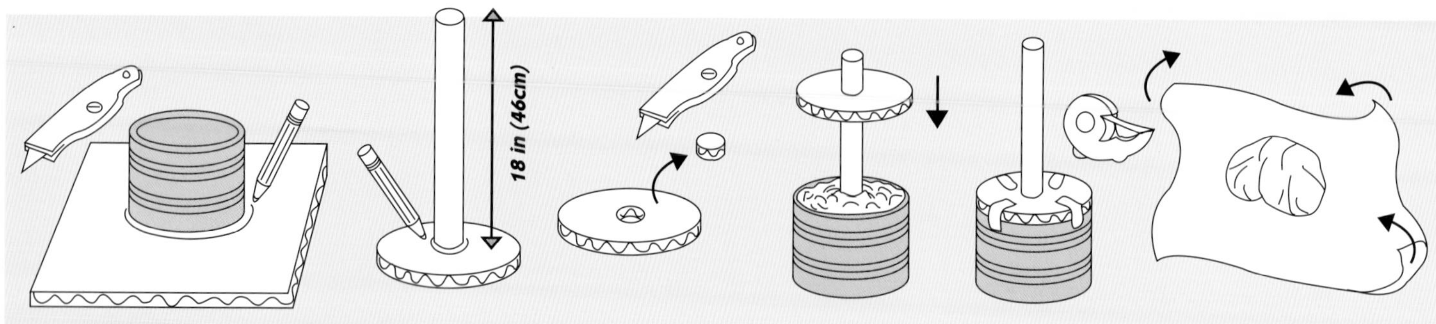

1 Place the open end of a plastic tub or can on a piece of cardboard and trace around it.
2 Cut out the cardboard circle. Place a cardboard tube in the center of the cardboard circle and trace around it, as shown.
3 Carefully cut out the smaller circle.
4 Place the cardboard tube upright in the center of the can. Fill can with stones or rice for weight, holding tube in place. Slide the cardboard circle over the tube, as shown and push it right down to the can.
5 Tape in place.
6 Crumple a sheet of newspaper into a loose ball. Wrap more sheets of newspaper around the ball.

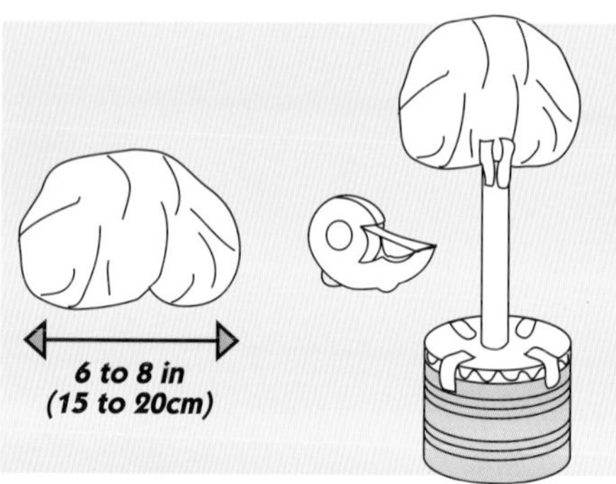

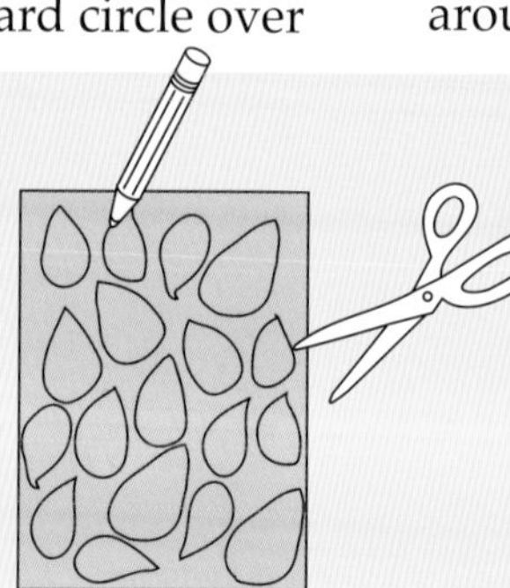

7 Ball should be 6 to 8 in (15 to 20cm) in diameter. Tape loose edges to hold the shape.
8 Place ball on top of the tube and tape in place.
9 Cover entire structure with strips of newspaper dipped in wallpaper paste. The newspaper ball and tube should have 3 to 4 layers of paper strips. The can needs only 2 layers. When dry, paint the topiary tree, as desired. Shellac.
10 Cut many 2-in (5-cm) -long leaf shapes from green construction paper.
11 Gently curl each leaf shape around your finger.
12 Glue leaves to green ball.

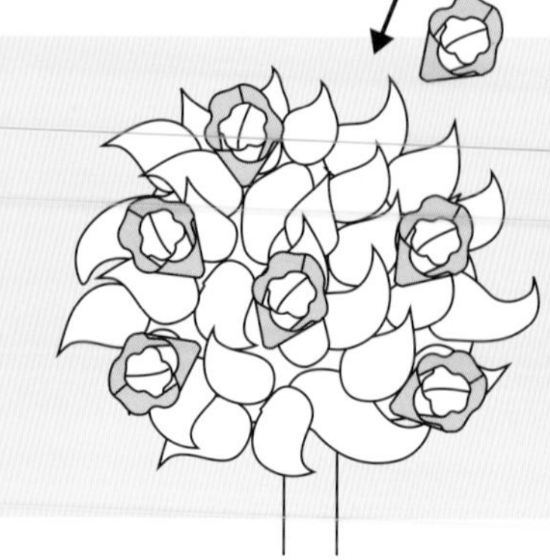

13 Make circles of orange construction paper. Cut each to the center, as shown, and form into a cone. Glue edges. Cut the open end into petal shapes. Make circles of yellow construction paper and form cones in the same way. Glue yellow cone in center of each orange cone.
14 Glue flowers to the tree. Add a paper bow, if desired, see p66.

Giant Easter Eggs

1 Blow up a round balloon and tie end. (When full of air, balloon becomes egg-shaped.)

2 Cover balloon with strips of newspaper dipped in wallpaper paste. Push knotted end of balloon inward and cover with more strips and paste. Make the covering 4 to 5 layers thick. Set aside to dry.

3 Make an egg cup from a plastic container (sour cream or margarine tub). Cover container inside and out with strips of newspaper dipped in wallpaper paste. Make 3 layers thick.

4 When dry, paint and shellac the egg and egg cup.

Egg- or Rabbit-Shaped Paper Boxes

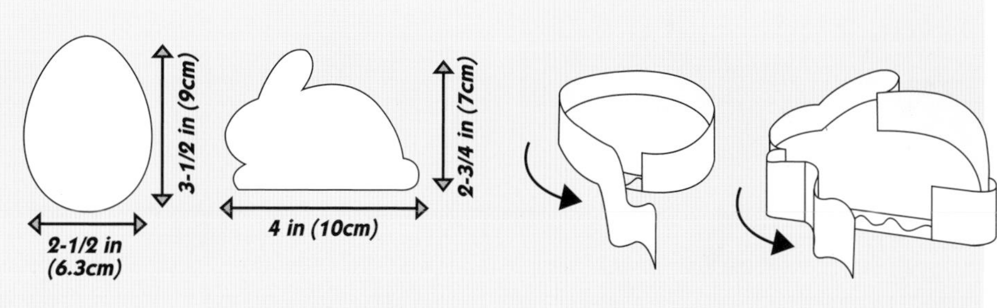

Make simple box shapes without too many bends in the outline. Use the same technique as for the heart-shaped box on p9.

1 Make 2 identical egg shapes or rabbit shapes in the dimensions shown.

2 Make the side of the lid 1/2 in (1.3cm) high, and the side of the bottom 2 in (5cm) high.

Note: When making the rabbit or any other non-symmetrical shape, remember to face the top and the bottom in opposite directions when attaching the sides. If you attach them both facing the same way, the lid will be backwards.

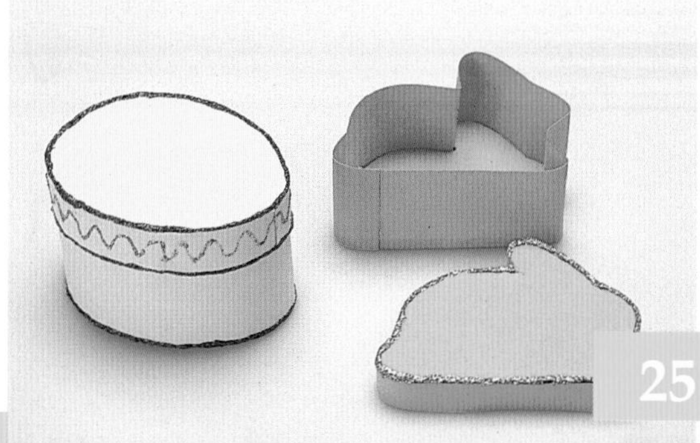

Woven Easter Basket

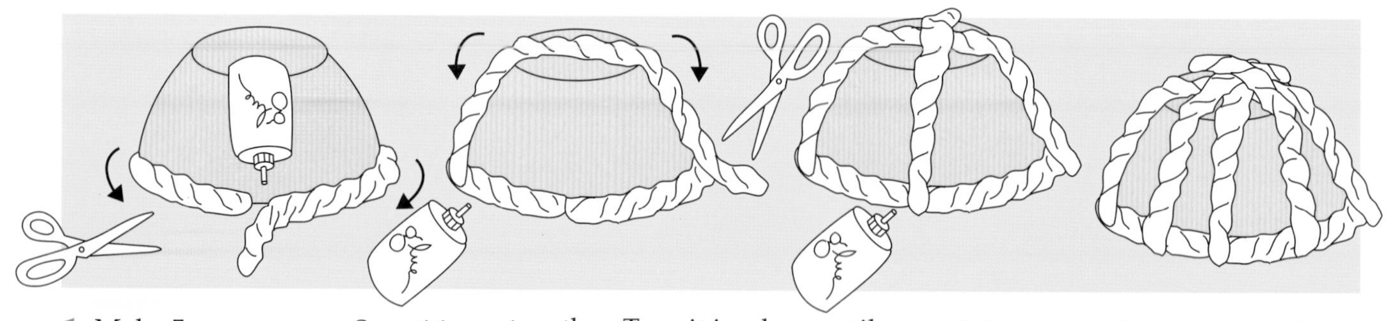

1 Make 5 paper ropes. See p16 for instructions.

2 Set a small mixing bowl upside down on a work surface. Wrap one rope around rim, as shown. Cut off any excess lengths and glue the 2 ends together. Tape it in place until glue dries.

3 Place another paper rope over the bowl and drape ends down each side of the bowl, as shown. Trim ends to fit. Glue each end to the first rope, as shown.

4 Drape another rope over the bowl, across the rope you just finished. Attach in the same way.

5 Add 2 more ropes, laying them across the top of the bowl, and in between the ropes, as shown. Glue all loose ends to the rim rope. Set aside to dry.

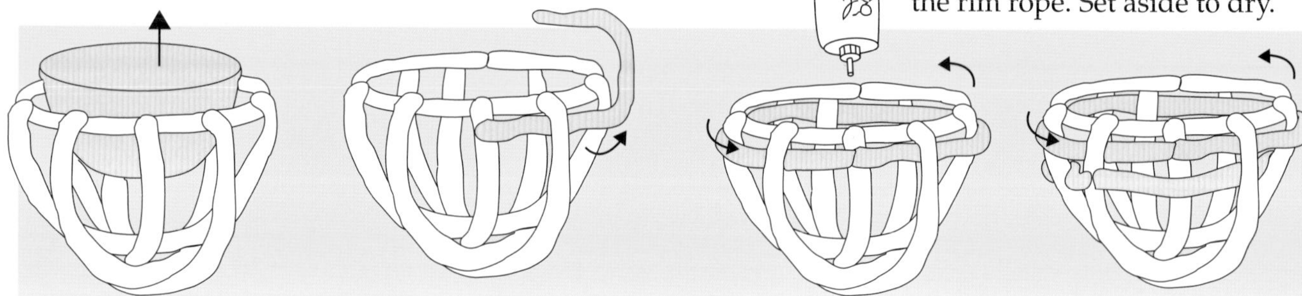

6 Make 10 more paper ropes.

7 When ropes are dry, remove the mixing bowl.

8 Glue one end of a new rope to one of the cross ribs, next to the top of the basket shape. Weave other end of this new rope in and out of the ribs, as shown. Attach another rope to the end of the new rope if more length is needed.

9 Trim any excess rope. Glue end in place.

10 Glue another new rope to a cross rib directly under the woven rope just completed. Continue this method until you have filled in the open spaces between the ribs.

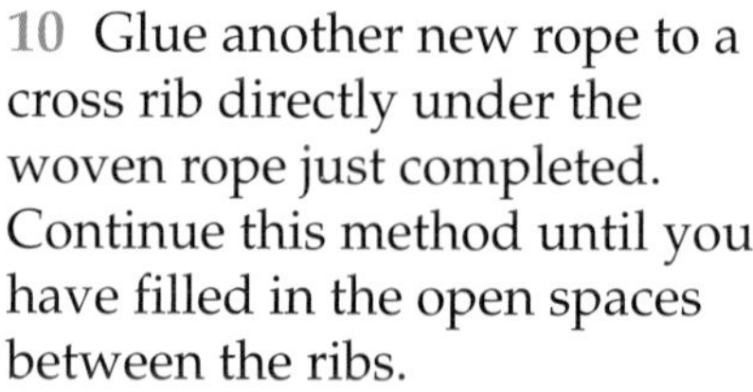

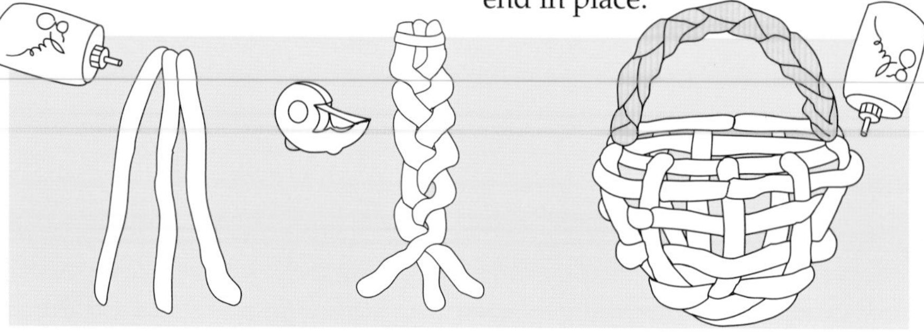

11 Make 3 more ropes. Lay them side by side on the work surface, and glue and tape ropes together at one end.

12 Braid the ropes. Glue other ends together.

13 Glue ends of the braided rope to top of basket, as shown. This is the handle.

Covered Balloon Easter Basket

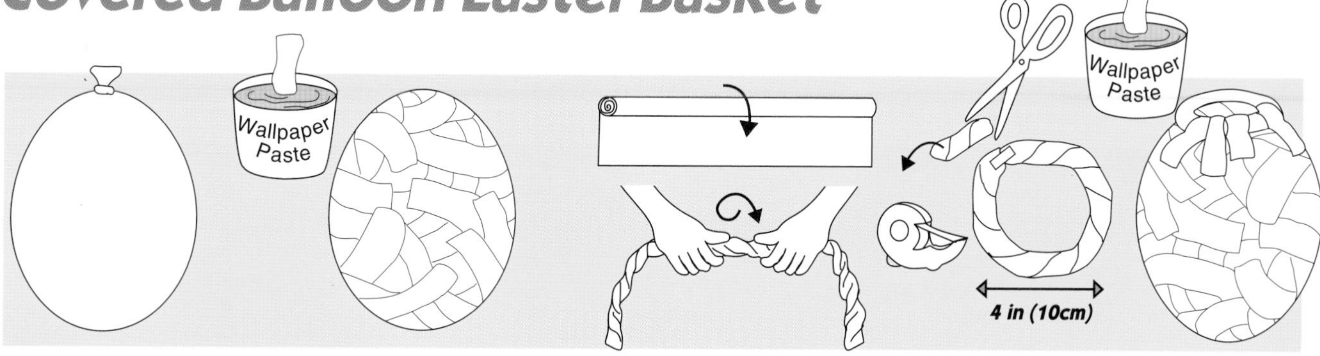

1 Blow up a round balloon and knot the end. When full of air balloon becomes egg shaped.

2 Cover the balloon with strips of newspaper dipped in wallpaper paste. Make 5 layers.

3 Roll a half sheet of newspaper into a tube, rolling from long side. Twist into a rope.

4 Form rope into a circle, as shown. Cut off excess paper. Tape in place.

5 Place circle on one end of the paper-covered balloon. Attach it with more strips of newspaper dipped in wallpaper paste. This ring forms the base of the basket. Set aside to dry.

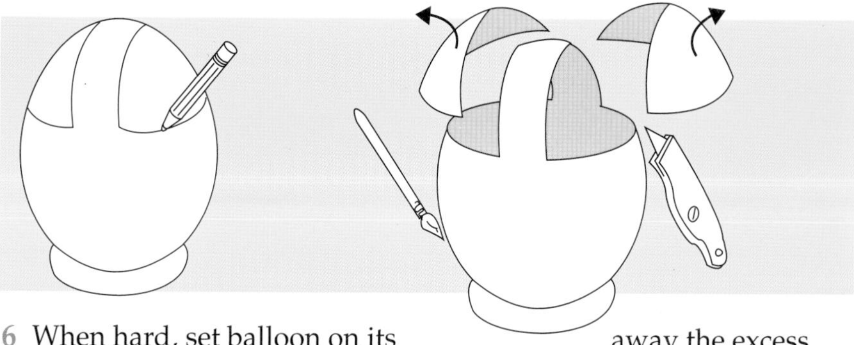

6 When hard, set balloon on its base. Draw a handle across the middle, as shown.

7 With a knife, carefully cut away the excess paper. Remove balloon from inside the paper. Paint and shellac.

Simple Folded Baskets

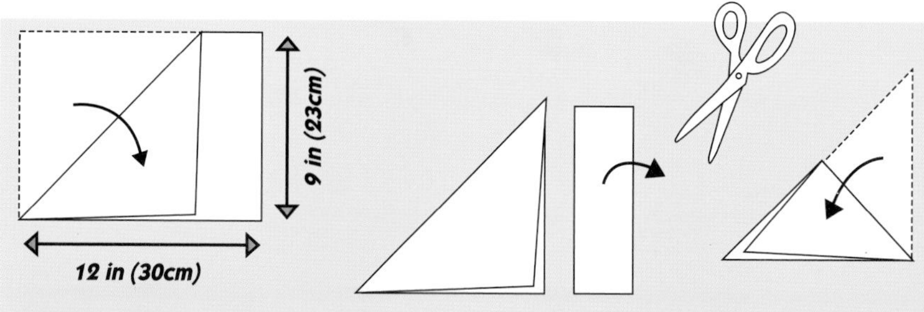

1 Fold a piece of construction paper into a square, as shown. Cut off extra paper leaving a folded triangle. Set aside extra paper.

2 Fold the triangle in half again, the two folded corners together, as shown.

3 Place open sides at the top and folded corner at the bottom, as shown. Crease the bottom 2 in (5cm) of the triangle and smooth flat again.

4 Draw a chicken, bunny, or egg shape across top of triangle.

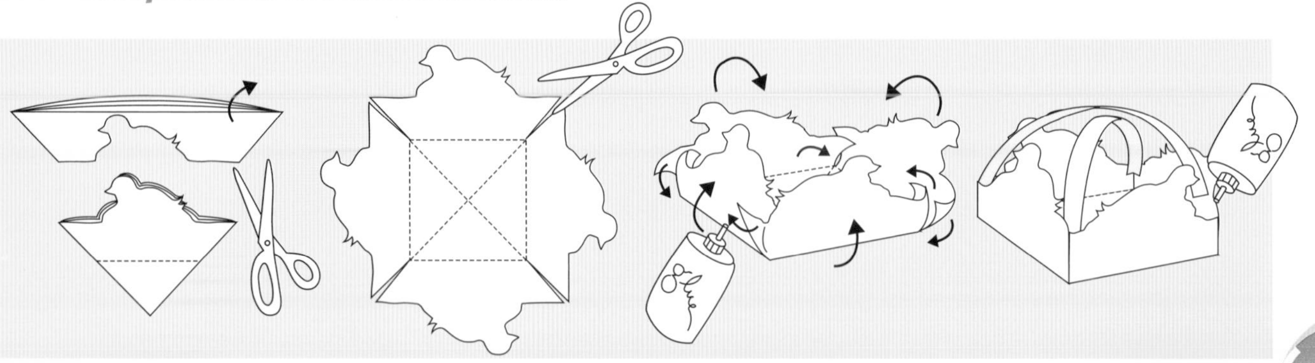

5 Cut out.
6 Unfold the paper. Snip corners of paper up to the folded square, as shown.
7 Fold sides up, overlap corners and glue in place.
8 Cut 2 strips 1/2 in (1.3cm) wide from the reserved paper (step 1). Glue ends of one strip into 2 opposite corners. Glue ends of remaining strip into the remaining opposite corners, as shown. Glue strips together where they cross in the center.

Bunny Place Cards

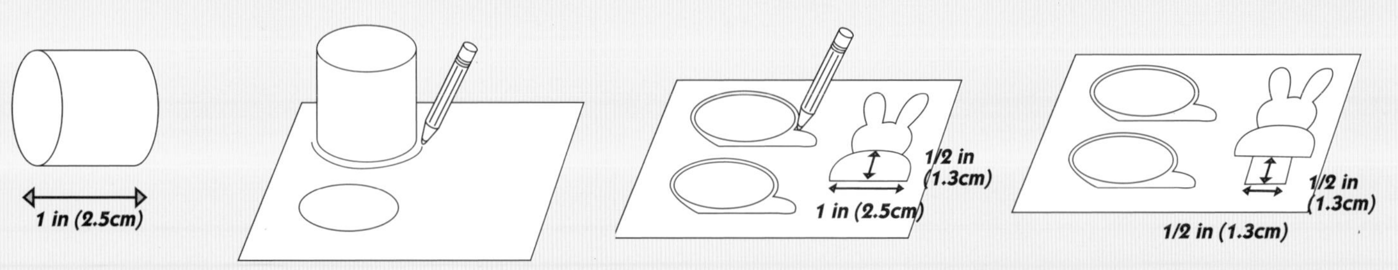

1 Cut a length of toilet tissue tube, as shown.
2 Place the open end on a piece of smooth cardboard (cereal box) and trace around it. Make 2 circles this way.
3 Draw around circles to make 2 legs with feet.
4 Draw a half circle to make bunny shoulders in dimensions shown. Add a head, ears.
5 Add a square tab along the bottom, as shown. Cut out around 3 shapes.

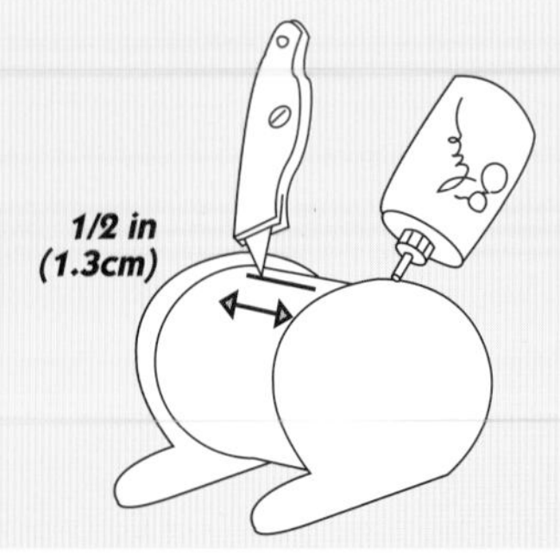

6 Glue a leg to each tube end.
7 With a sharp knife, carefully make a cut along top of the tube.
8 Glue the tab into the cut. Paint. Write person's name on bunny's tummy.

Block Puzzle

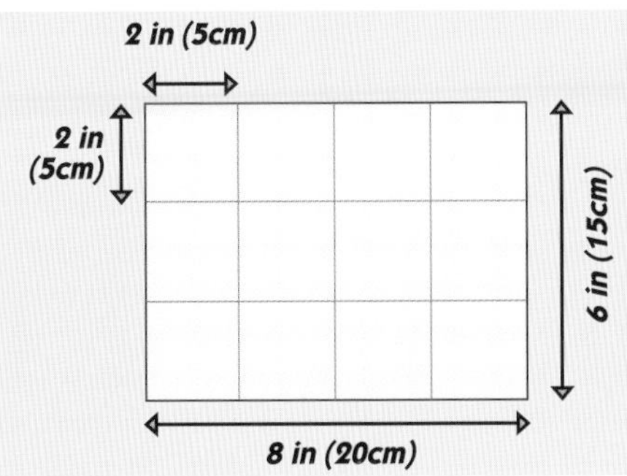

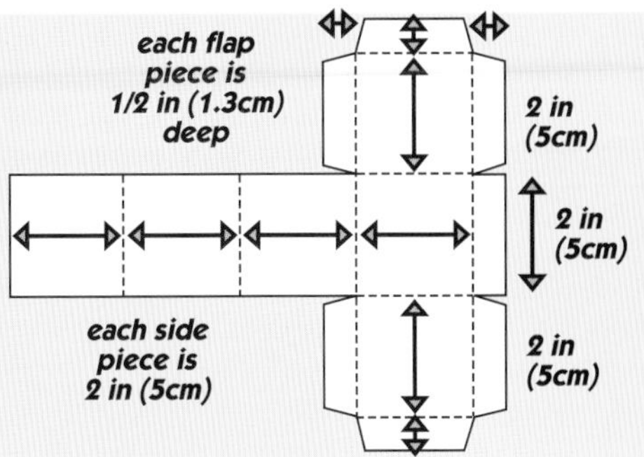

1 On a sheet of construction paper measure and draw 12 squares, as shown.

2 Draw and color a picture over the squares on this large rectangle using crayons, markers, or pencil crayons. Make 5 more pictures in the same way using different colors of construction paper. Set aside.

3 To make blocks use the pattern provided and draw it to scale on stiff paper. Cut out. Make creases where indicated.

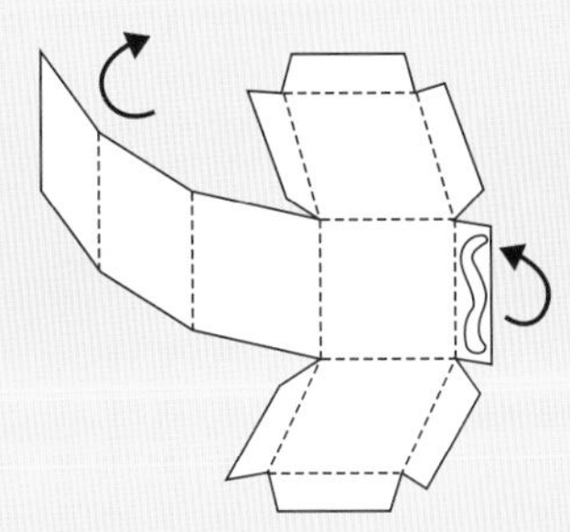

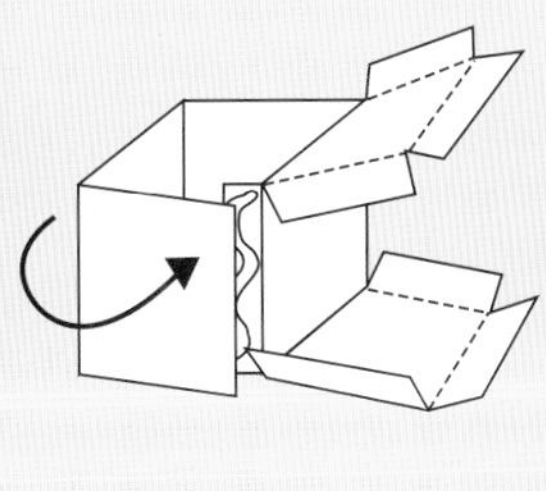

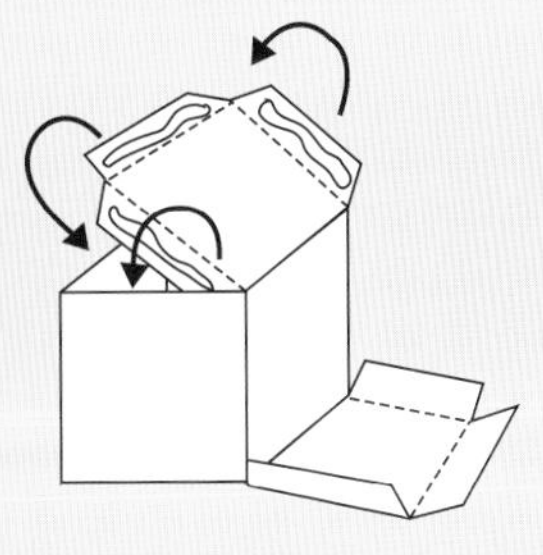

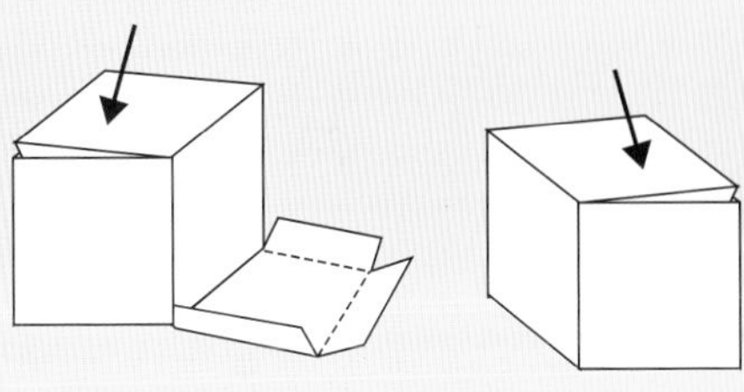

4 Spread glue on the center flap at the wide end, as shown.

5 Bring the opposite end over and onto the glued flap, making a square.

6 Spread glue on the flaps inside the square.

7 Gently press them in place.

8 Spread glue on the flaps of the other loose side and tuck these inside the cube. Make as many blocks as your drawing has squares.

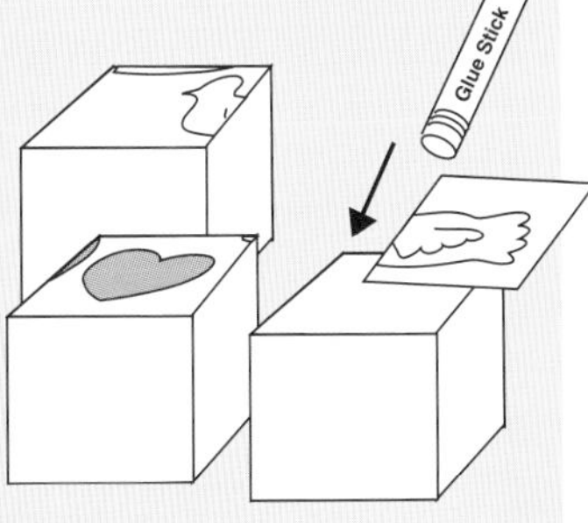

9 Cut out the squares of one drawing.

10 Glue one square to each paper block to reconstruct the picture. Turn all the blocks over. Cut squares of another drawing and glue one square to each block.

Continue until the blocks are covered on all sides with different drawings.

Paper Flowers Bouquet & Vase

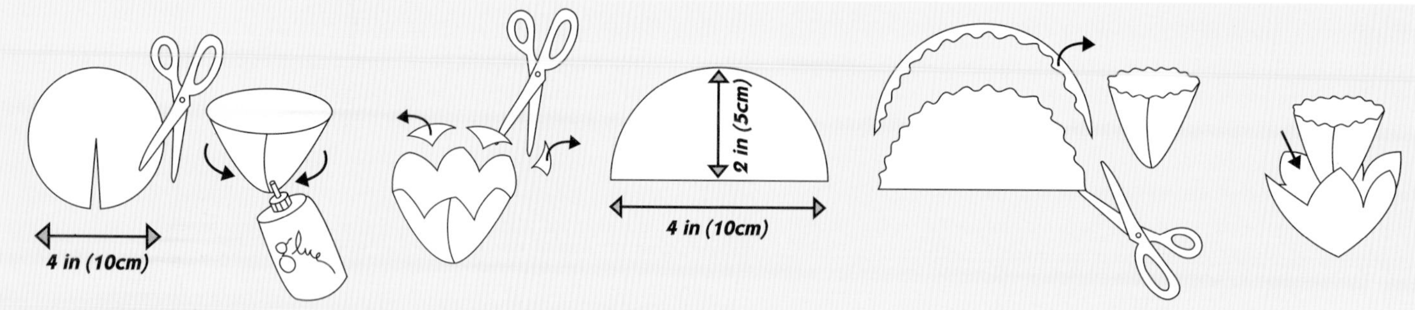

1 For each daffodil, cut out a circle of white construction paper, as shown. Make a cut from the edge of the circle to the center. Overlap the edges and glue in place to make a cone.

2 Cut triangles out of the edge of the cone leaving 6 petal shapes, as shown.

3 Cut out a half circle of yellow construction paper, as shown.

4 Cut a rippled edge.

5 Roll into a cone and glue in place, as shown.

6 Put a drop of glue in the center of the white cone, and press the tip of the yellow cone into the glue. Set aside.

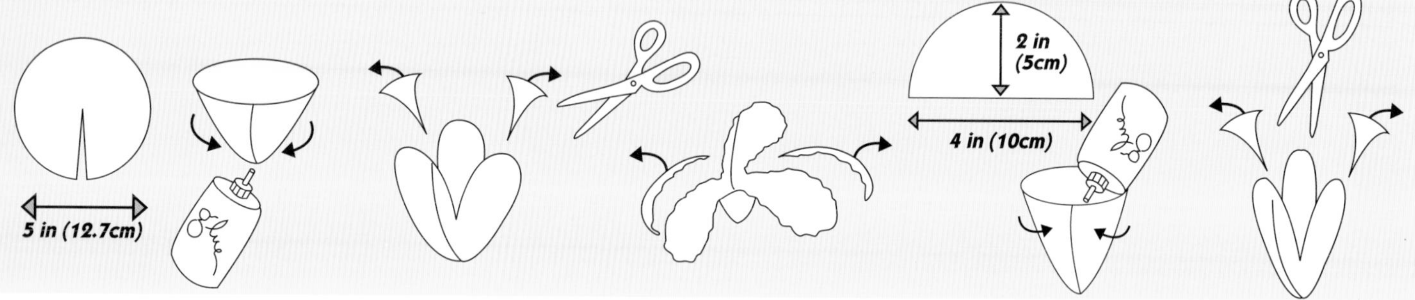

1 For each iris, cut a circle of purple or blue construction paper, as shown. Make a cut from the edge to the center. Overlap the edges and glue in place to make a cone.

2 Cut out 3 wedges from the cone, leaving 3 petals. Iris petals are wide at the tip and narrow at the bottom, as shown.

3 Bend the petals back slightly, and cut a rippled edge on petals.

4 Cut a half circle of purple or blue construction paper 4 in x 2 in (10cm x 5cm). Roll into a cone and glue.

5 Cut wedges out of this cone to leave 3 petals, as shown.

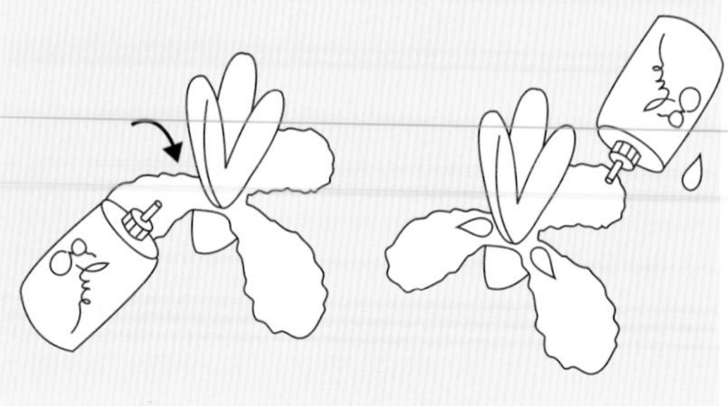

6 Put a drop of glue in the center of the first cone, and press second cone into glue.

7 Cut 3 small teardrop shapes from yellow construction paper. Glue one to each rippled petal. Set aside.

1 For each tulip, cut a circle from red construction paper, as shown. Make a cut from the edge to the center. Overlap the edges to form a cone and glue.

2 Cut triangle shapes from the edges of the cone, leaving petals, as shown. Set aside.

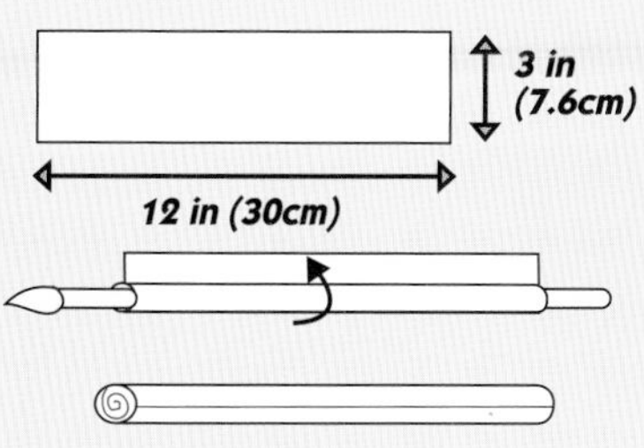

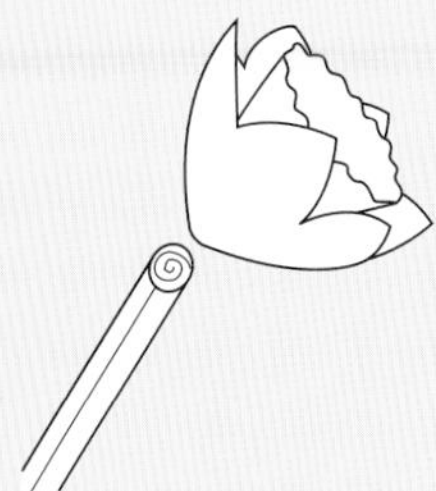

Stems for flowers
1 Cut a piece of green construction paper, as shown. Roll paper from the long side around a paint brush handle. Rremove brush and glue edge down.

2 Make one stem for each flower and glue on flower head, as shown.
3 Cover small can with scraps of construction paper. Glue on. Place flowers in this vase.

Hair Clips

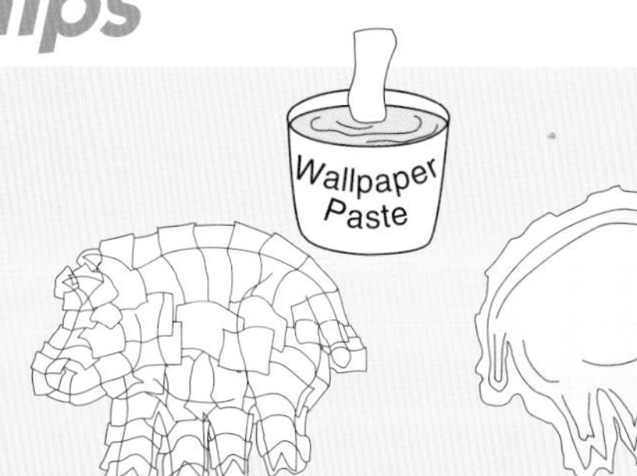

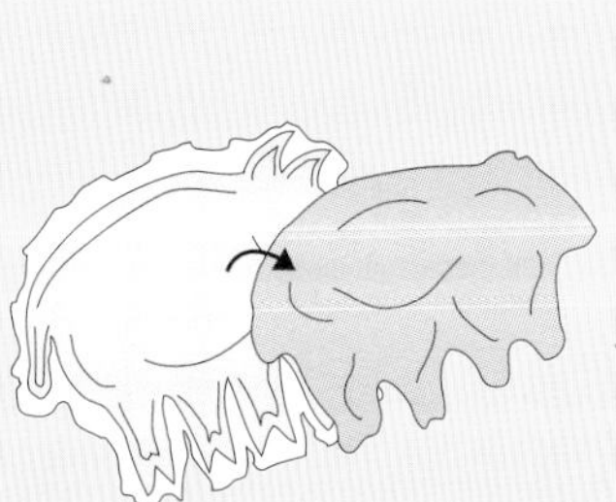

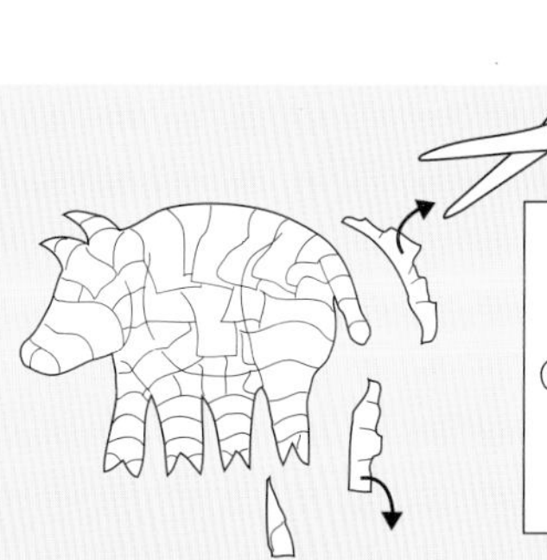

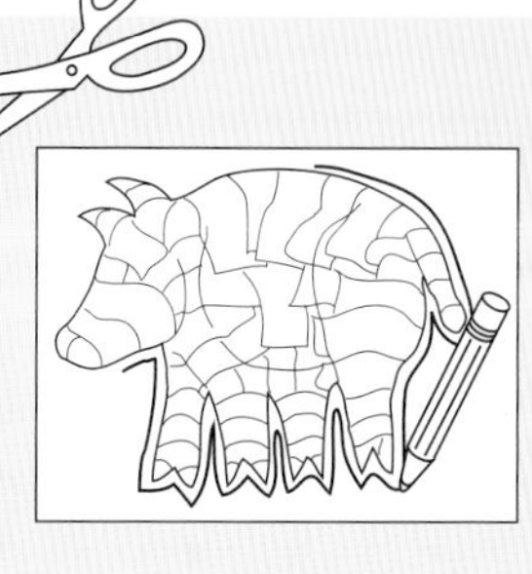

1 To make a pig hair clip, form a pig shape out of plasticine. Make the back of the shape flat.
2 Cover top of plasticine with small pieces of newspaper dipped in wallpaper paste. Set aside to dry.
3 When dry, turn shape over, and pull the plasticine out of the back, leaving the hollow paper shape.
4 Trim edges of shape.
5 Set pig shape on thin card-board and trace around it.

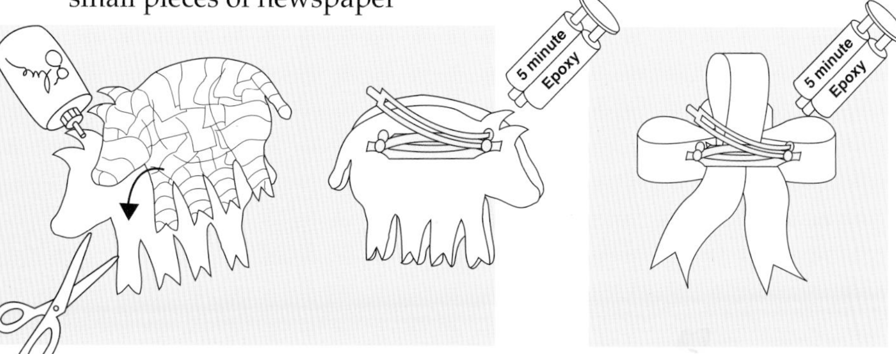

6 Cut out cardboard shape and glue it to the back of the pig shape. Paint and shellac.
7 Epoxy a purchased hair clip to back cardboard.

1 To make paper bow hair clip, make paper bow on p66.
2 Epoxy a purchased hair clip to the back.

Egg Tree & Blown Eggs

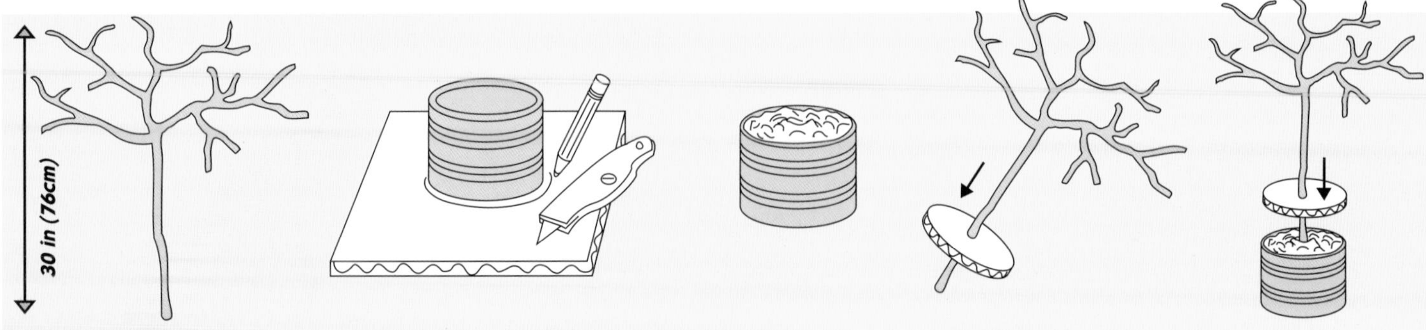

1 Cut a branch about 30 in (76cm) high from a tree. Choose one with spreading branches. Remove leaves. Set aside.
2 Turn an empty tin can upside down on a piece of smooth heavy cardboard. Trace around can, and cut out the circle.
3 Fill can with gravel or sand.
4 Poke a hole through the center of the cardboard and push the stem through the hole, as shown.
5 Push the end of the branch into the gravel, down to the bottom of the can. Slide cardboard circle down the stem and onto the can.
6 Tape circle to the can. Secure the stem in place with tape.

7 Paint the entire branch white and gold. Allow to dry.
8 Cut 3 pieces of different colored tissue paper in dimensions shown.
9 Lay the pieces one on top of another, and place can in the center.
10 Bring paper up and around can, tie in place with a ribbon. Tie in a bow.
11 To empty eggs, carefully scratch an X on one end of egg with a darning needle.
12 Poke the needle through the center of the X.
13 Carefully chip a hole in the end of the egg. Turn egg around and make a hole in the other end in the same way.

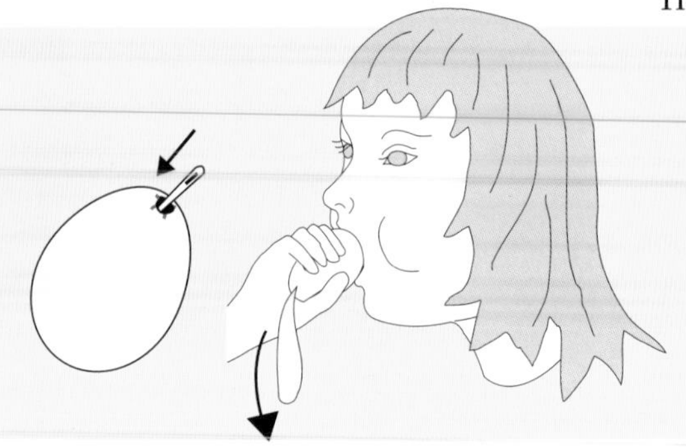

14 Push needle into the egg to break the yolk. Remove needle.
15 Place your lips around one end of egg, making a tight seal, and blow egg contents into a bowl. When eggshell is empty hold it under the tap and allow some water to run into the shell. Shake water around in the shell and then blow the water out.

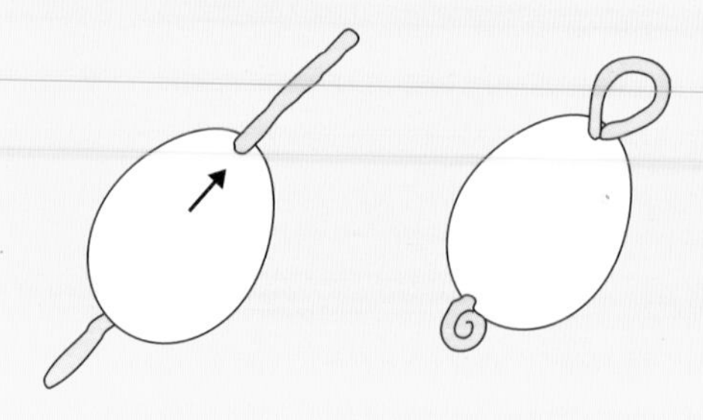

16 To make a hook for hanging, push a chenille stem through one end of the egg and out the other end.

17 Make a loop in chenille stem at one end. Pull loop tight against bottom of egg. Make a loop or hook out of the chenille stem sticking out the other end of egg.

18 Paint eggshell with water-based paints. Glue on ribbon, chenille stems, tissue paper, or wrapping paper. Hang decorated eggshell on tree.

Bunny Bank

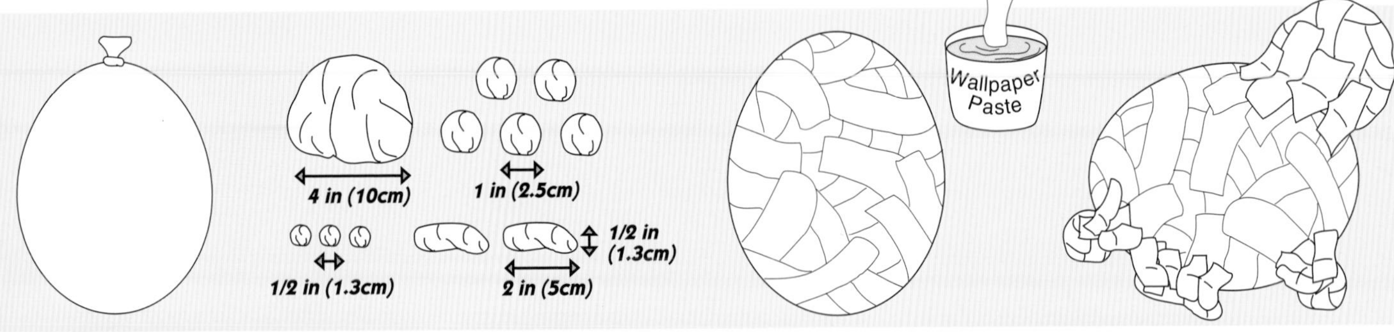

1 Blow up a round balloon and tie end. Set aside.

2 To make bunny feet and head, crumple up sheets of newspaper. Tape loose edges to hold the shape. Make as many balls as shown in the dimensions given above.

3 Cover balloon with strips of newspaper dipped in wallpaper paste. Cover with 5 to 6 layers of paper strips.

4 Place the paper balls in position one at a time for feet, tail, and head covering with strips of newspaper and wall-paper paste. Extend strips over paper balls and onto the body to hold in place.

1/2 in (1.3cm)

2 in (5cm)

5 When head is secure on the body, add cheeks, eyes, and nose in the same way.

6 Cut out ears from thin card-board (cereal box) and attach to the head with more newspaper strips dipped in wallpaper paste. Set aside to dry in a warm place for 2 to 3 days.

7 When hard, turn rabbit up-side down. Draw a rectangle on the stomach, as shown. With a utility knife carefully cut out the rectangle. Remove the balloon.

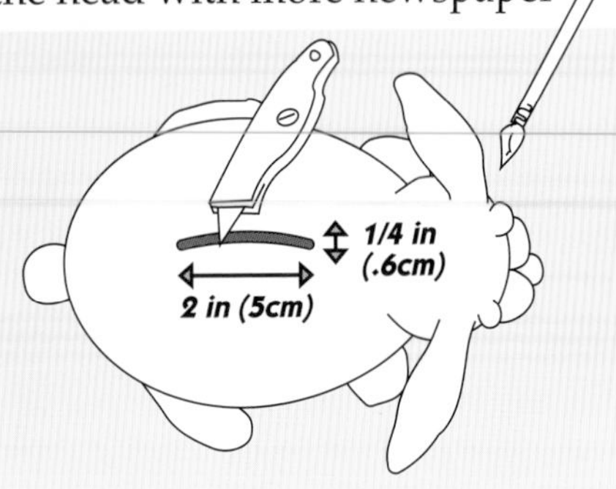

8 Turn the rabbit right side up. With knife, carefully cut out slot indicated in rabbit's back. Paint and shellac. Cover hole in the bottom of the bank with tape.

Bracelets—Rope Bracelet

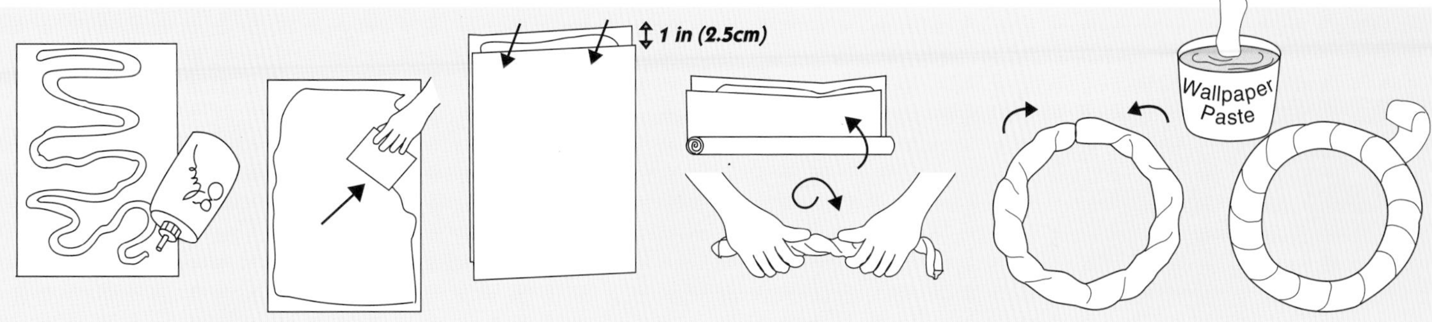

1 Drizzle glue over a single sheet of newspaper.
2 Spread glue to cover the entire sheet.
3 Place another single sheet of newspaper on top of glue. Leave 1 in (2.5cm) at top of glued sheet uncovered.
4 Roll up into a tight tube, as shown. The glued strip at the top will hold the edge down.
5 Twist the tube into a rope.
6 Shape rope into a bracelet. Cut off excess. Tape ends together.
7 Wrap bracelet with pieces of newspaper dipped in wallpaper paste, as shown. Allow to dry. Paint and shellac.

Narrow Bracelet

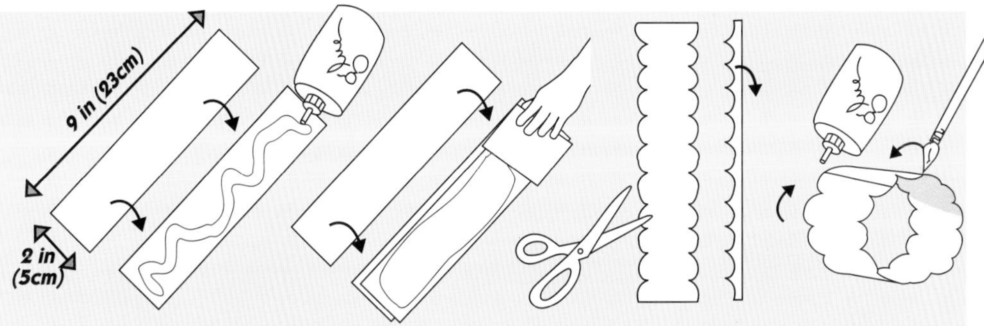

1 Cut 3 pieces of newspaper in the dimensions given.
2 Spread one piece with glue and place other piece on top of glue. Smooth out. Repeat with third piece of newspaper to make one strip 3 layers thick.
3 Cut a scalloped edge along both long sides.
4 Overlap the 2 short ends. Glue together. Paint and shellac.

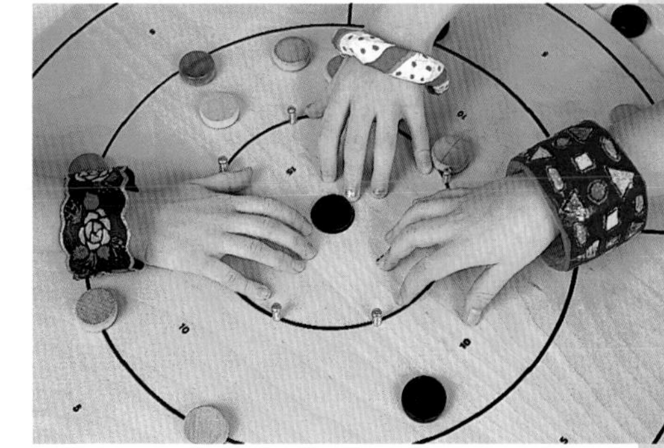

Wide Bracelet

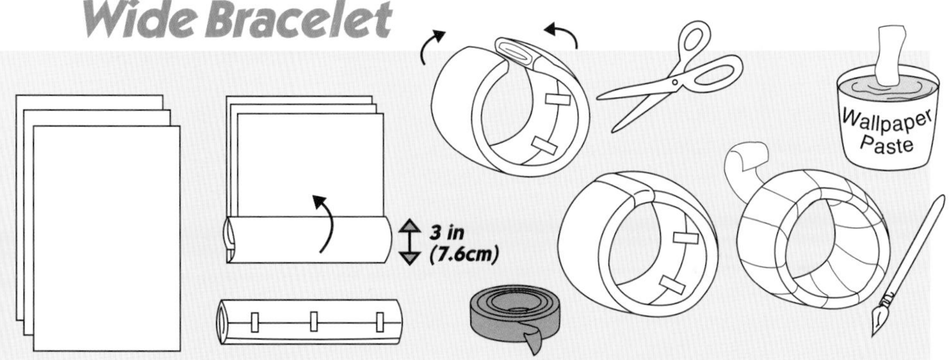

1 Place 3 single sheets of newspaper one on top of another.
2 Starting at short end, fold the sheets together, over and over, as shown. Tape free ends in place.
3 Bring short ends together, as shown, to make a bracelet.
4 Cut off excess and firmly tape ends together.
5 Wrap bracelet with strips of newspaper dipped in wallpaper paste. Allow to dry. Paint and shellac.

Papier-Mâché Pulp Earrings

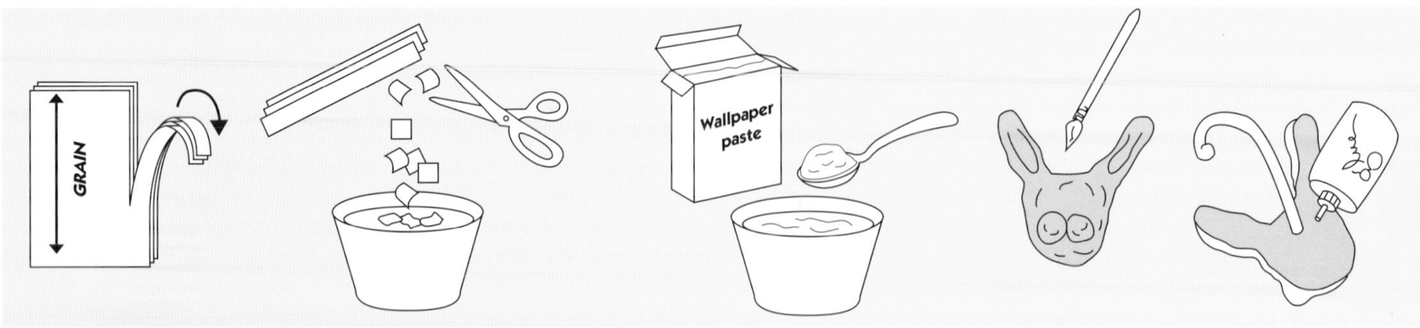

1 **To make papier-mâché pulp** stack several sheets of newspaper and tear along grain into 1/2 in (1.3cm) strips.

2 Use scissors to cut strips into 1/2 in (1.3cm) pieces. Place the small pieces of paper in a bucket and add enough water to cover. Soak for several hours (overnight).

3 Add powdered wallpaper paste to the mixture and combine. Add more water or more paper to adjust the consistency. It should resemble clay or cookie dough.

4 Mold pulp into bunny head, egg, peacock, or fish shapes. When dry, paint and shellac.

5 Glue a 4 in (10cm) piece of chenille stem to the back of the earring. Bend stem into a loop, as shown, and hang over the top of the ear.

Spider Web Door

1 Cut newspaper in strips 1/2 in (1.3cm) wide. Make catstairs from the strips (p66). You will need 40 to 50 feet (12 to 15m) of catstairs for this project.

2 Tape one end of catstairs to the top of the door, let it hang down to the bottom. Cut off excess. Tape this end to the bottom of the door, as shown.

3 Glue both cut ends together.

4 Starting at a top corner, attach another length of catstairs to the door and bring it down to the opposite bottom corner, as shown. Cut off excess and tape in place. Re-glue cut ends as before.

5 Attach another length in the opposite direction, taping in place.

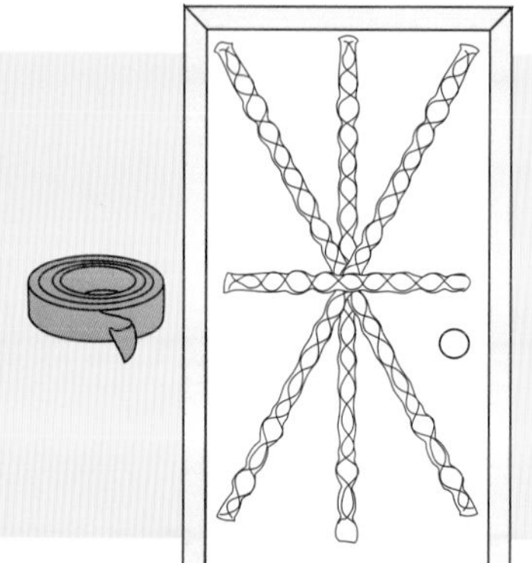

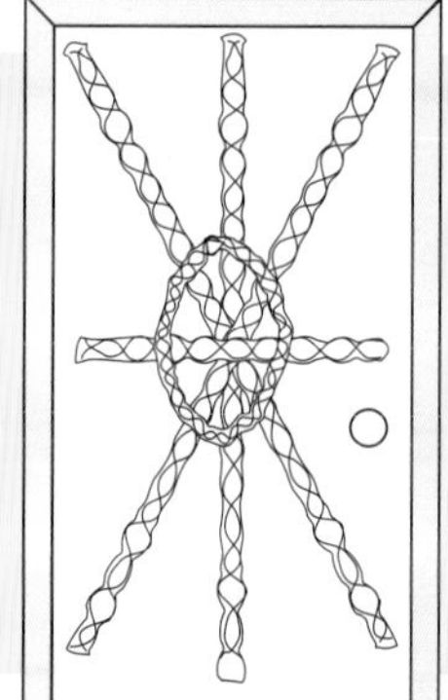

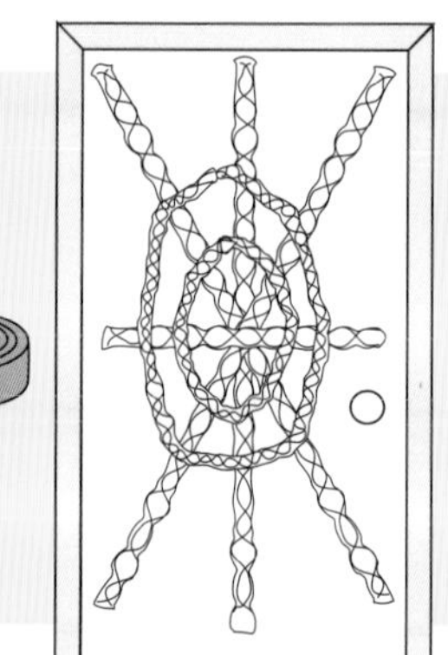

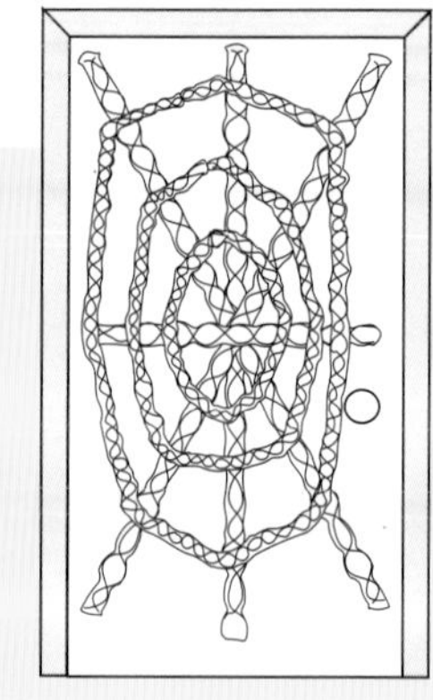

6 Attach a short strip sideways, across the middle.

7 Starting in the center of web, make a small catstair circle. Tape in place where it crosses each of the straight lines of catstairs, as shown.

8 Start again farther from the center and make another circle in the same way.

9 Make a third circle around the second circle, as shown.

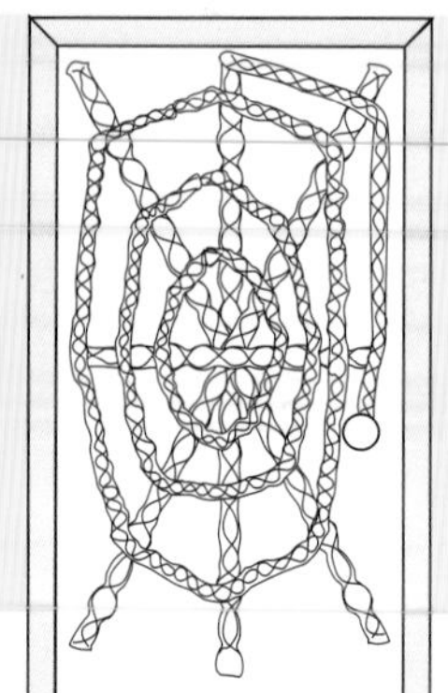

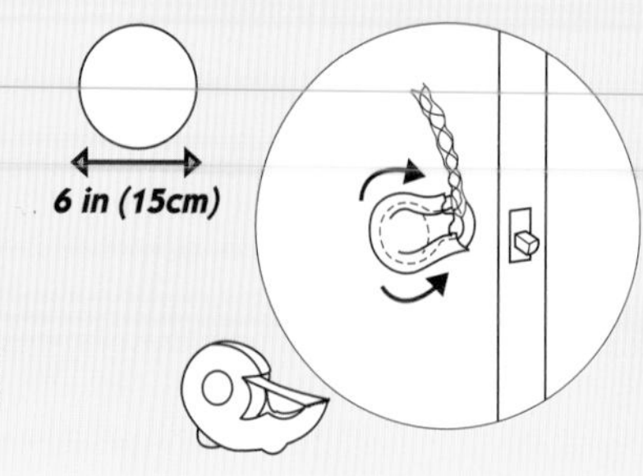

10 Attach another length of catstairs from the top of the web down to the doorknob.

11 Cut a circle of newspaper 6 in (15cm) in diameter. Fold it over the doorknob and tape in place at the base of the knob.

12 Glue or tape chenille stems to the underside of the knob for spider legs.

13 Glue eyes on the top of the paper-covered spider knob.

Halloween Wreath

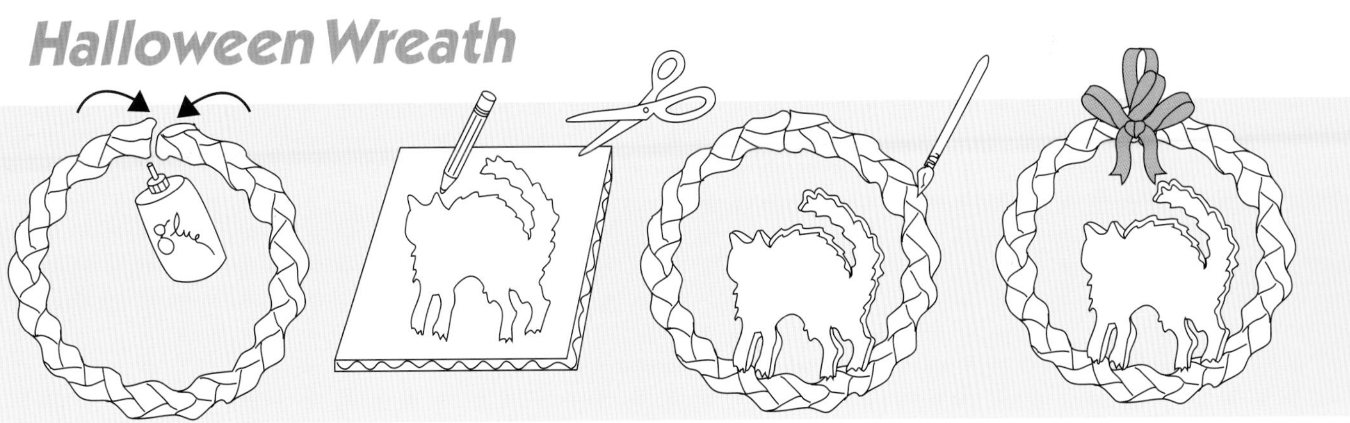

1 Make 9 newspaper ropes and braid them together, see p16.
2 Glue ends together to form a circle.
3 Lay wreath flat for a day or two to dry and stiffen.
4 Draw a cat shape on smooth cardboard to fit inside the wreath. Use pattern on p40 as a guide.
5 Cut out and glue in the center of the wreath. Paint the wreath and the cat. Shellac.
6 Tie a ribbon around the top and hang the wreath.

Skeleton Mobile

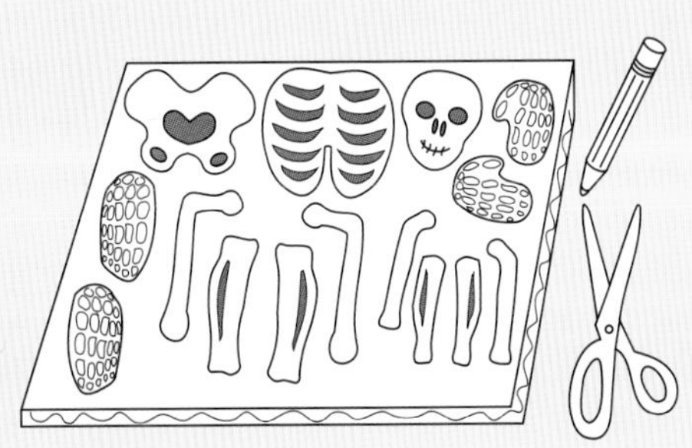

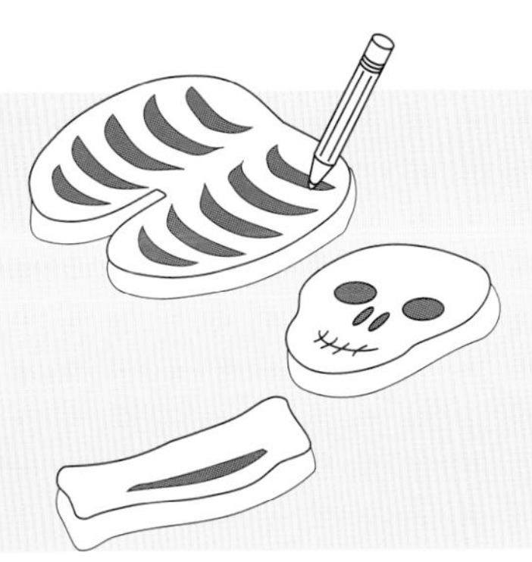

1 From the pattern provided (p40), draw the bone shapes on smooth cardboard. Cut out. Paint white.
2 Draw and fill in the black spaces on the shapes, as indicated on the pattern.

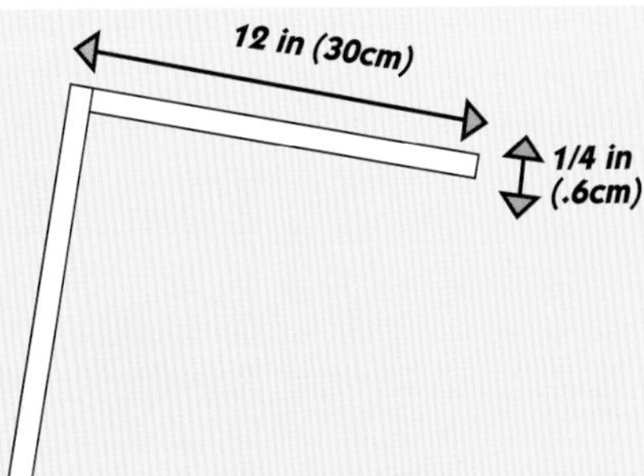

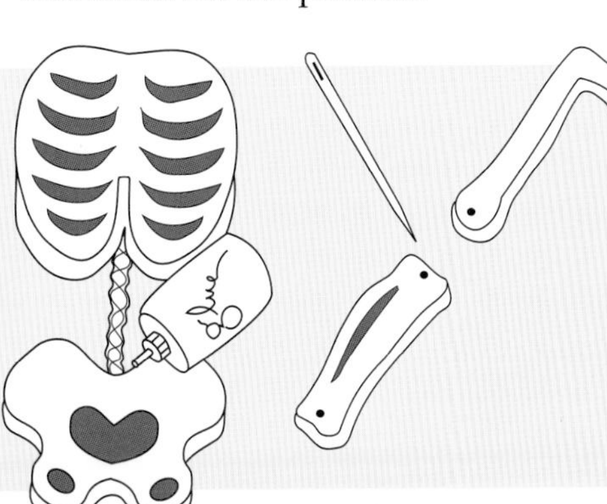

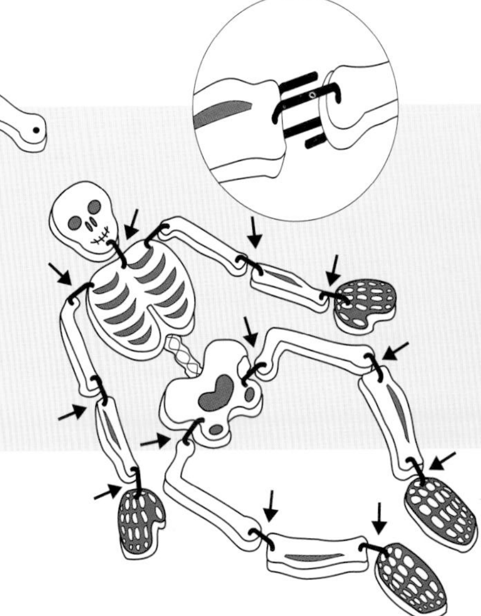

3 Cut out 2 strips of white paper, as shown. Make a catstair (p66).
4 Glue one end of catstair to bottom of rib cage piece, and the other end to top of pelvis piece, as shown.
5 With a darning needle, carefully punch holes in ends of bones as indicated.
6 Hook up bones with paper clips, as shown.

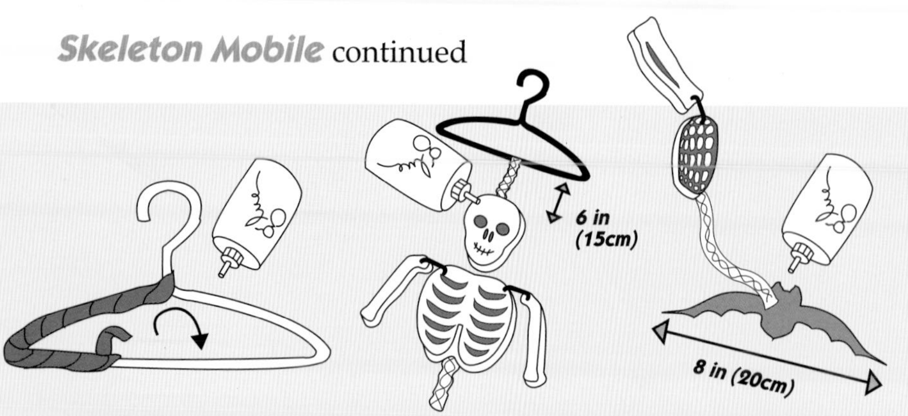

7 Cut strips of black tissue paper and wrap around a coat hanger, completely covering the metal. Glue in place.

8 Lay coat hanger on a work surface, and spread skeleton out beneath it, as shown.

9 Cut many strips of black construction paper 12 in x 1/4 in (30cm x .6cm) and make into catstairs (p66). Make 2 catstairs long enough to reach from coat hanger to legs, 2 catstairs to reach from hanger to elbows, one catstair to connect head to hanger, and one catstair to connect pelvis to coat hanger, see photograph. Glue catstairs in place.

10 Draw a bat on black construction paper in dimensions indicated and cut out. Glue one end of catstair strip to skeleton foot and one end to bat, as shown.

11 Hook coat hanger from ceiling or curtain rod and let skeleton dangle on catstairs in a window.

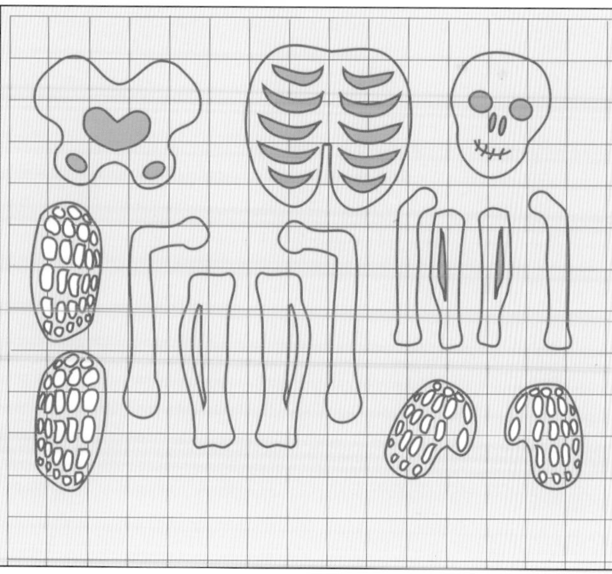

Skeleton Mobile pattern p39

Scale 1 square = 1 in (2.5cm)

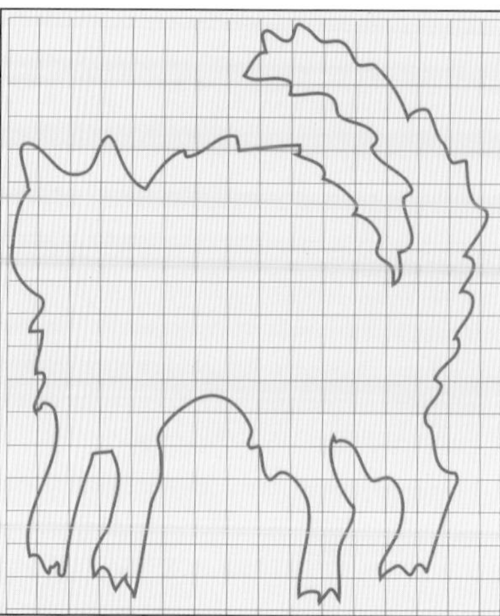

Halloween Wreath cat pattern p39

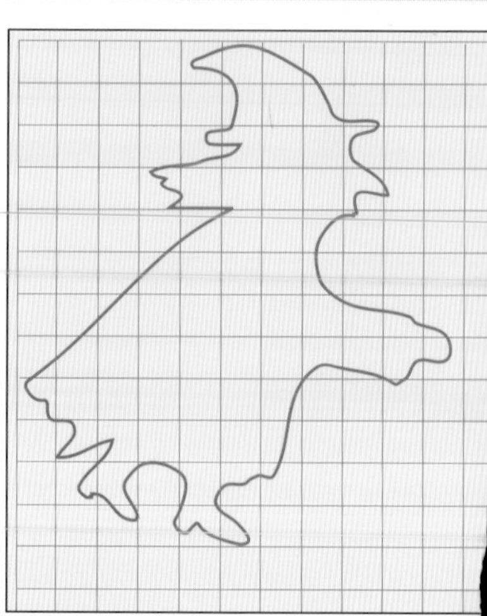

Witch Mobile pattern p41

Witch Mobile

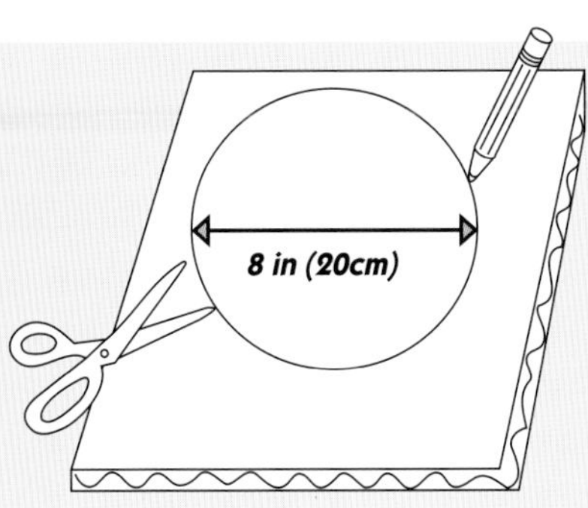

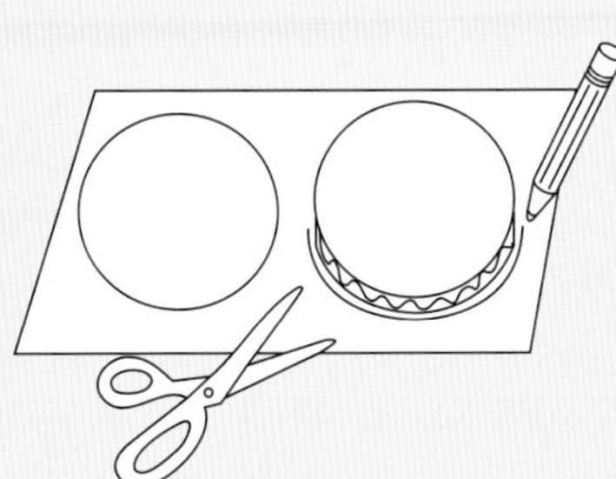

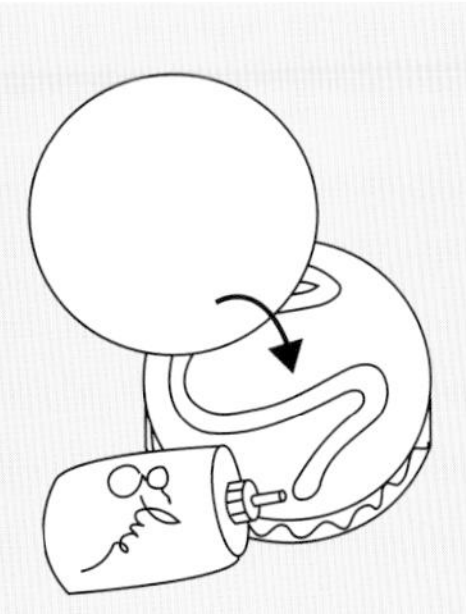

1 Draw a circle on smooth heavy cardboard, as shown, and cut out.
2 Trace around cardboard circle on yellow construction paper. Repeat. Cut out the 2 yellow circles.
3 Glue one paper circle to each side of cardboard circle. Set aside.
4 On smooth cardboard draw a witch, as shown, see pattern p40. Cut out.

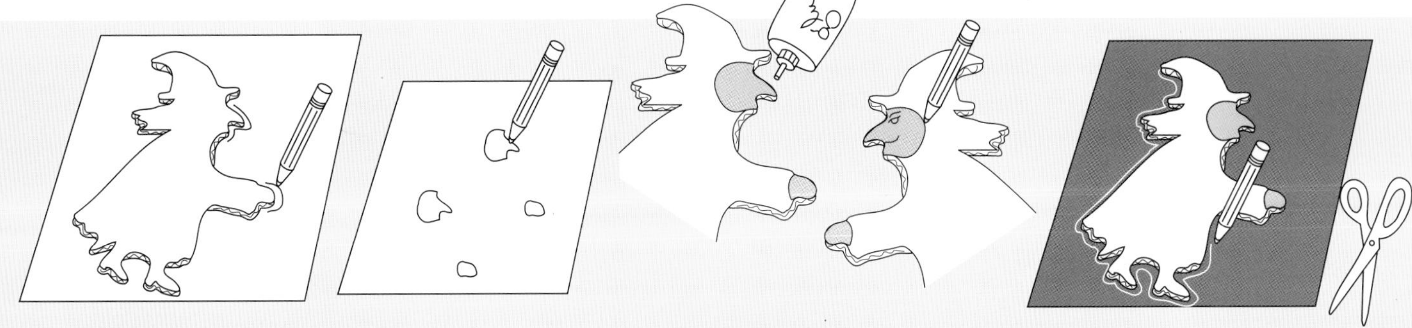

5 Lay cardboard witch on green paper and trace around face and hand. Repeat.
6 Remove cardboard, and draw the inside edge of face and hand, as shown.
7 Cut out and glue in place, one on each side of the cardboard witch.
8 Draw on face with marker.
9 Place cardboard witch on black construction paper and trace around it. Repeat.
10 Remove cardboard, and cut out, omitting face and hand.

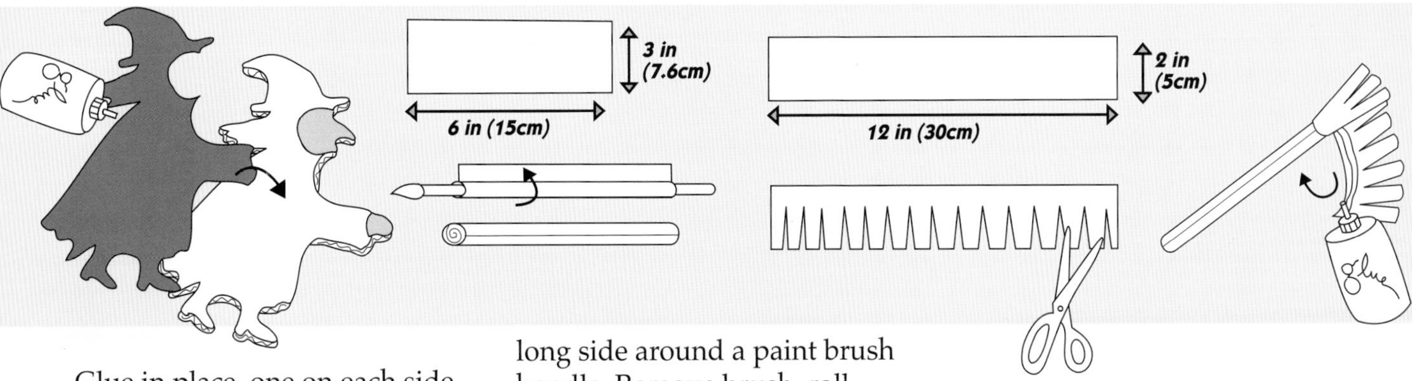

Glue in place, one on each side

11 Make a broom. Cut out a piece of brown construction paper, as shown. Roll up from long side around a paint brush handle. Remove brush, roll again to make a tight tube, as shown. Glue the edge down.
12 Cut a piece of yellow construction paper. Fringe one side with 1 in (2.5cm) cuts.
1… …read glue along uncut side a… …fringe around one end o… …e.

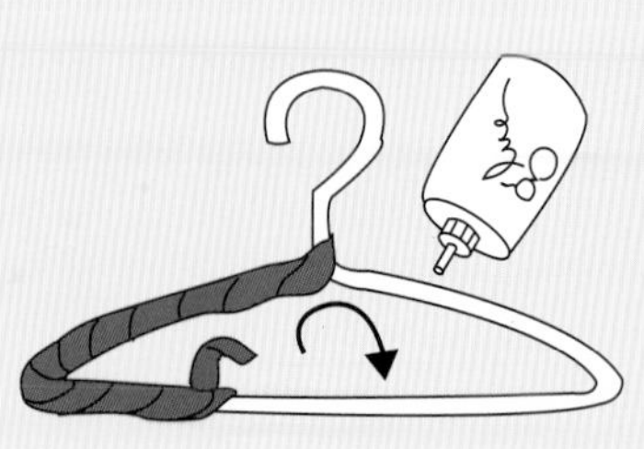

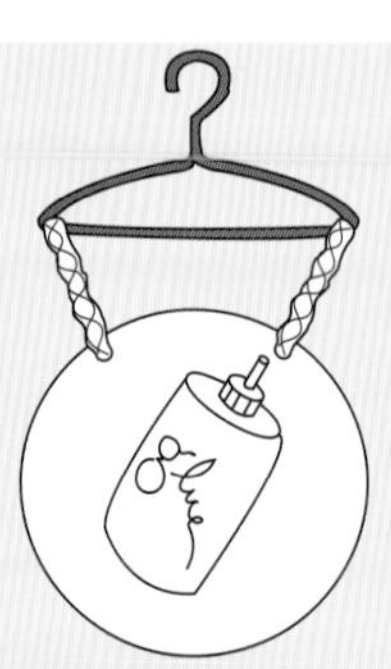

14 Cut strips of black tissue paper and wrap a coat hanger, completely covering metal. Set aside.

15 Cut strips of yellow construction paper 12 in x 1/4 in (30cm x .6cm). Make 3 catstairs 12 in (30cm) long, see p66. Glue one end of catstairs to top of yellow circle and glue other end to coat hanger, as shown.

16 Glue remaining catstair to witch's hat and center of coat hanger.

17 Glue broom in place on top of witch. Cover middle of broom handle with a scrap of black construction paper.

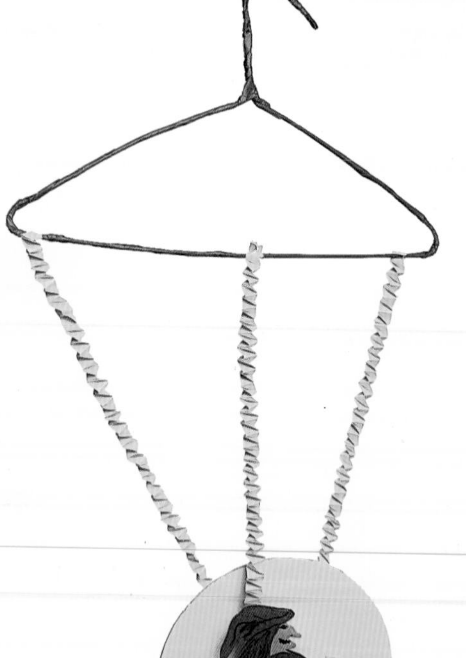

Pumpkin Light

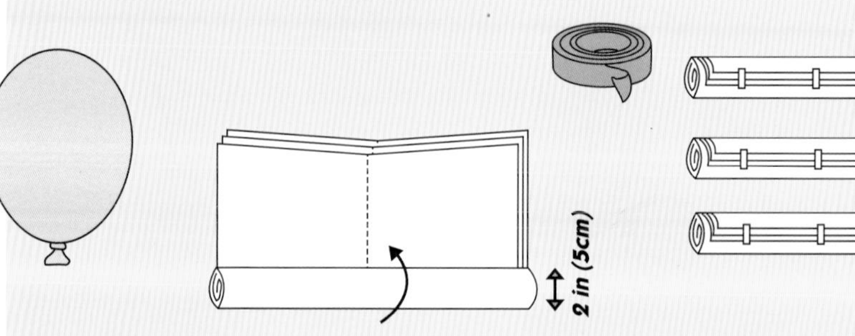

1 Blow up a round balloon and tie end. Set aside.

2 On a flat surface, spread out 3 full-sized sheets of newspaper, one on top of the other. Fold up, over and over, as shown. Tape in place.

3 Make 3 more folded lengths in the same way.

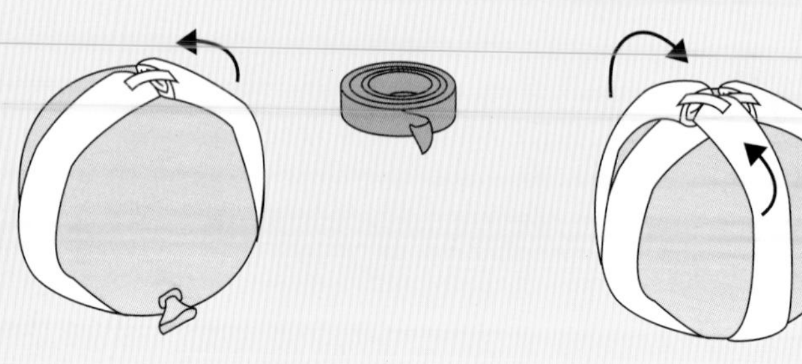

4 Starting at the top of balloon, wrap one folded length of newspaper around balloon. Tape ends together.

5 Starting at the top again, wrap another folded length of newspaper around balloon, crossing first strip, as shown, and tape.

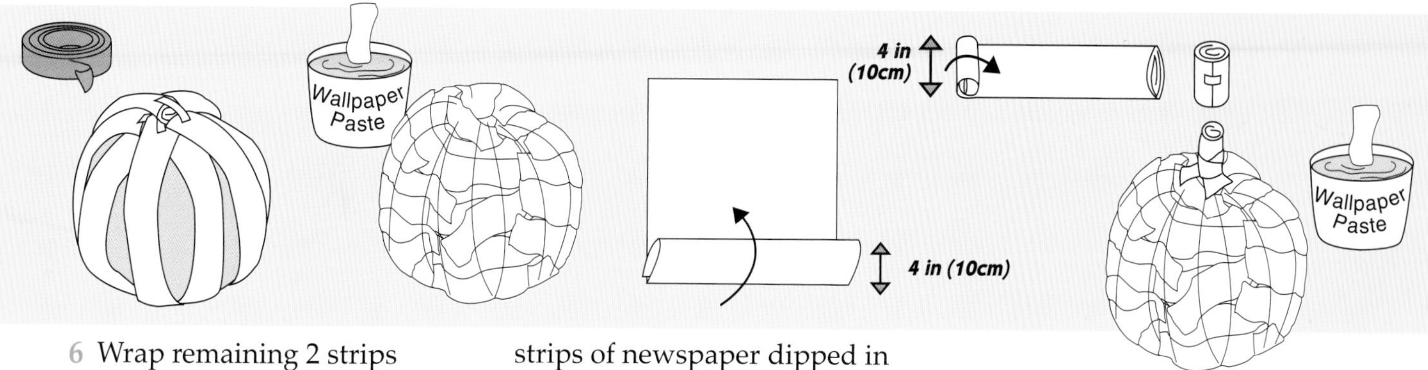

6 Wrap remaining 2 strips around balloon in the same way, filling in between the first strips, as shown.

7 Tear up many strips of newspaper. Cover entire project with strips of newspaper dipped in wallpaper paste. Use at least 5 to 6 layers.

8 Fold up a single sheet of newspaper, as shown.

9 Roll up from short end and tape. This is the stem.

10 Attach to top of pumpkin with more strips of newspaper and wallpaper paste. Set aside to dry.

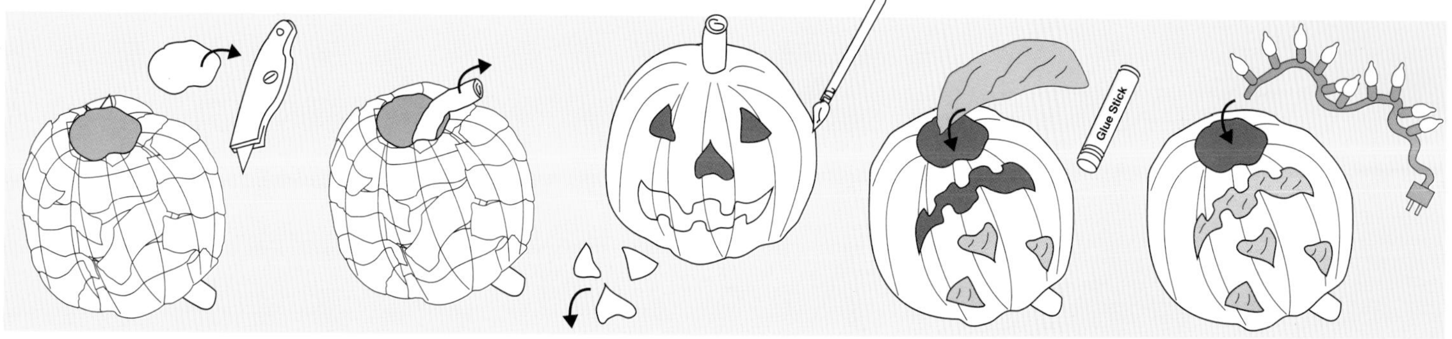

11 On the bottom draw and cut out a circle large enough to fit your hand. Remove the circle, balloon, and folded newspaper lengths, leaving the thin paper shell.

12 Draw eyes, nose, and mouth,as shown. With utility knife, cut out eyes, nose, and mouth. Paint and shellac.

13 Cut pieces of yellow tissue large enough to cover these holes and attach tissue with glue to inside to cover holes in the face.

14 Mini Christmas lights may be placed inside the pumpkin to light it up. Bring cord in through hole in bottom. Do not paint or shellac the tissue.

Note Use mini lights that do not get hot, or use a flashlight. When unattended, pumpkin or skull interior lights should be unplugged.

Skull Light

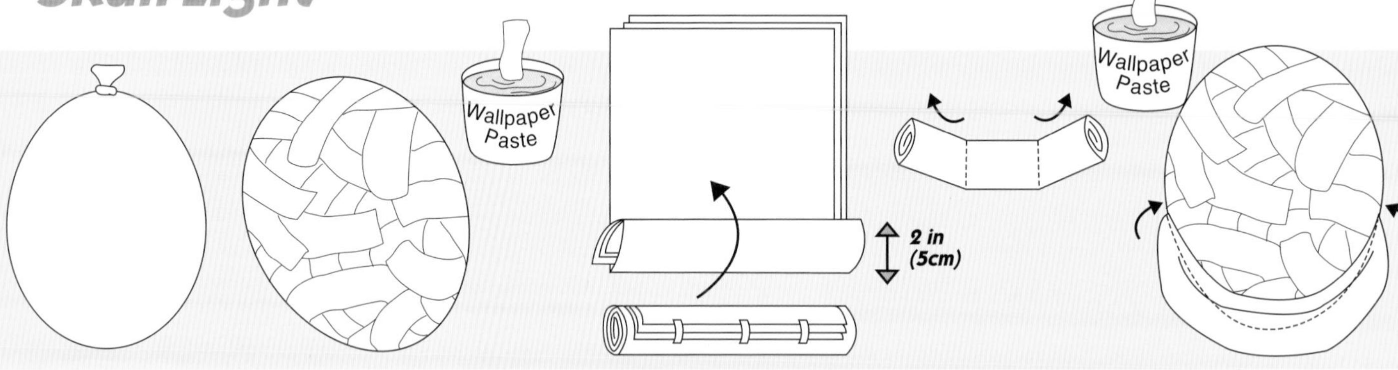

1 Blow up a round balloon and tie end.
2 Cover balloon with strips of newspaper dipped in wallpaper paste.
3 On a flat surface lay 3 single sheets of newspaper one on top of another. Fold up all 3 sheets together, over and over, as shown, starting at the narrow side. Tape.
4 Fold into 3 equal sections, as shown.
5 Attach this folded strip to the balloon along the bottom, one end on each side of the balloon, as shown. Attach with several newspaper strips dipped in wallpaper paste.

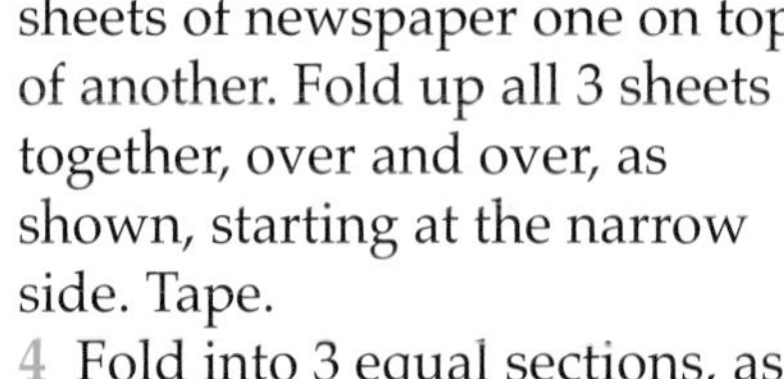

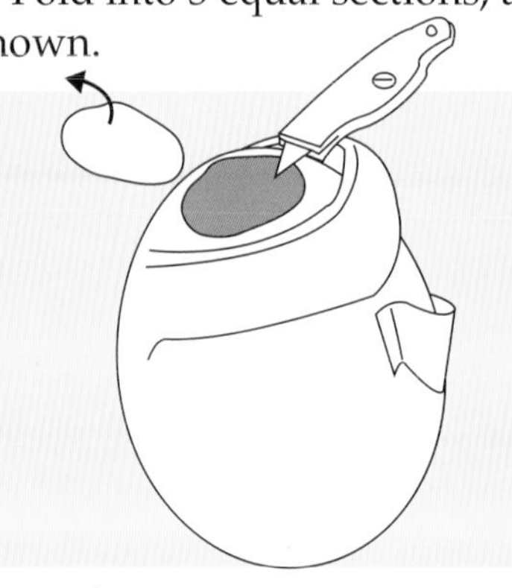

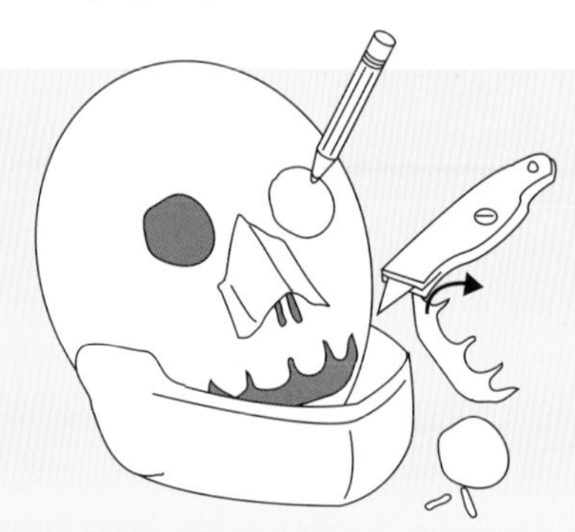

6 Cover folded piece with strips of paper and wallpaper paste as well. This forms the jawbone. Cut a piece of paper, as shown. Fold in half and glue to face for a nose.
7 On the bottom draw a circle large enough to fit your hand. With a utility knife, carefully cut out the circle. Remove the circle and the balloon, leaving the thin paper shell.
8 Draw eye and nose holes on the skull. Draw teeth on balloon shape just above the jawbone. Carefully cut out with a utility knife.

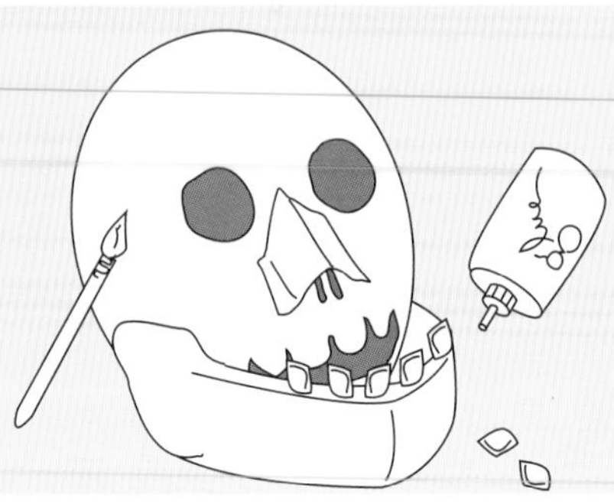

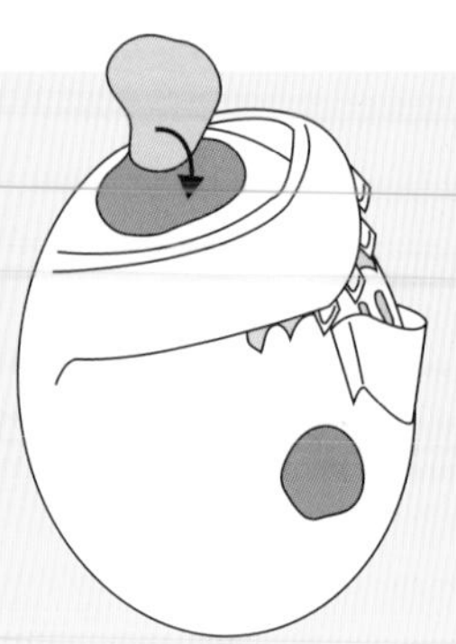

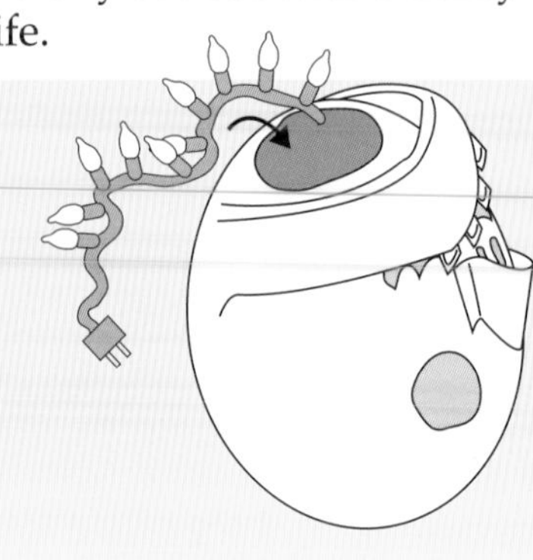

9 From cut-out scraps, cut out teeth and glue them to the top edge of the jaw bone, as shown. Paint the skull white and shellac.
10 If desired, glue or tape blue tissue paper to inside of skull to cover holes in face.
11 Place mini Christmas lights that do not get hot or a flashlight inside the skull through the bottom circle to light it.

Fishing for Apples Game

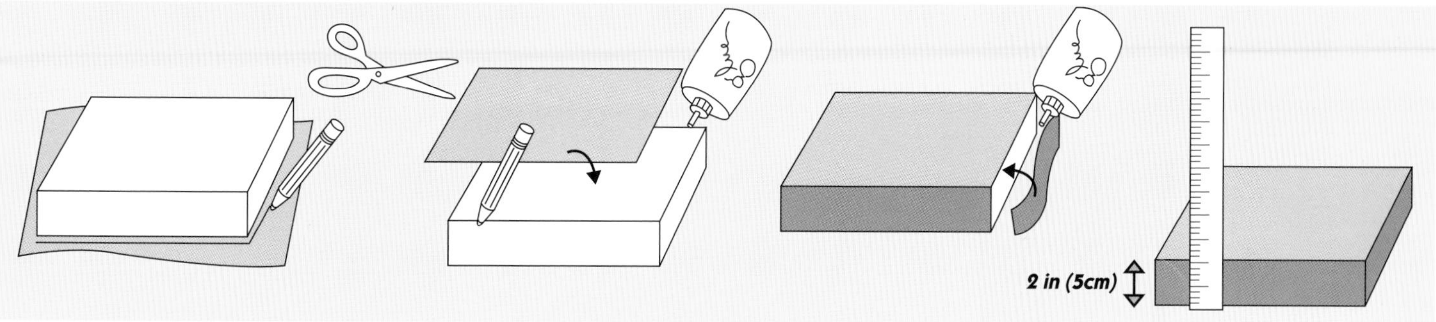

1 Set a cereal box on colored construction paper and trace around the bottom.

2 Cut out the shape and glue to the box.

3 Cover all 6 sides of the box this way.

4 Measure the thickness of the box.

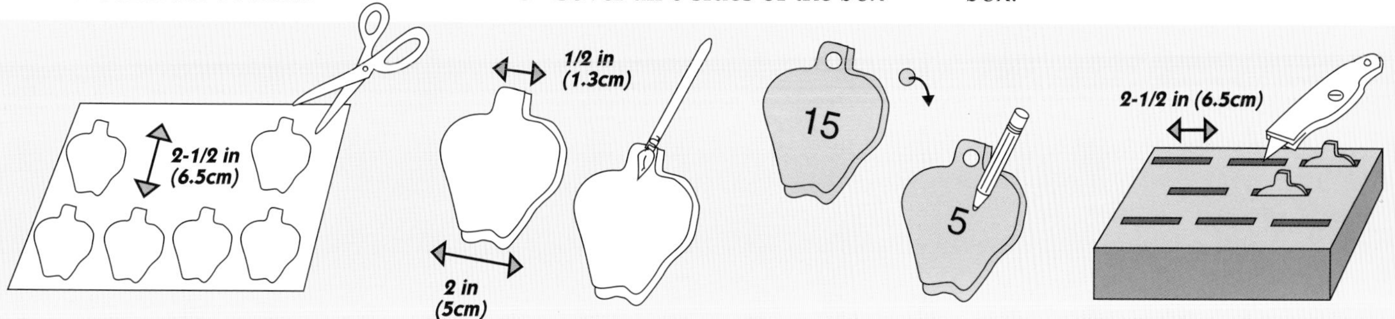

5 On smooth, thin cardboard (another cereal box), draw apple shapes that are 1/2 in (1.3cm) taller than the thickness of the box.

6 Cut out. Paint apples red with a brown stem. (If apples curl as they dry, lay them under a board overnight with a weight on top to flatten them.)

7 With a single-hole punch, make holes in the middle of the apple stems. Mark apples with different point values—5, 10, 15 points.

8 On one side of the box use a utility knife to cut narrow slits, as shown.

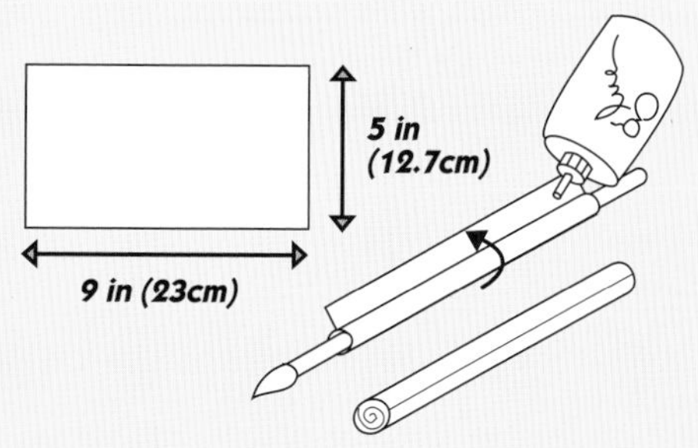

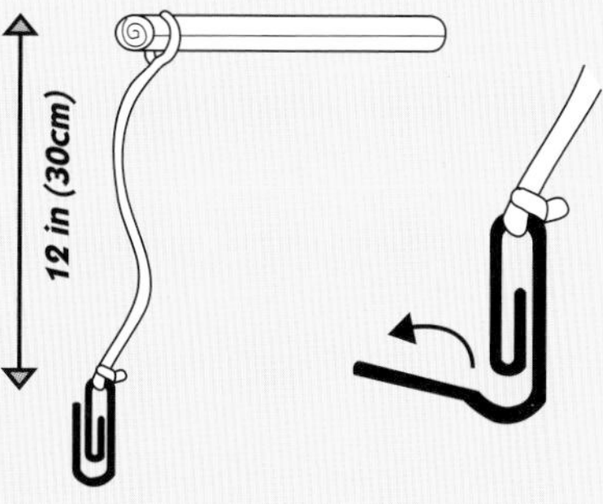

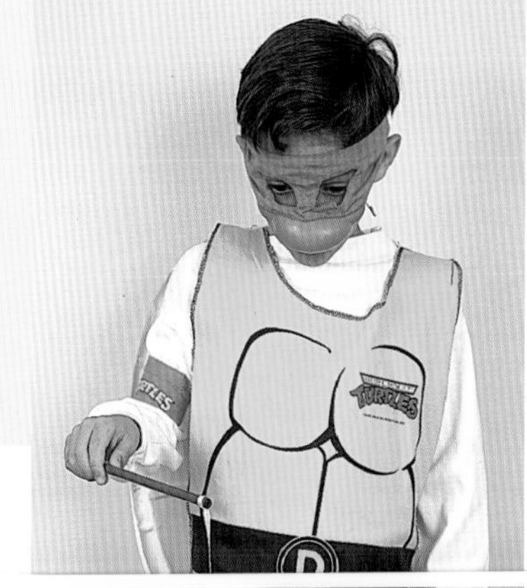

9 Roll up a piece of paper, as shown, into a tight tube 9 in (23cm) long. Glue edge down.

10 Cut a piece of string, as shown. Tie one end to the paper tube. Tie the other end to a paper clip.

11 Unbend one section of the paper clip to make a hook.

To play the game, put the apples in the slots in the box, numbers at the back. Adjust the angle of the hook so that it will hook onto the apple stem. Each player takes 3 turns. Add up each score. The most number of points wins.

Catch-a-Penny Hippo Game

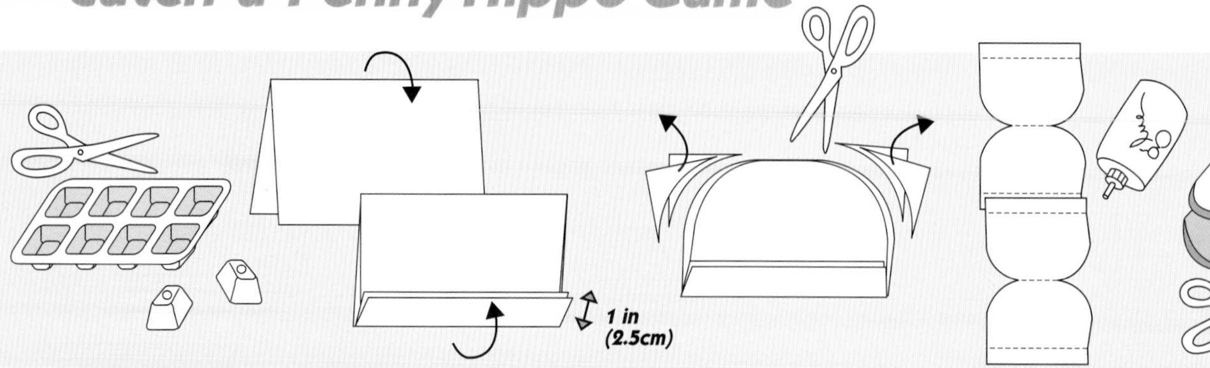

1 Cut out 15 cups from egg cartons. Paint the outside of the cups white and set aside.
2 Fold a piece of pink construction paper in half, short ends together.

3 Fold over 1 in (2.5cm) of the open sides.
4 Round off corners of folded side with scissors, as shown. Repeat with another piece of pink construction paper.

5 Unfold both pieces. Overlap folded ends of each piece of paper, as shown. Glue together.
6 Fold each sheet in half again, as before. Cut off the extra 1 in (2.5cm) folded end.

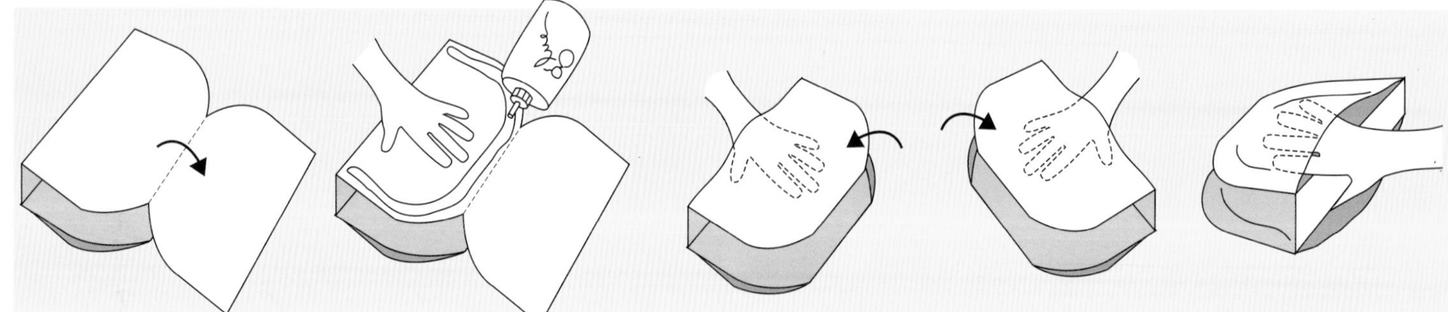

7 Unfold the top sheet.
8 Spread glue around the edges of this sheet and place hand flat on project, as shown.

9 Fold other half of top sheet, press glued edges, making a pocket for your hand.
10 Turn project over, and glue other layer of paper together in the same way, making 2 pockets that open in the middle, like a mouth.

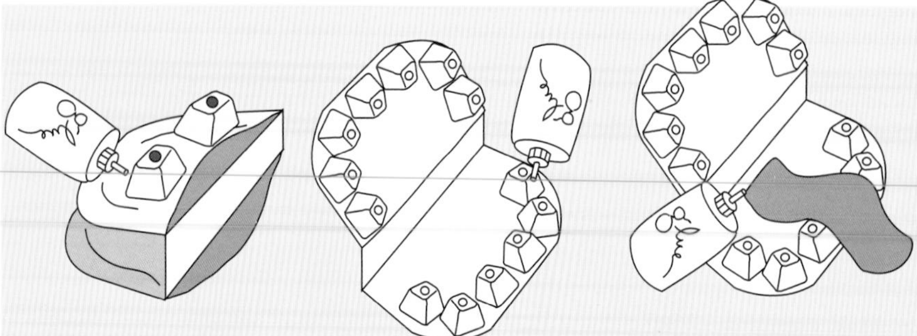

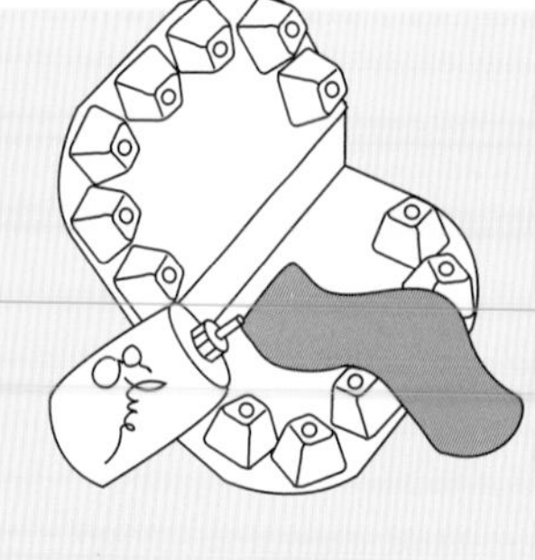

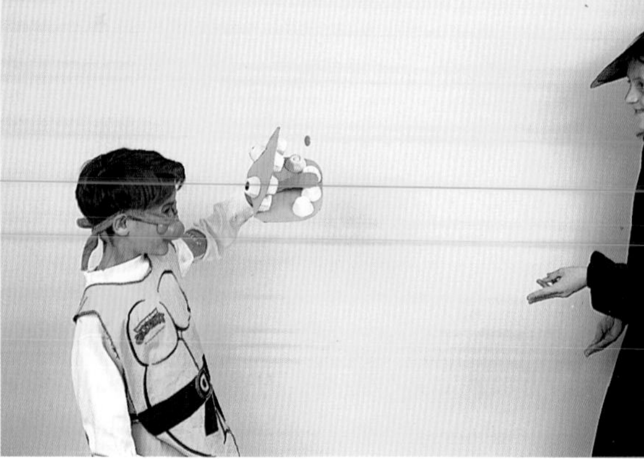

11 Glue 2 white egg cups to top of mouth for eyes. Add black pupils.
12 Glue remaining egg cups inside mouth for teeth. On bottom section of mouth leave spaces at the very back of mouth to allow it to close, as shown.

13 Add a red paper tongue to the bottom half of mouth.

To play the game, one player holds hippo mouth and tries to catch pennies thrown by one or more tossers. Player catching pennies keeps coins caught in hippo's mouth.

Place Cards

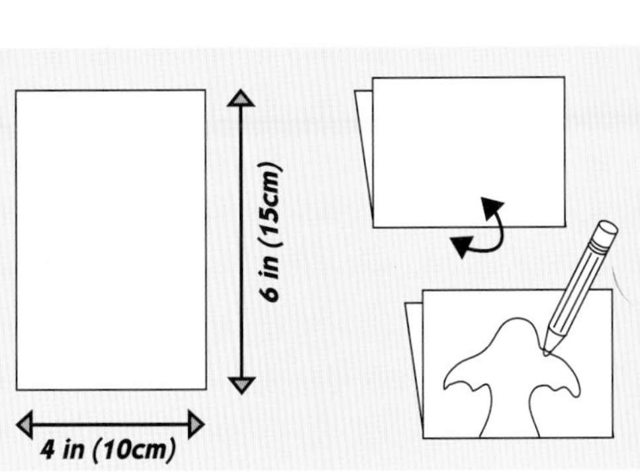

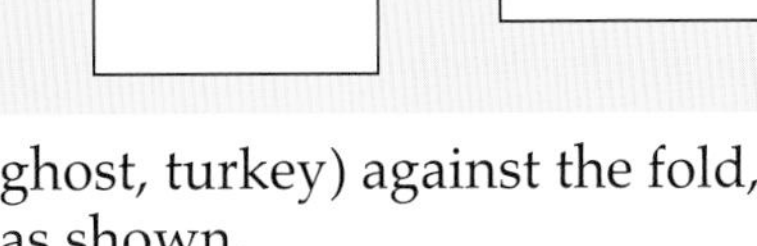

1 Cut pieces of colored construction paper, as shown.
2 Fold in half, short ends together.
3 With fold at the bottom, draw a holiday subject (heart, daffodil, ghost, turkey) against the fold, as shown.
4 Unfold. Starting at top edge cut down to and around the drawing. Do not cut along fold!
5 Tape top cut together.
6 Re-fold the card, allowing drawing to stand up, as shown.
7 Write names on bottom half, or draw and cut out letters to glue on the place card.

Place Mats

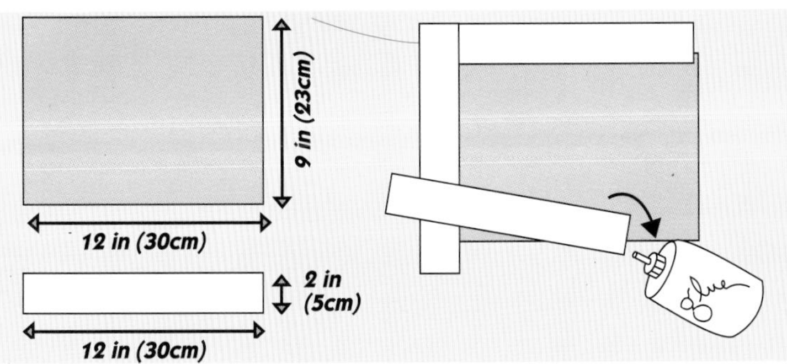

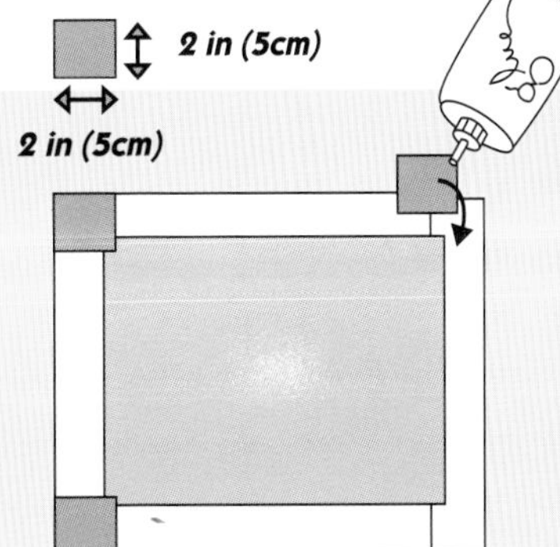

1 Start with a sheet of colored construction paper, as shown. Cut out strips of paper in a contrasting color in dimensions shown and glue around edges.
2 Cut out 4 squares in a third color. Glue one in each corner.
3 Draw and cut out holiday subjects from construction paper. Glue in center of mat. Draw and cut out more decorations from colored paper. Glue around the border.
4 Decorate with crayons and markers.

Haunted House Surprise Box

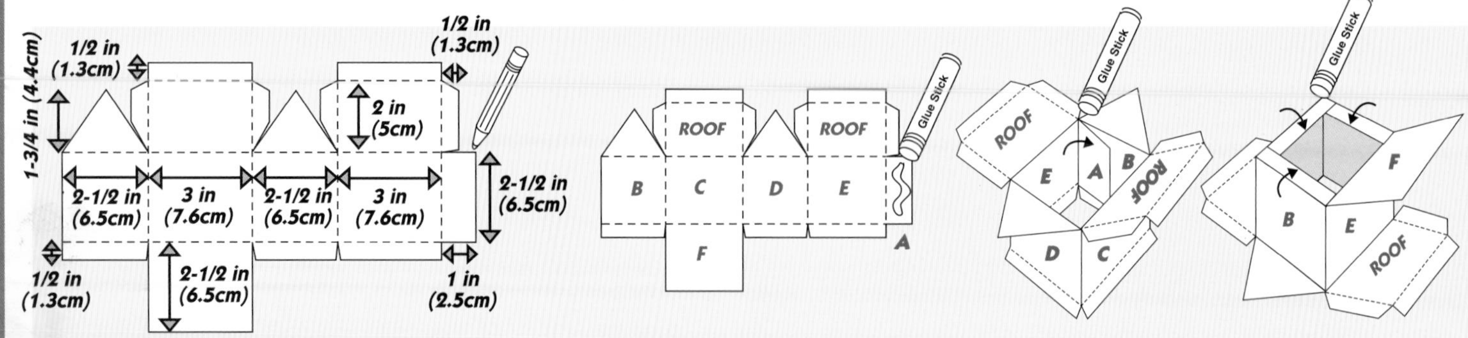

1 On a 9 in x 12 in (23cm x 30cm) piece of black construction paper measure and draw out house pattern, as shown. Use a light colored pencil crayon to make the marks. Cut out. Make cuts along solid lines and folds along dotted lines.

2 When all dotted lines have been creased, spread glue on end flap A.

3 Bring flap A to opposite end, forming a rectangle. Glue flap A to inside of B.

4 Turn house upside down. Fold 3 flaps inward and spread glue stick on, as shown.

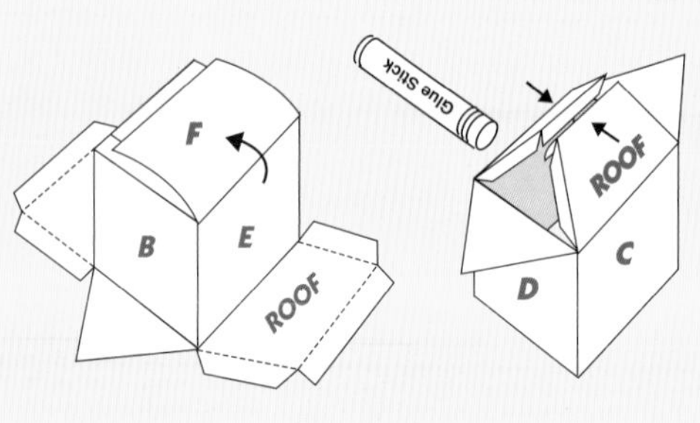

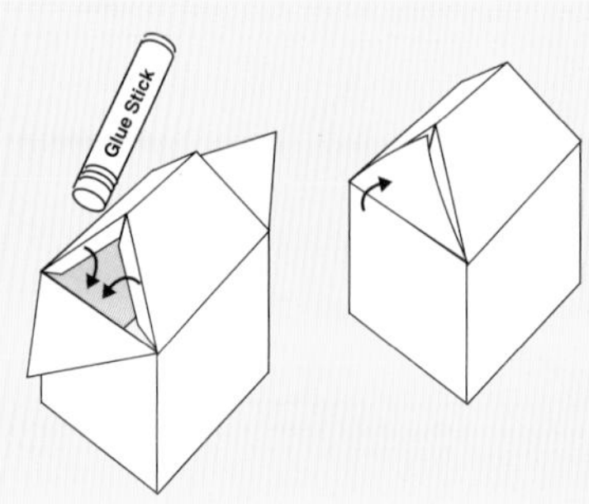

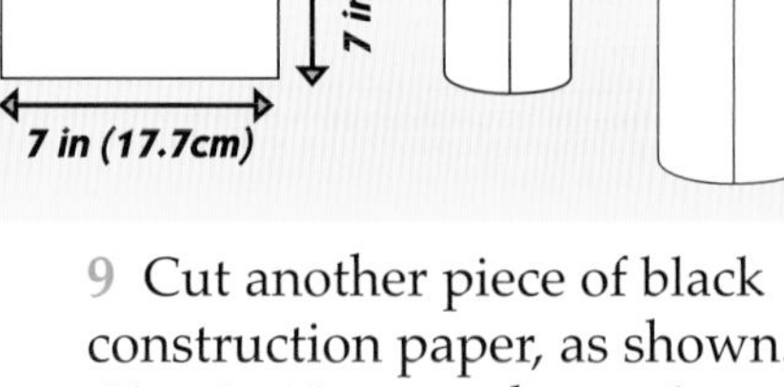

5 Fold F onto glued flaps.

6 Turn right side up. Bend ROOF flaps inward. Put in party surprises. Glue flaps together at top, as shown.

7 Spread glue on ROOF flap sides, as shown.

8 Press triangle-shaped side pieces onto glued flaps.

9 Cut another piece of black construction paper, as shown. Glue 2 sides together to form a cylinder.

10 Make cuts around one end.

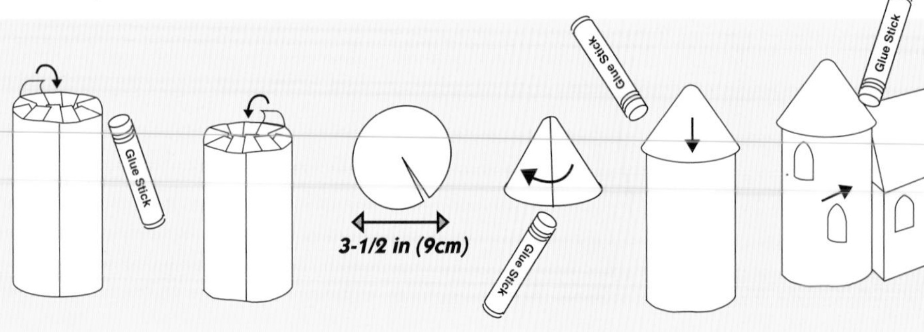

11 Fold flaps inward. Glue on top of each other to close end.

12 Turn over and close other end in the same way.

13 Cut a circle from green paper, as shown. Make one cut from edge of circle to the center. Overlap cut edges and glue to make a cone.

14 Glue cone to one end of the black cylinder to make a tower.

15 Glue tower to one end of the haunted house.

16 Cut out windows and a door from scraps of green and yellow paper and glue to house, see photograph.

Halloween Picture Frame

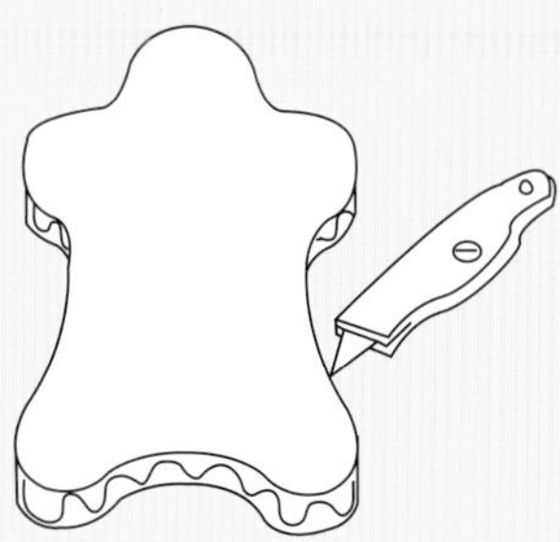
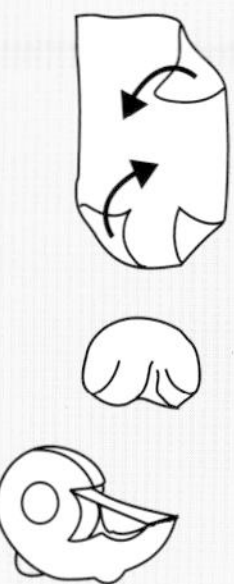
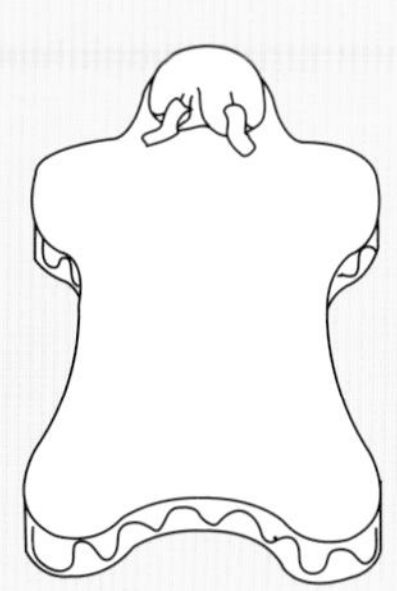
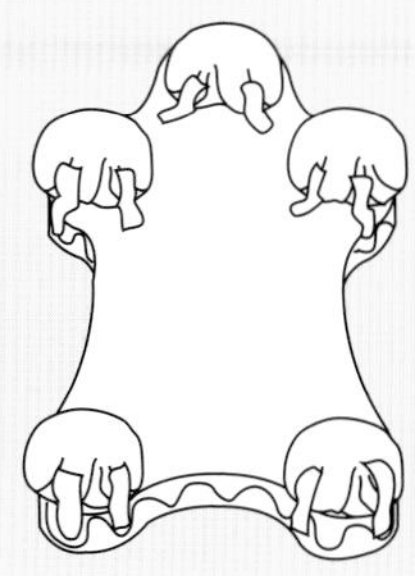
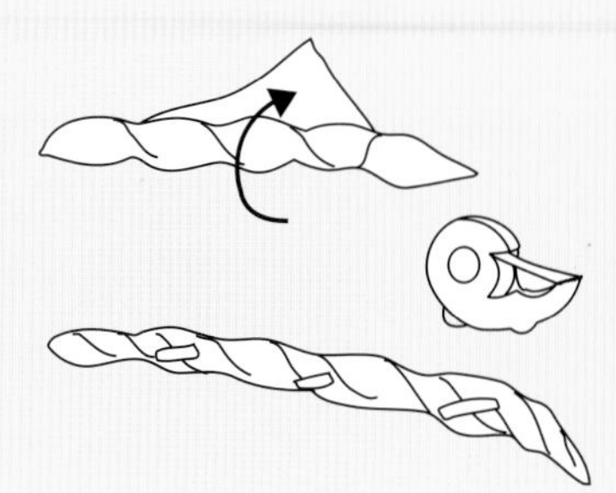

1 Cut decorative shape pattern below from heavy cardboard.
2 Crumple a single sheet of newspaper into a ball and tape. Tape onto cardboard for a medallion.
3 Make 4 more paper balls and attach, as shown.
4 Twist a double sheet of newspaper into a rope and tape in a few places to hold the shape.

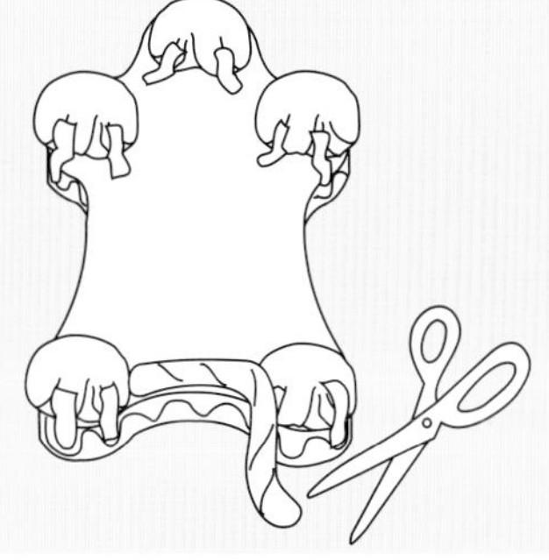
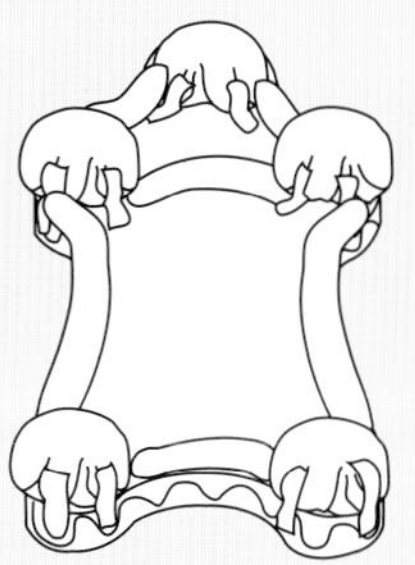
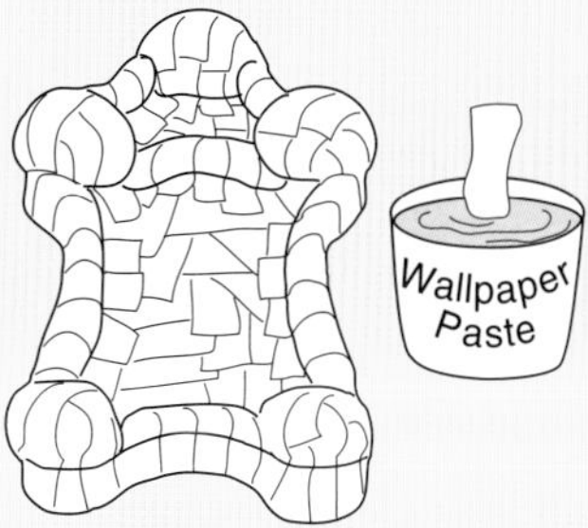

5 Place along edge of frame between medallions and cut to fit. Tape in place.
6 Make more twisted paper ropes to complete a border on the frame.
7 Cover entire frame with strips of newspaper dipped in wallpaper paste. Set aside to dry.
8 Glue the ends of a 6 in (15cm) piece of ribbon on the back of the frame to form a hanging loop. Paint and shellac. Tape a picture at the center of the frame.

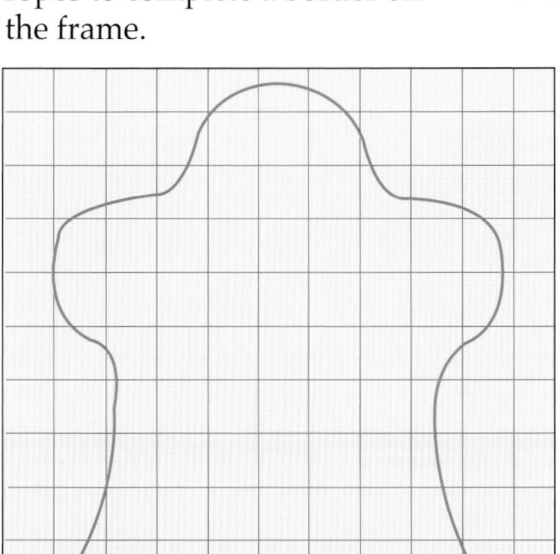

Scale
1 square = 1 in (2.5cm)

Harvest Time

Chicken Bowl Holder & "Straw" Plate Holder

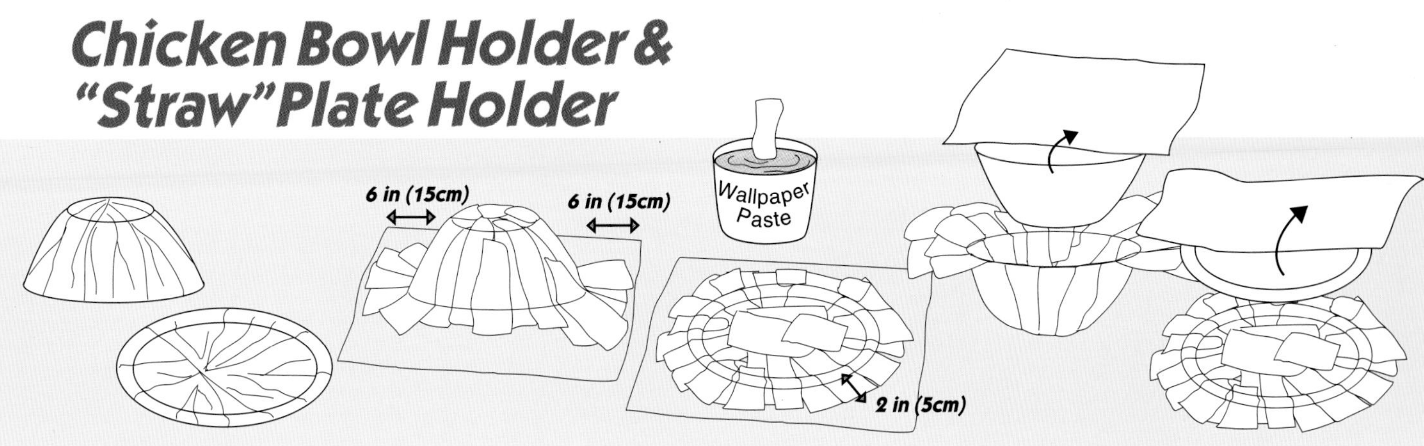

1 Wrap a plate and a soup bowl, separately, with plastic wrap.
2 Place bowl and plate upside down on several sheets of newspaper. Cover bottom of each with strips of newspaper dipped in wallpaper paste. Extend layers of paper past edge of bowl on 2 opposite sides and all around plate, as shown.
3 Use 6 to 8 layers of paper. Set in a warm place for 2 to 3 days.
4 When dry, peel off newspaper sheets under the projects, and remove the plate and bowl.

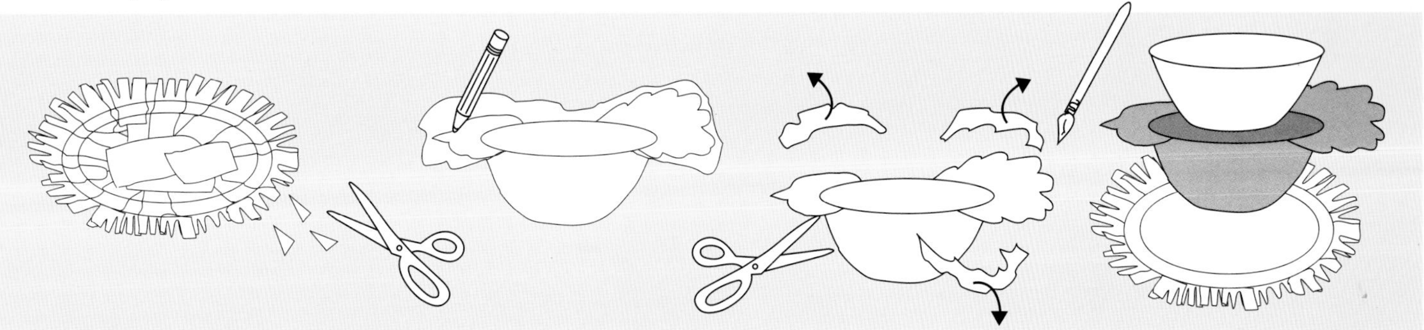

5 Trim edges of paper plate to look like straw.
6 Draw a head and tail on the extra paper at the sides of bowl, as shown.
7 Cut out the head and tail, and trim the sides.
8 Paint the chicken bowl and "straw" plate and shellac.

To use, set plate and bowl in the paper shapes. Make several to decorate dinnerware for a festive meal.

Place Mats & Place Cards

1 Follow same technique as in Halloween instructions, p47. Decorate place mats and place cards with Harvest time subjects.
2 Catstair garland technique is on p66. Use orange and gold colored construction paper.

Bread Loaves

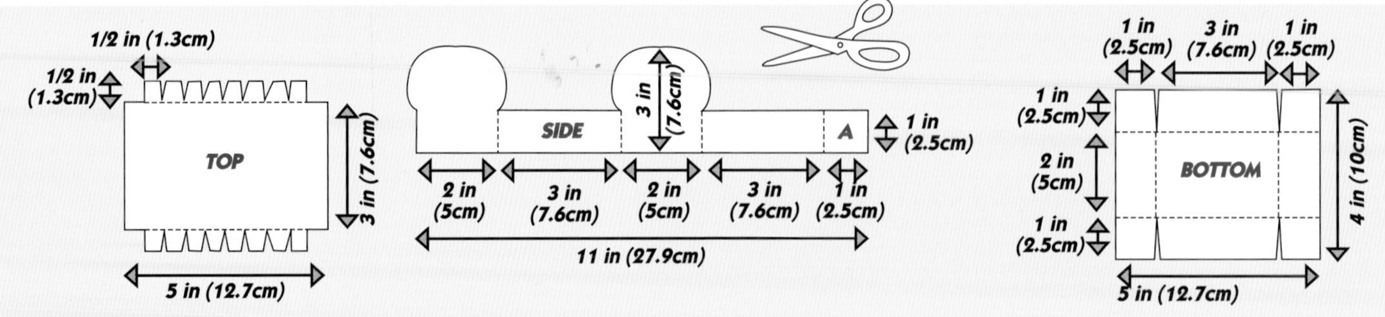

1 On a piece of brown construction paper, measure and draw out patterns, as shown. Use a light-colored pencil to make marks easier to see. Cut out the pieces. Make cuts along solid lines and fold along dotted lines.

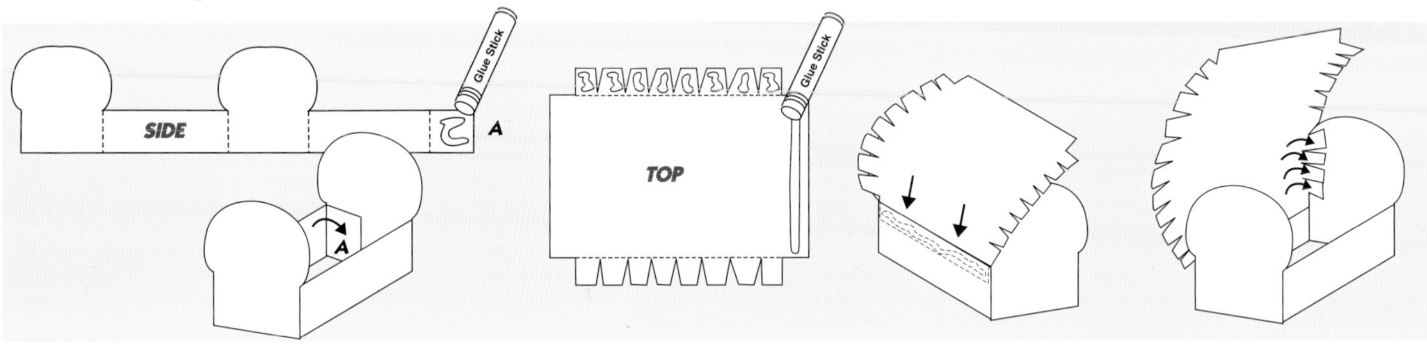

2 When all dotted lines have been creased, begin with section marked SIDE. Spread glue on end flap A and bring flap A to the inside of opposite end, as shown, forming a rectangle.

3 Spread glue on tabs of one side of TOP piece and one end, as shown.

4 Press glued end to the inside of the SIDE piece you just made, as shown.

5 Fold glued tabs inward, and stick them to the inside of the rounded end. As you work your way around, the top will bend to form the top of the loaf.

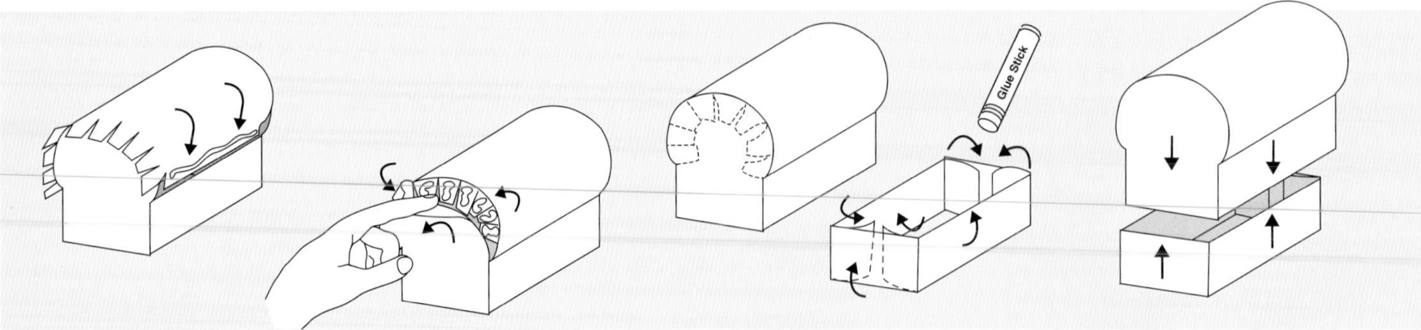

6 Tuck other end of top inside the opposite side. Glue in place.

7 Spread glue on remaining tabs. Gently bend back loaf side and tuck tabs inside, as shown. Glue in place.

8 To make the bottom for the bread loaf, spread glue on corner flaps of the piece marked BOTTOM. Fold sides and ends up, overlapping corner pieces. Press glued flaps inside open box, as shown.

9 Slide together, as shown. Fill box with treats, as desired.

Wheat Sheaves

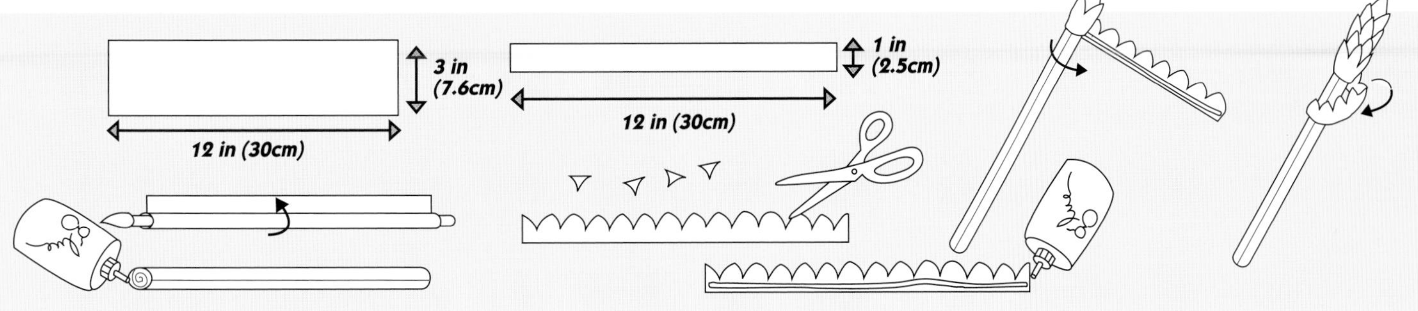

1 Cut a piece of yellow construction paper, as shown. Roll paper around a long paint brush handle until the paper holds its shape. Remove brush, roll paper up again tightly, and glue. This makes the stem.

2 Cut another piece of yellow paper, as shown. Cut one side of the strip into points. Spread glue along uncut side of paper, as shown.

3 Starting at top of stem, wrap strip around stem, gradually moving down the stem. This makes one wheat ear.

4 Make many of these and tie together with a green piece of ribbon to form a wheat sheaf.

We Give Thanks Banner

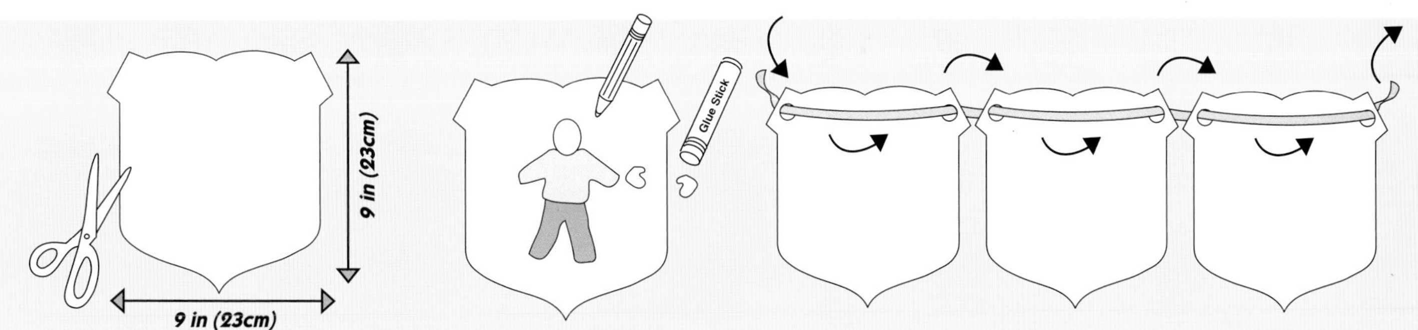

1 Using pattern on p92, cut a piece of colored construction paper into a shield shape. Make identical shapes for each child in different colors of construction paper.

2 Each child chooses something to be thankful for, and depicts it on a shield. Draw subjects on pieces ofcolored construction paper and glue together. Use crayons and markers to make additional decorations.

3 When completed, make a hole in each corner of each shield and string shields on a ribbon across the top of the wall, as shown.

Cornucopia

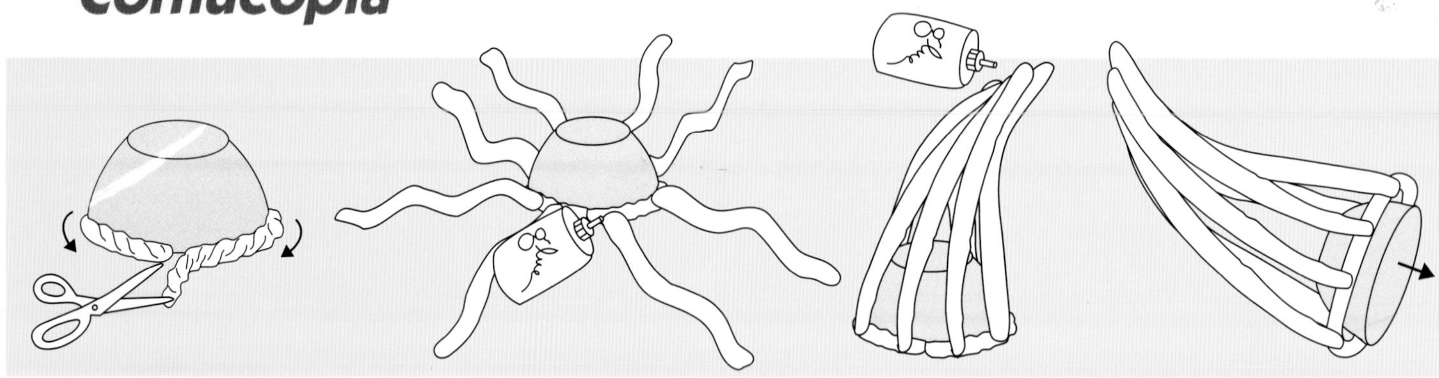

1 Cover work surface with plastic or paper. Set a small bowl upside down on the work surface. Make 9 newspaper ropes, see p16. Wrap one rope around bowl rim, as shown. Cut off any excess length and glue ends together. Glue and tape in place until glue dries.

2 Glue one end of another paper rope to ring around bowl, leaving other end free. Attach 7 more ropes around ring in the same way, spacing them evenly.

3 Bring free ends together over bowl. Pull them off center to form a curved horn shape, and glue in place. Set aside to dry. When glue is dry, remove bowl.

4 Make 15 more paper ropes to weave into the cornucopia.

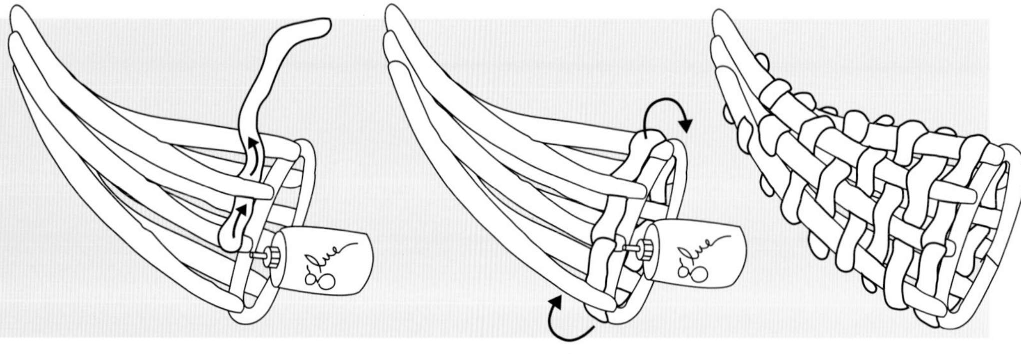

5 Glue end of a new rope to one of the cross ribs, as shown, right next to top of basket. Weave other end of this new rope in and out of ribs, as shown.

6 Attach another rope to end of new rope if it is not long enough to go all the way around. Trim excess rope when a circle is completed. Glue end in place.

7 Glue another new rope to a cross rib directly under woven circle just completed. Continue this method until you have filled in the open spaces between the ribs.

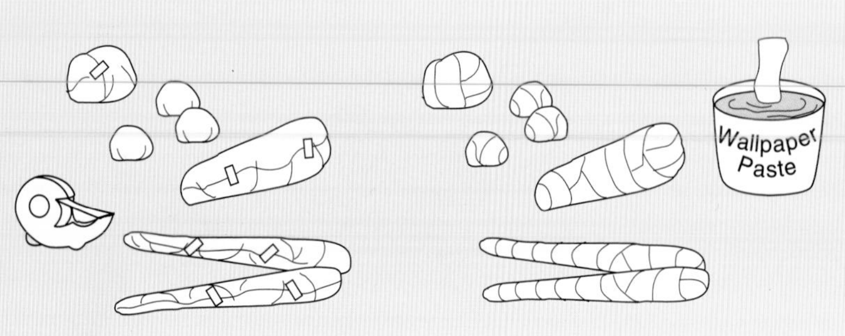

8 To make fruit and vegetables, crumple sheets of newspaper into balls and long thin shapes and tape in place. Tape the loose edges to hold the shape.

9 Cover shapes with 2 to 3 layers of strips of newspaper dipped in wallpaper paste. Set in a warm dry place to harden. Paint and shellac.

Turkey Window Hanging

1 On red construction paper, draw a turkey head and neck shape and turkey wattle (see patterns, p93). Cut out. Draw a 1/4 in (.6cm) border inside the edge of the shapes and cut out in one piece.
2 Spread glue stick on borders and press on red tissue paper. Cut out around head and neck.
3 Fold shape in half (see illustration). For a beak, cut out a piece of the red tissue along the fold. Unfold. On yellow construction paper draw a shape slightly larger than the hole, draw a 1/4 in (.6cm) border, and cut out in one piece.
4 Glue this shape to yellow tissue and cut out. Glue the yellow shape over the hole in the red tissue. Proceed using this technique to construct turkey.
5 Make eye from green construction paper and tissue paper, body and wings (pattern, p93) from brown construction paper and tissue paper, feet (pattern, p93) from yellow construction paper and tissue paper, and feathers (pattern, p93) on light brown construction paper and orange tissue paper.
6 Glue legs, wings, head, and feathers to the body. Use small pieces of tape to hang turkey in window for Thanksgiving.

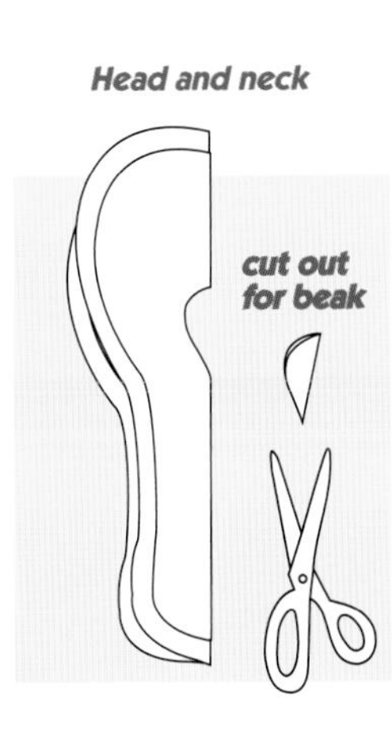

Dog Bone Parcel

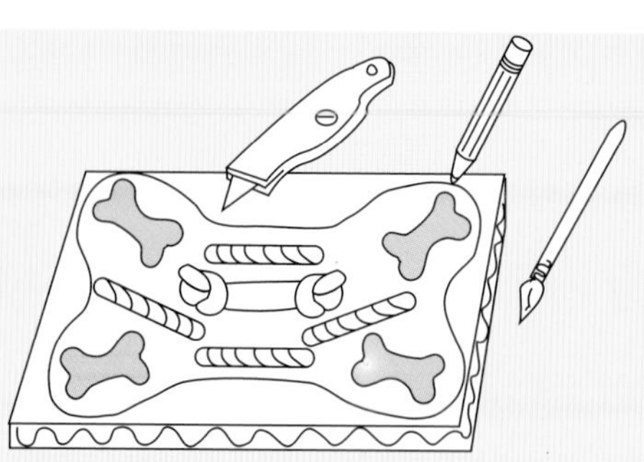

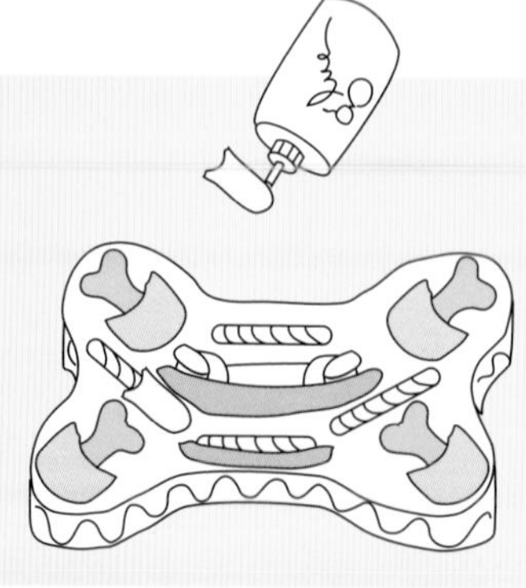

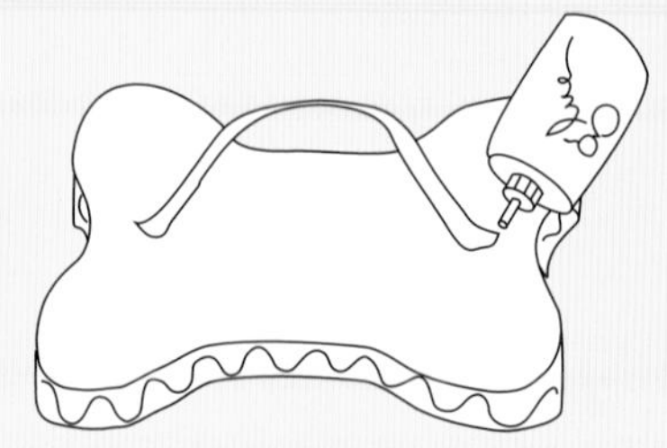

1 Arrange purchased pet treats on a piece of smooth cardboard. Draw a dog bone shape around the treats, as shown.

2 Remove treats and cut out cardboard shape with utility knife. Paint and shellac.

3 When dry, place treats in position again. Cut out pieces of colored construction paper to cover the bottom half of each treat. Glue paper over treat to make a pocket to hold treat in place.

4 Glue ends of a strong piece of ribbon 16 in (41cm) long to top of cardboard "bone" to hang out of pet's reach.

Pet Food Tray

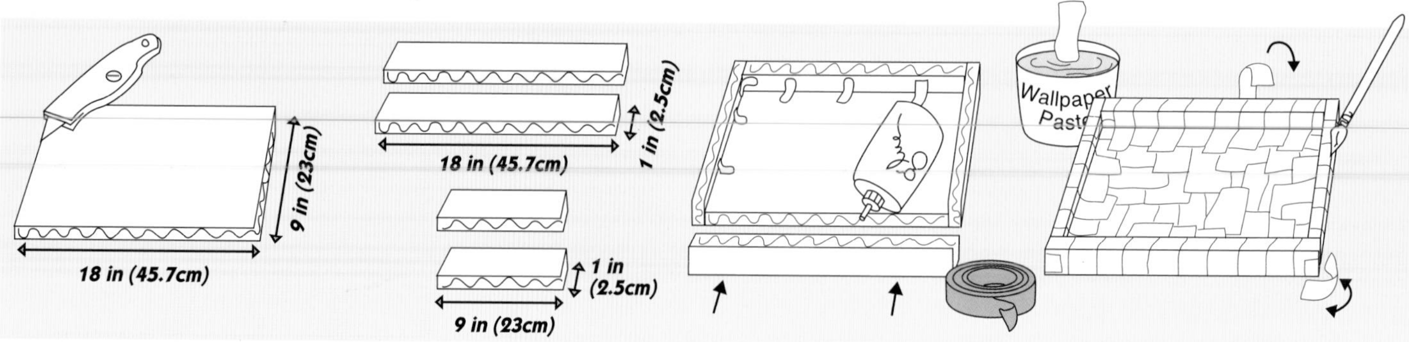

1 Cut out illustrated pieces from cardboard— a base and 4 sides. The finished tray should be large enough to hold water dish and food dish.

2 Glue strips to sides of base and tape in place.

3 Cover entire tray with 4 to 5 layers of strips of newspaper dipped in wallpaper paste.

Reinforce corners with more strips and paste. Set aside to dry. When dry, paint and shellac.

Tree Ornaments–Basic Cone

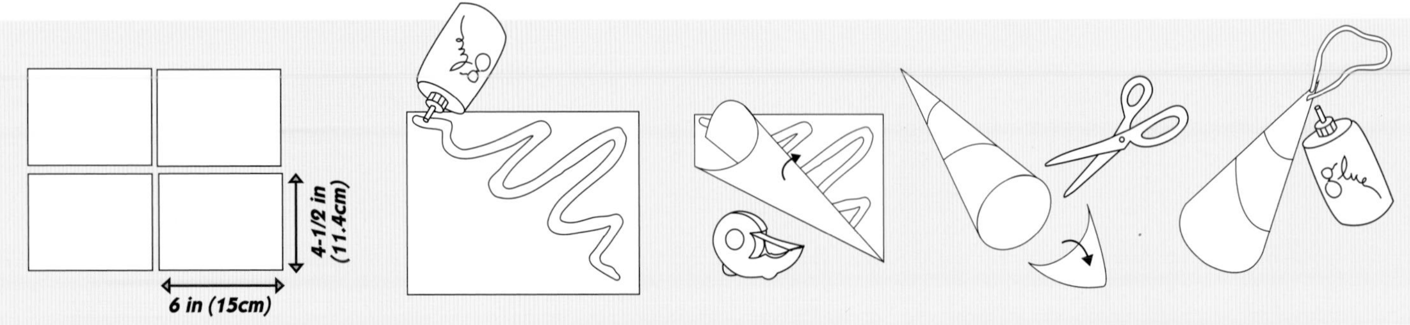

1 Cut a standard 9 in x 12 in (23cm x 30cm) sheet of colored construction paper in 4, as shown.
2 Spread glue over one diagonal half of one piece.

3 Roll paper from unglued corner into a cone, as shown. Tape until glue dries.
4 Trim the open end to make it even.

5 After decorating cone, glue ends of a 6 in (15cm) piece of string or ribbon to the back of the pointed end of cone. Hang string loop on Christmas tree.

Elf

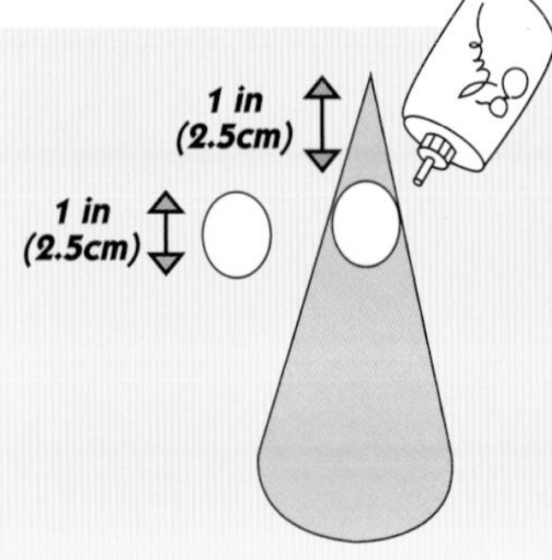

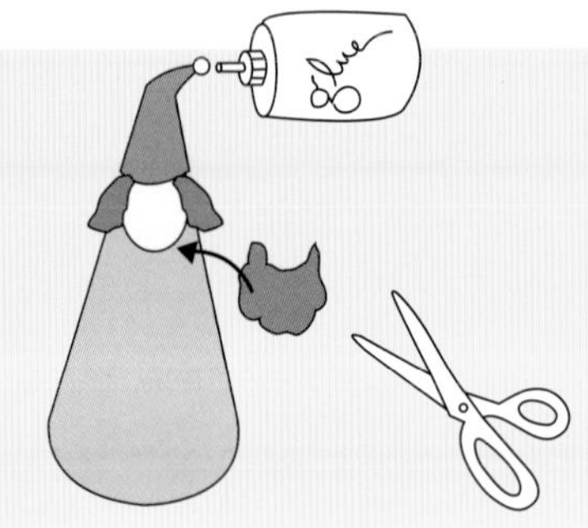

1 Make a basic cone (above) from green construction paper. Cut an oval face from beige paper and glue to top of cone, as shown.

2 Cut a triangle from red paper to make a hat. Wrap triangle around top of cone, overlapping face, as shown. Glue in place.

3 Bend top of hat over. Glue a colored circle to end of hat.
4 Cut out hair and beard from colored paper and glue on.

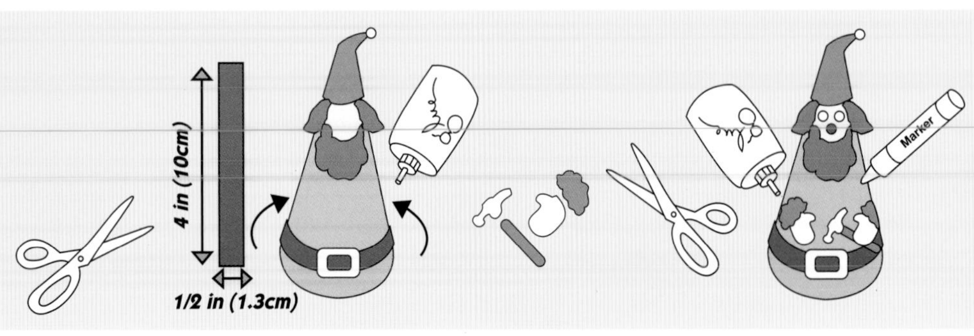

5 Cut a belt from blue paper. Glue around body. Add a belt buckle cut from yellow paper.
6 Draw a hammer head from grey paper. Draw and cut out a handle for the hammer from brown paper. Glue them together. Cut out 2 hands from beige paper. Glue one hand onto tool handle. Cut out cuffs from red paper. Glue to edge of hands.
7 Attach hands and tool to sides of body cone. Add eyes and nose from paper circles. Draw mouth and arms with markers.

Santa

1 Make a basic cone from red construction paper (p58). Cut a piece of beige paper into an oval shape, as shown. Glue on front of cone for the face.
2 Cut a strip of black construction paper, as shown, for a belt. Glue around cone.
3 From white construction paper draw and cut out hair, a beard, mitts with cuffs, and hat trim. Glue in place.
4 Cut out a belt buckle from yellow paper and glue in place. Glue on eyes, nose, cheeks, and a pompom from paper circles. Draw mouth and other decoration with colored markers.

Angel

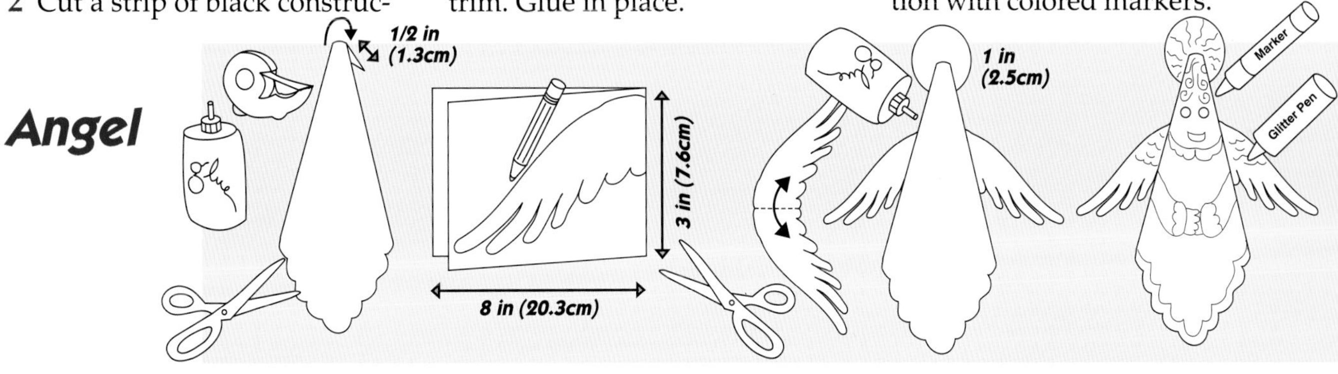

1 Make a basic cone from white construction paper (p58), but *do not trim bottom edge*. Scallop edge, as shown. Fold top of cone over to the back, as shown. Glue and tape until dry.
2 Fold a piece of yellow construction paper in half, short end to short end, as shown. Draw a wing shape with base of wing along fold, as shown. Cut out. Do not cut folded edge.
3 Unfold. Glue wings to back of cone. For a halo cut out a yellow circle and glue to top of cone at the back, as shown.
4 Draw hair, face, and gown decorations with markers. Glue on paper circles for eyes. With a glitter pen, draw feathers and halo rays.

Christmas Tree

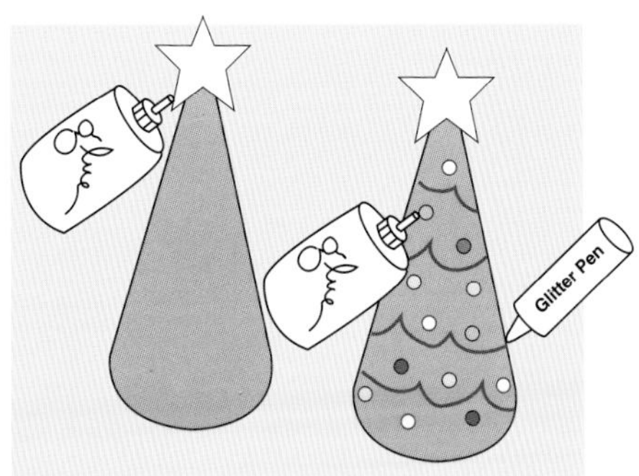

1 Make a basic cone from green construction paper (p58). Cut out a yellow star and glue to top.
2 Glue different colors of paper circles made from paper scraps all over tree for ornaments.
3 Use glitter pen to draw on garlands around tree, and add glitter to star at top.

Teddy Bear

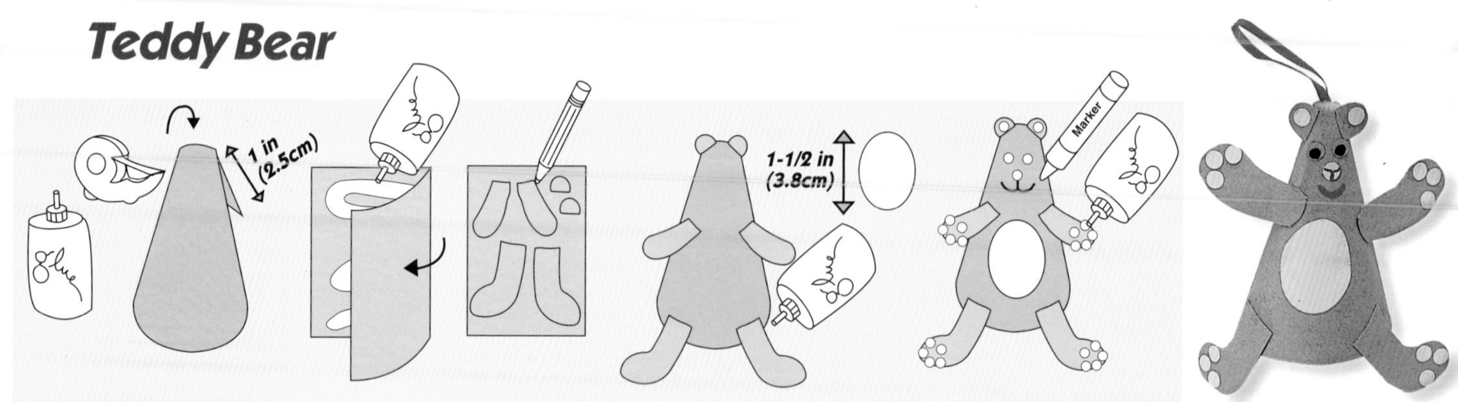

1 Make a basic cone from brown construction paper (p58). Fold top down, as shown. Glue and tape until dry.

2 Spread glue over another piece of brown paper. Fold in half. Press together to make a double sheet. Draw and cut out 4 legs with paws and 2 ears.

3 Glue legs to body cone and ears to top of cone, as shown.

4 Cut an oval from yellow construction paper and glue to bear's tummy. Add paper circles made from yellow paper scraps for bear's toes and inside of ears. Glue on 2 blue paper circles for eyes, and a pink paper circle for a nose. Draw on mouth with markers.

Fireplace

1 Make a basic cone from white construction paper (p58). Cut out 3 strips of grey construction paper, as shown. Glue on front of cone to frame a fireplace.

2 Draw a brick pattern on rest of cone with markers.

3 **Version 1** Draw a fire with orange and yellow markers and fill in rest of hearth with black markers.

Version 2 Fill in hearth with a black marker *(do not draw a fire)*. Cut out stockings from red and green paper. Cut out cuffs for stockings from white paper. Glue cuffs to top of stockings. Glue stockings to top of fire-place, as shown.

Bell

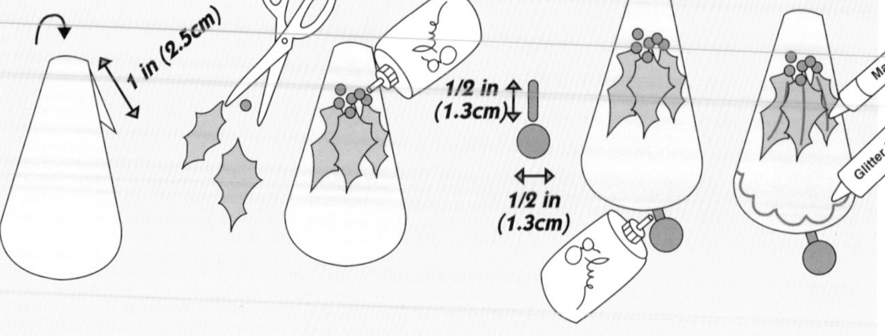

1 Make a basic cone from colored construction paper (p58). Fold down the top, as shown. Glue and tape.

2 Draw and cut out holly leaves from green paper. Glue to front of cone. Glue on red paper circles for berries.

3 Cut a circle from colored paper, as shown. Glue to a small strip of paper. This is the clapper. Glue end of strip inside bell, as shown.

4 Decorate with markers or glitter.

Reindeer

1 Make a basic cone from grey construction paper (p58). Fold point down, as shown. Glue and tape until glue dries.
2 Spread glue over a piece of brown construction paper and fold in half to make a strong double sheet. Draw and cut out 2 antlers and 2 eyes.
3 Glue in place on cone.
4 Draw and cut out 2 ears from grey paper. Glue onto head below antlers, as shown. Cut out a red circle and glue on face for nose. Use a black marker to draw mouth and hair. Cut out a tongue from pink paper and glue in place, as shown.

Pleated Star Ornament

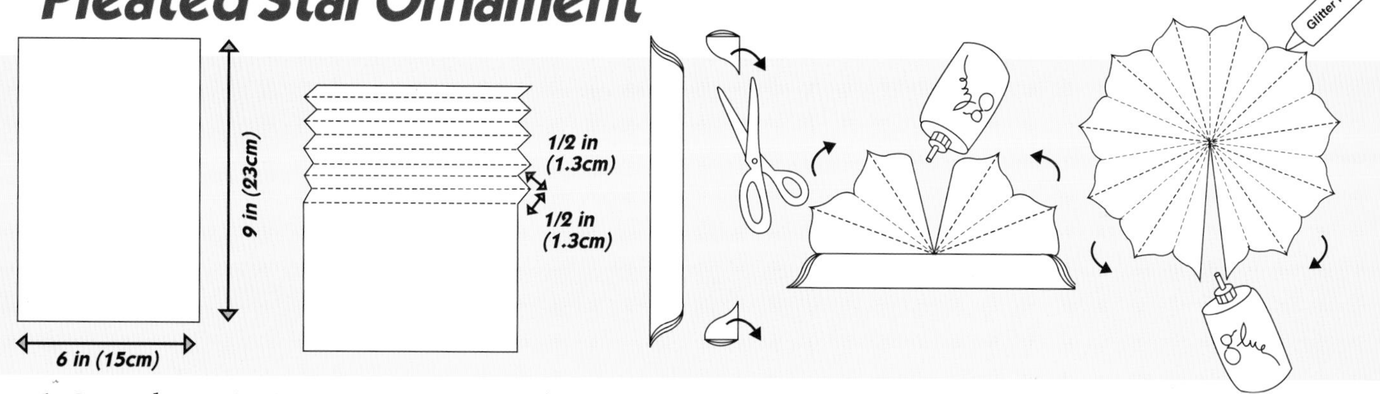

1 Cut a sheet of colored construction paper, as shown.
2 Pleat the sheet in folds starting at the short side, as shown.
3 While folded, cut a decorative edge at each end, as shown.
4 Bring the 2 corners on one long side together and glue, as shown.
5 Repeat on the other long side to make a circle.
6 Decorate edges with liquid glitter.

7 Cut a piece of ribbon 6 in (15cm) long. Glue both ends to edge of ornament to make a loop for hanging.

House Tree Ornament

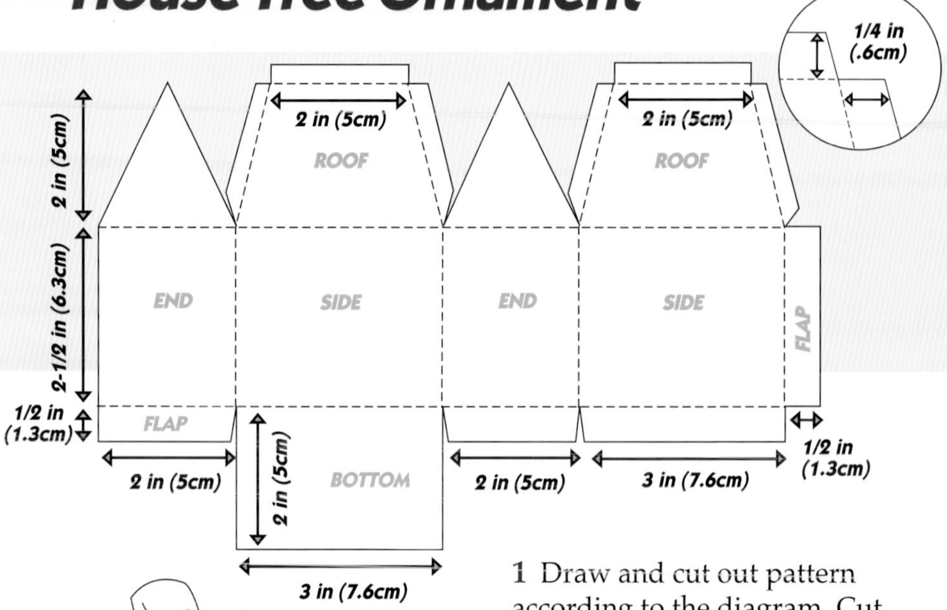

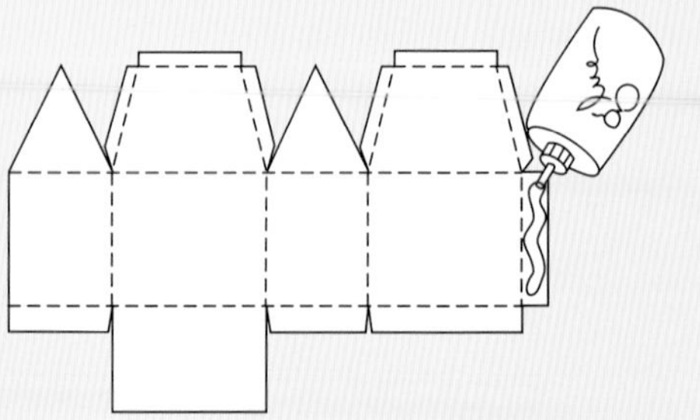

ROOF
ROOF
END
SIDE
END
SIDE
FLAP
FLAP
BOTTOM
2 in (5cm)
2 in (5cm)
2 in (5cm)
2-1/2 in (6.3cm)
1/2 in (1.3cm)
2 in (5cm)
2 in (5cm)
2 in (5cm)
3 in (7.6cm)
3 in (7.6cm)
1/2 in (1.3cm)
1/4 in (.6cm)

1 Draw and cut out pattern according to the diagram. Cut along solid lines and fold along dotted lines. To make a sharp fold, place a ruler along a dotted line and fold paper up against it.

2 Spread glue on the flap along one SIDE section, as shown.

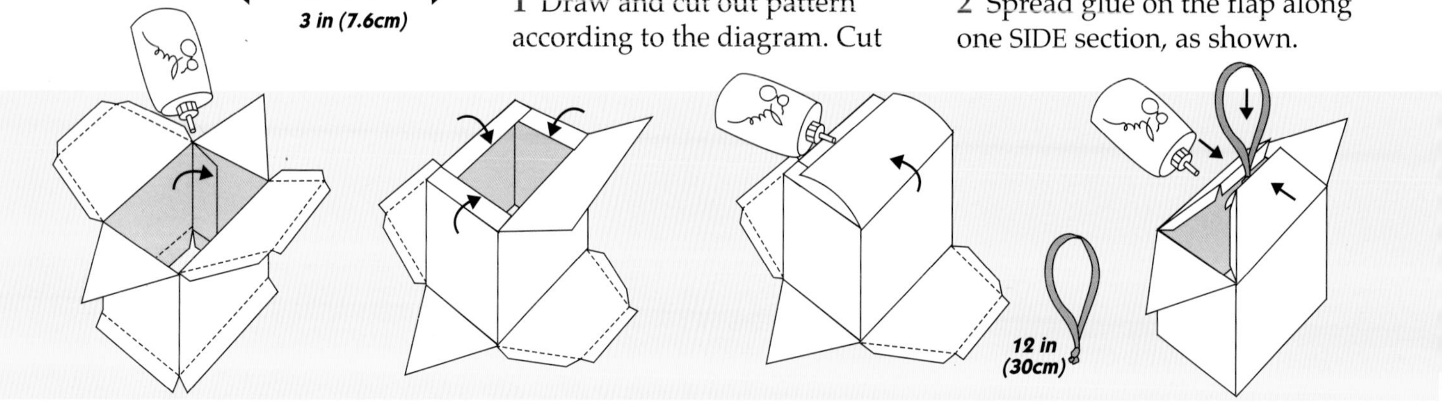

12 in (30cm)

3 Bend house into a rectangle and attach glued flap to the END section, as shown. Tuck flap inside the rectangle.

4 Turn house upside down.

5 Fold over flaps along the lower edge of the house. Spread glue on these flaps and fold the BOTTOM piece onto the flaps. Gently press in place.

6 Turn house right side up. Make a loop from a 12 in (30cm) piece of ribbon. Fold top flaps along ROOF inward and spread with glue. Drop knotted end of ribbon between roof sections and press glued flaps together, as shown.

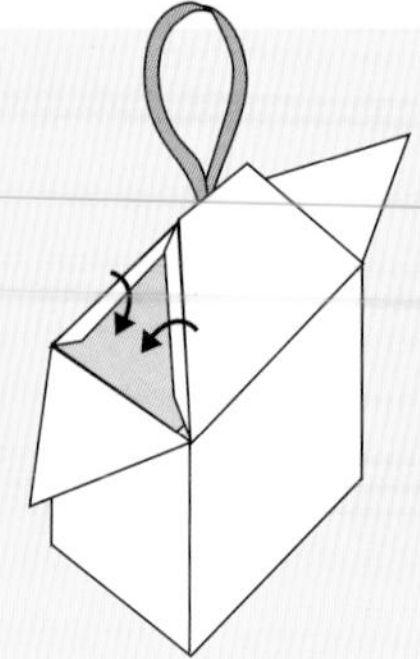

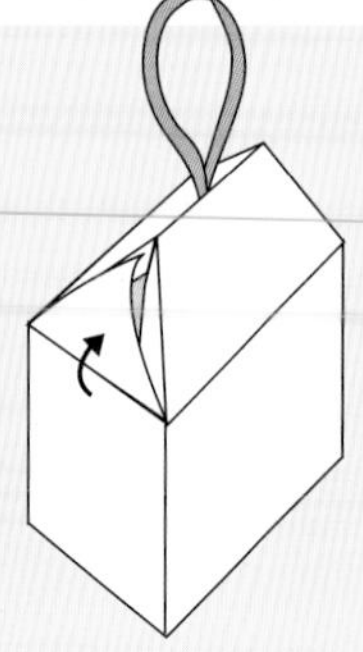

7 Fold flaps along the angled roof section inward.

8 Spread with glue. Fold the triangular end roof section onto the glue and gently press in place. Close both ends of the roof in this way. Decorate the house with markers.

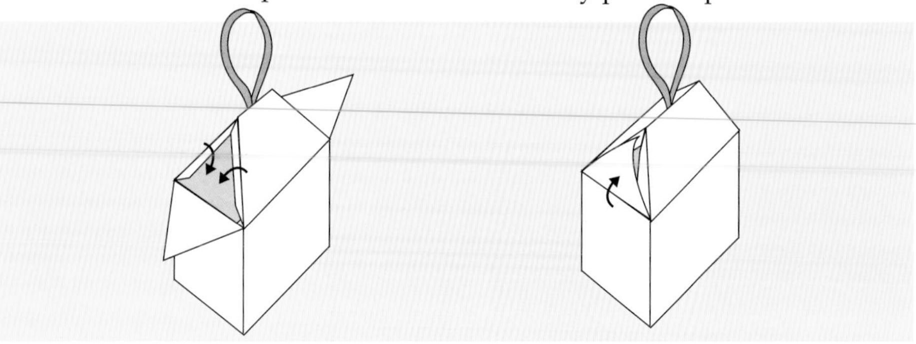

Church Tree Ornament

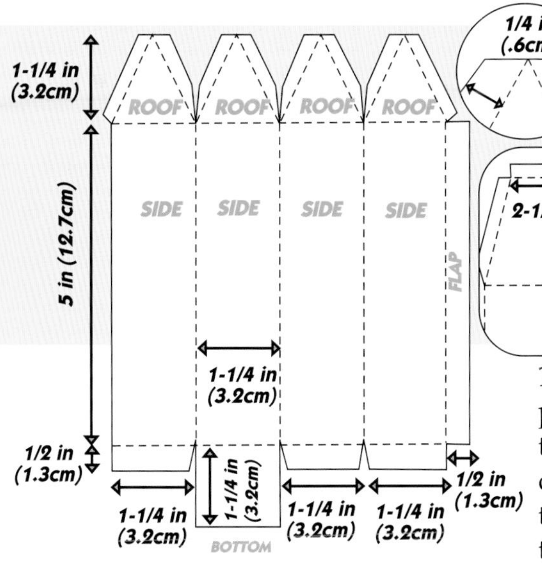

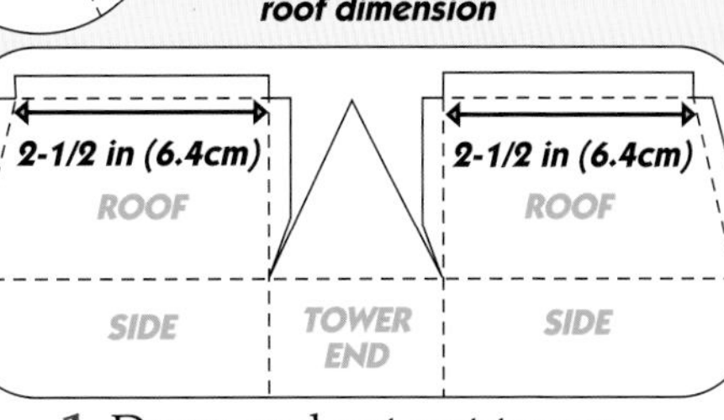

1 Draw and cut out tower pattern above and house pattern (p62) using building roof detail above for roof side with tower. Assemble building in the same way as the house.

2 Place ribbon loop close to flat end (not sloped end) of roof, for balance when tower is added.

Tower

3 Spread glue on the flap along one SIDE section. Bend tower

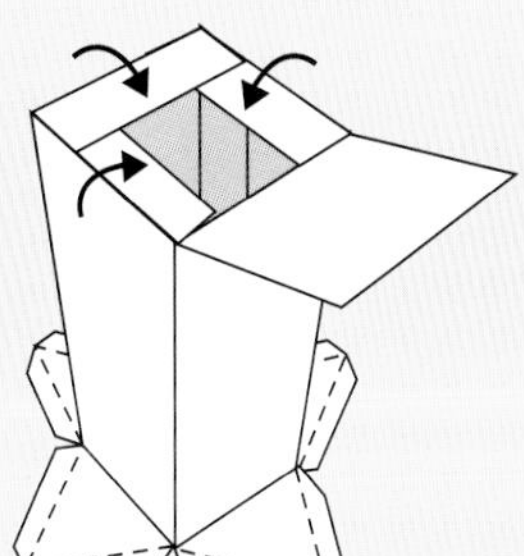

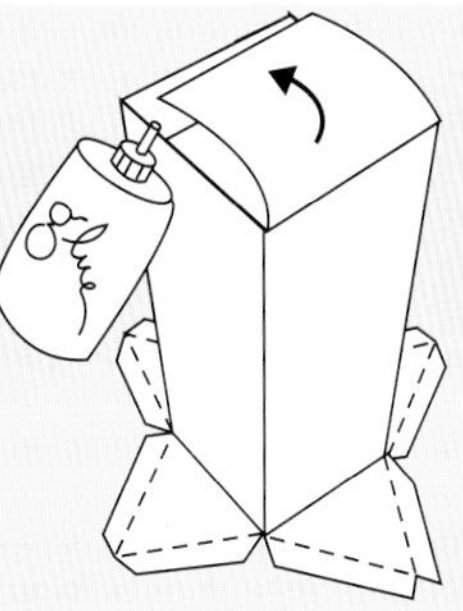

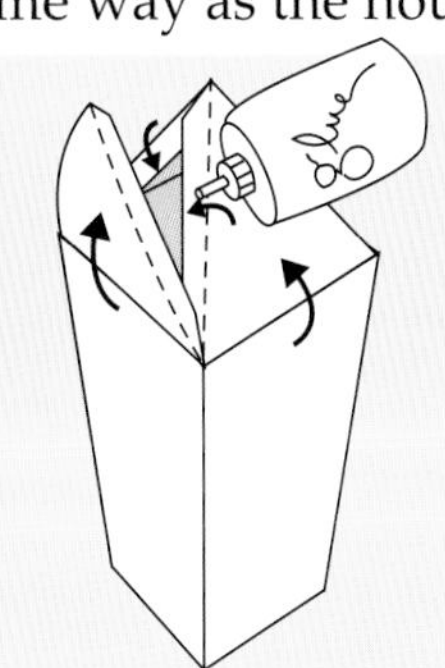

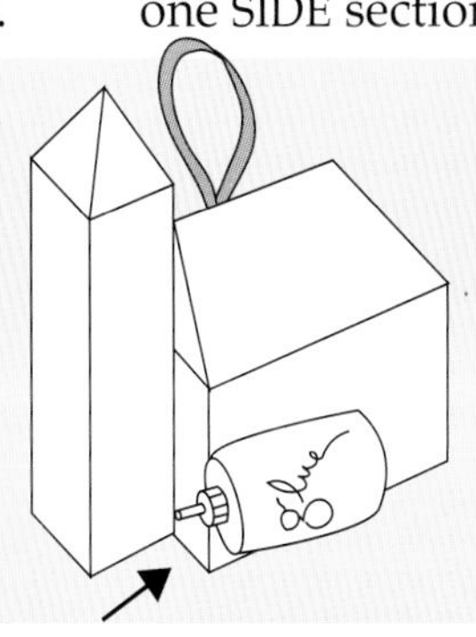

into a rectangle and attach glued flap to opposite SIDE, as shown. Tuck flap inside tower.

4 Turn tower upside down. Fold over flaps along the lower edge of the tower. Spread glue on these flaps and fold BOTTOM piece onto the flaps. Gently press in place.

5 Turn tower right side up. Fold flaps along ROOF sections inward and spread with glue.

6 Press all ROOF sections inward, glued flaps together inside the roof.

7 Glue tower to the flat roof side of the church building, as shown. Decorate with markers.

Egg Carton Basket

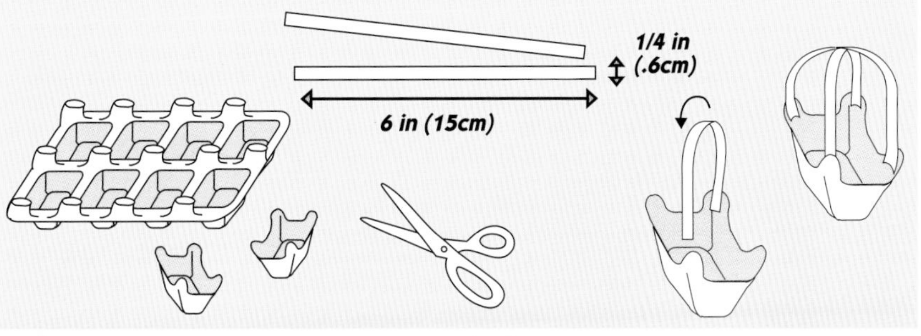

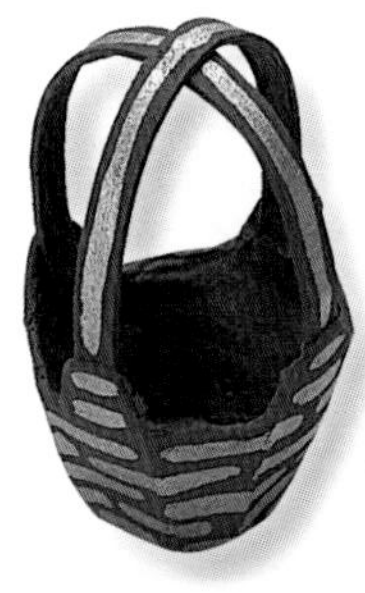

1 Cut out the cups from a paper egg carton. Trim the top of the cup to make 4 high corners, as shown.

2 Cut the lid of the egg carton into strips, as shown.

3 Glue one end of a strip to one corner of the cup. Curl strip over the top of the basket and glue other end of strip to the opposite corner, as shown.

4 Glue another strip to remaining 2 corners of the cup in the same way. Glue the 2 strips together where they cross above the basket. Paint and shellac. Fill basket with small candies and hang on the tree.

Doily Ornament

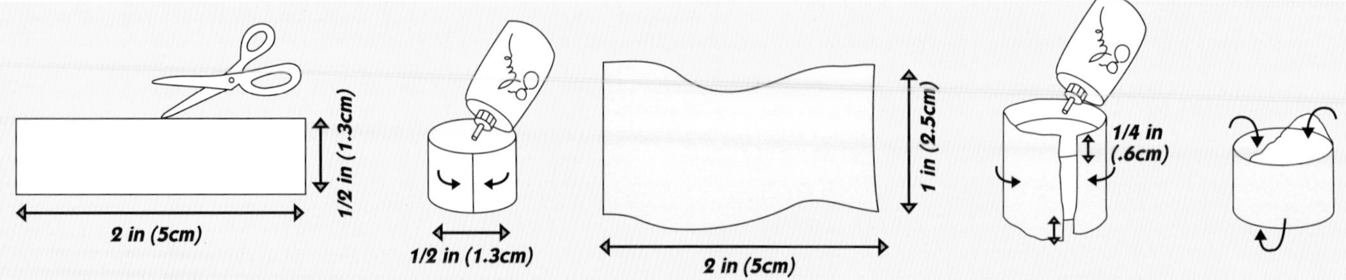

1 Cut a strip of cardboard (cereal box), as shown.
2 Glue one end over the other to form a circle, as shown.
3 Cut a strip of gold foil wrapping paper in dimensions given.
4 Spread glue over the back of the foil.
5 Wrap foil around cardboard ring, leaving 1/4 in (.6cm) hanging over each end, as shown. Fold these edges under.

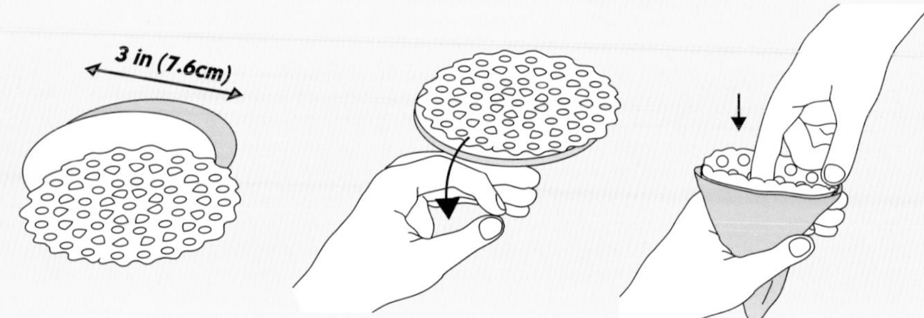

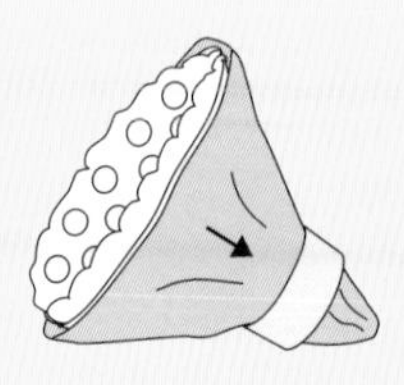

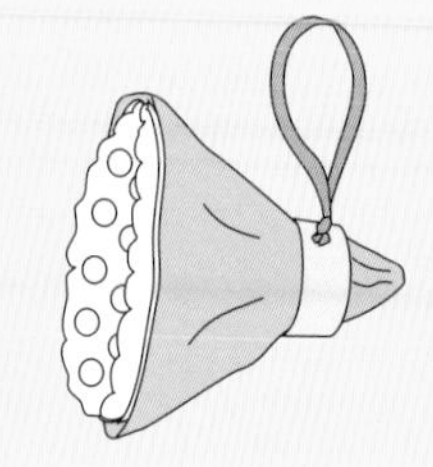

6 Cut 2 circles of tissue paper in contrasting colors the same size as a purchased paper doily. Stack the tissue paper circles with the doily on top.
7 Make a circle with your finger and thumb and lay the paper circles on top.
8 Poke center of circles with finger of your other hand, to push paper into a ruffled cone.
9 Push paper cone into the ring and glue in place. Fold back tissue slightly.
10 Cut a 6 in (15cm) piece of ribbon and glue both ends to the side of ring to make a loop for hanging.

Papier-Mâché Pulp Ornaments

1 Prepare papier-mâché pulp (p36).
2 Mold pulp with your hands into ball shapes and stack together to make a teddy bear, snowman, or Santa. Place in a warm dry place to harden. Allow several days to dry.

Goose Egg Ornament

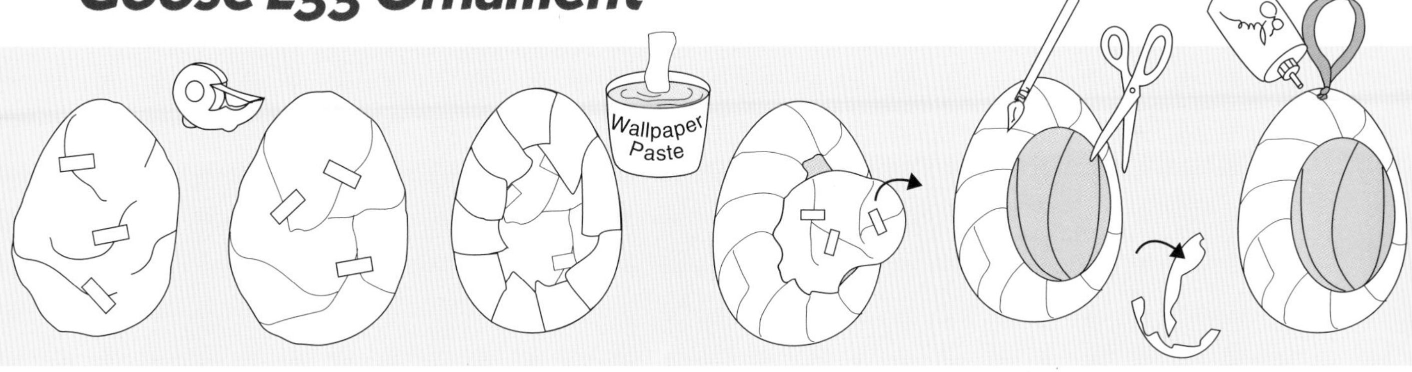

1 Crumple a double sheet of newspaper into an egg shape and tape.
2 Wrap with plastic wrap. Tape.
3 Cover egg with strips of newspaper dipped in wallpaper paste, leaving an oval area uncovered. Make a solid covering for the egg, using at least 6 layers of newspaper strips. Allow to dry in a warm place.
4 When quite hard, compress the crumpled paper inside the shell and remove.
5 Trim opening with scissors. Paint and decorate inside and out. Mark a particular event or date inside the opening, if desired. Shellac.
6 Glue a ribbon loop to the top of the egg for hanging.

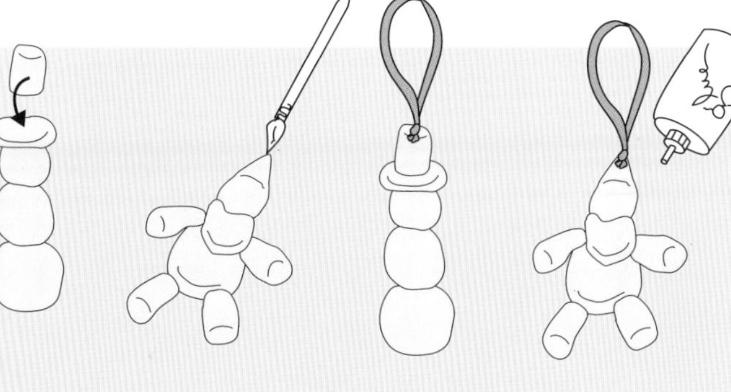

3 Paint and shellac.
4 Cut one piece of ribbon 6 in (15cm) long for each ornament to make a loop for hanging. Glue to the top of the ornament.

Bow Tree Ornament

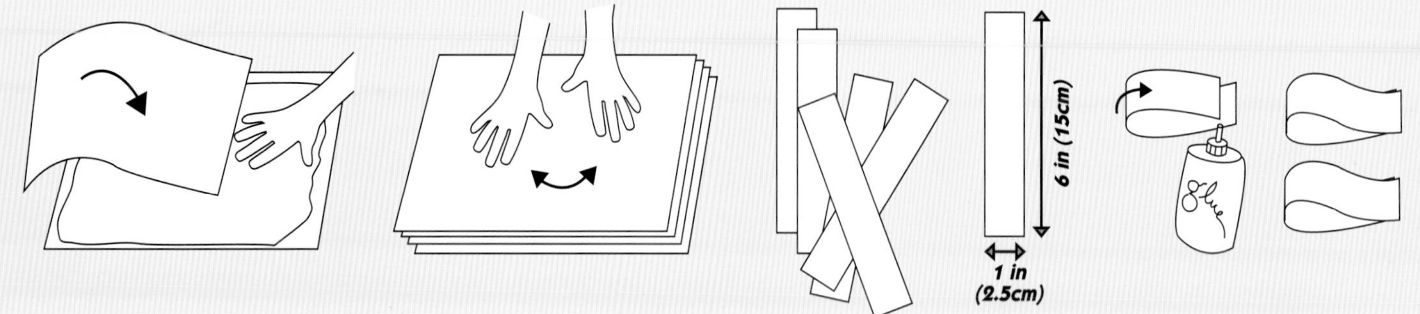

1 Lay a sheet of newspaper on a waterproof surface. Spread with wallpaper paste or glue. Lay another sheet of newspaper on top and smooth into place.

2 Add more paste, then more paper to make a sheet 4 layers thick.

3 Cut 6 strips, as shown, from the prepared sheet.

4 Bend one strip into a loop, gluing the 2 ends together, as shown. Repeat with 2 more strips, making 3 loops.

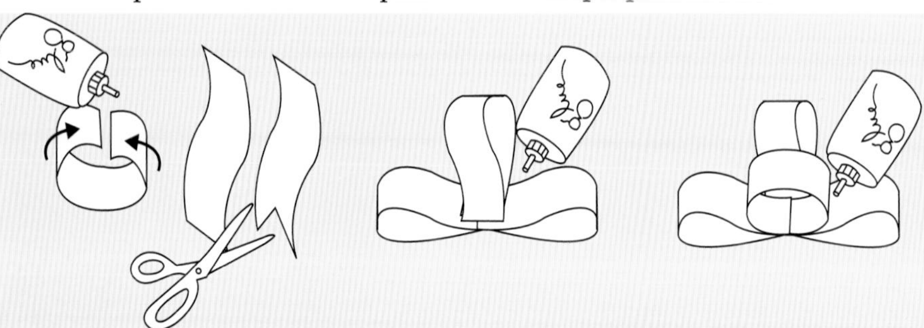

5 Curl another strip into a circle. Glue one end over another. Curl the last 2 strips over your finger to form "S" shapes, as shown. Cut a notch in one end of each "S"-shaped strip.

6 Glue first 3 loops together in a fan shape, as shown.

7 Glue circle in center of fan.

8 Glue the 2 S–shapes underneath, notched ends facing downward. Set aside to dry.

9 Paint and shellac. When dry, glue ends of a loop of ribbon to the top of the bow for hanging ornament on tree.

Catstair Candy Canes

1 Cut strips of red and white construction paper, as shown. With a green marker, draw a line down the center of each white strip, on both sides.

2 Glue one white and one red strip together at a right angle, as shown.

3 Fold one strip over the other, back and forth, maintaining the right angle.

4 Glue more strips to ends of folded strips as needed until you have used up 3 strips of each color. Glue ends together. When dry, gently pull apart. Hang strip over tree branches in a candy cane shape.

Cardboard & Paper Strip Ornaments

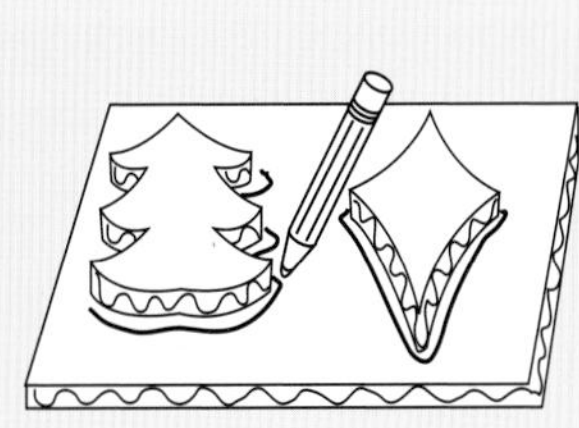

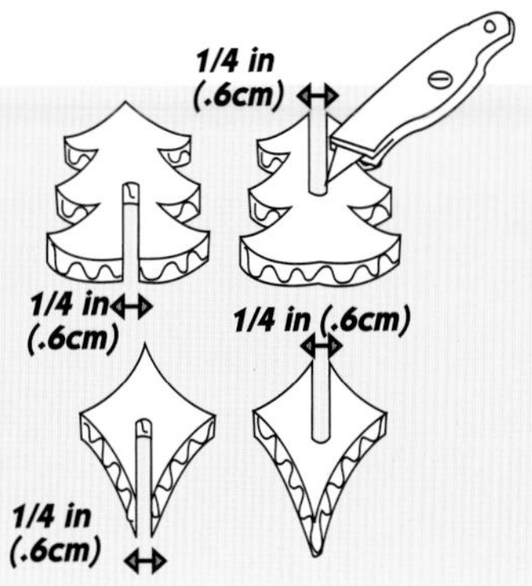

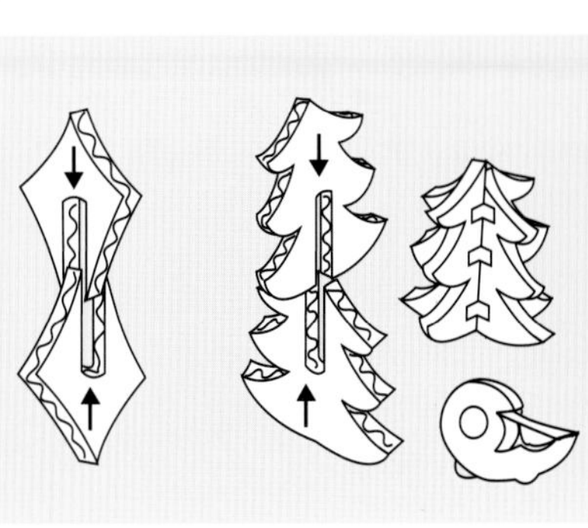

1 Draw shapes on stiff cardboard, as shown. Cut out.
2 Place each shape on more cardboard and trace around it. Cut out second identical shapes.
3 Make cut from bottom of each shape to the center. Make a cut in identical shape from the top down, as shown.
4 Slide the 2 identical shapes together, as shown. Tape in place.

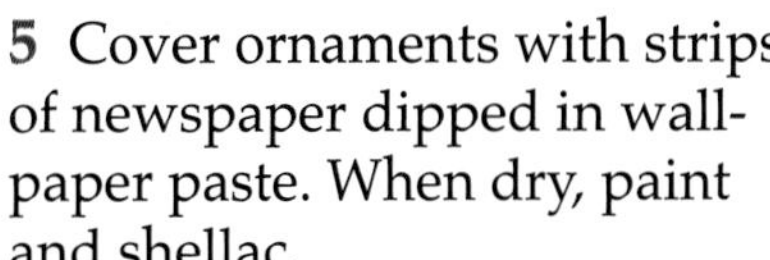

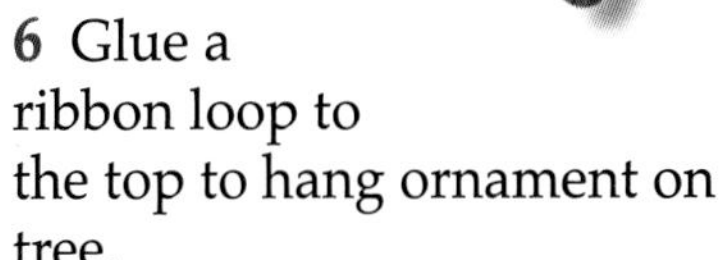

5 Cover ornaments with strips of newspaper dipped in wallpaper paste. When dry, paint and shellac.

6 Glue a ribbon loop to the top to hang ornament on tree.

Catstair Garland

1 Cut lengths of different colors of construction paper 1 in (2.5cm) wide. Proceed as for Catstair Candy Cane (p66), folding different colors together until desired length is reached. Choose colors to suit holiday season.

Rolled Bead Garland

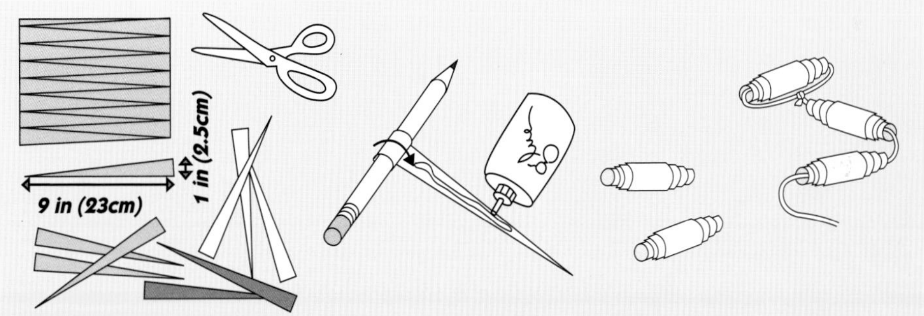

1 Cut sheets of different colored construction paper into triangles, as shown.
2 Wrap base of triangle around a pencil once. Spread glue over remainder of triangle and continue rolling it on pencil.
3 Slide pencil out. When you have made many beads, thread beads on a string to hang on tree.
4 Tie a knot around end beads to keep them on the string, as shown.

Stuffed Christmas Tree

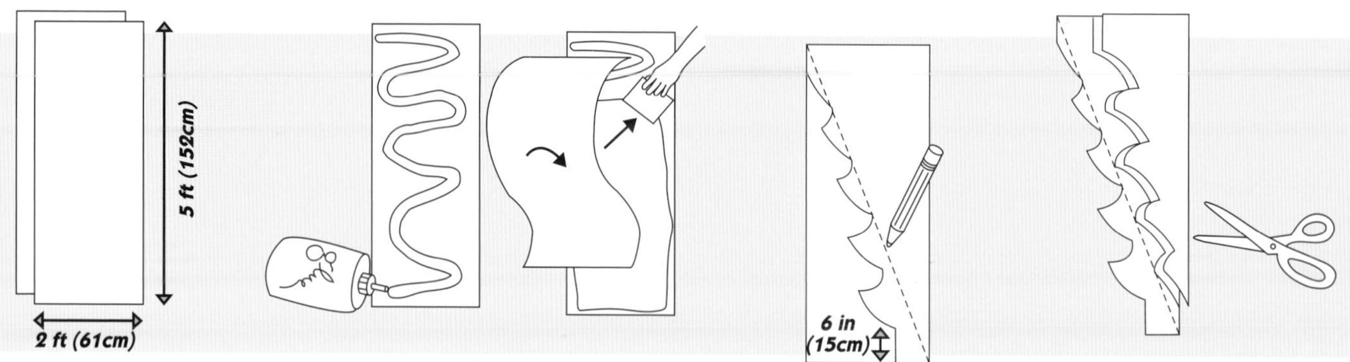

1 Cut 2 pieces of brown paper, as shown.

2 Spread glue over one sheet and lay the other sheet on top. Smooth in place. Make 4 more double sheets in the same way.

3 Draw a line from one corner of a sheet to opposite diagonal corner. Draw half a tree shape on one side, as shown. Square the bottom, as shown. Cut out tree shape.

4 Lay tree shape on other half of paper in opposite direction. Trace and cut out a second identical shape. Lay tree shape on other double sheets in the same way, cutting 2 shapes from each sheet for a total of 10 half tree shapes.

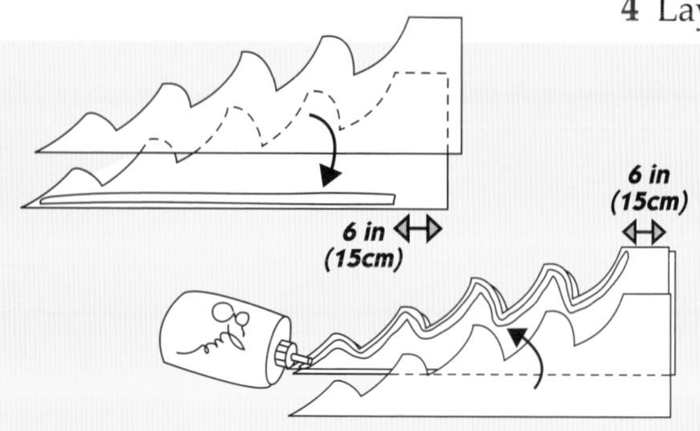

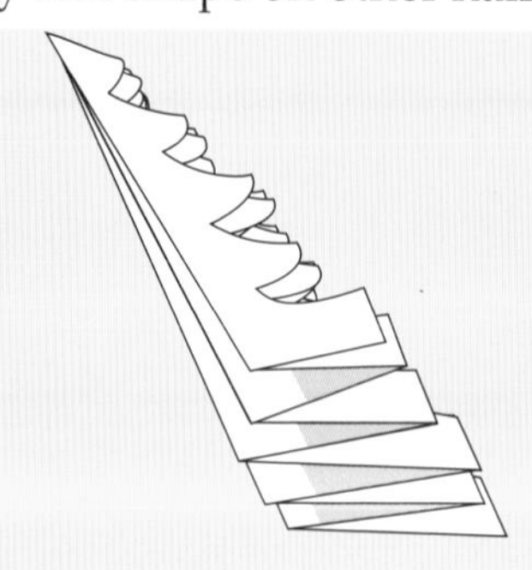

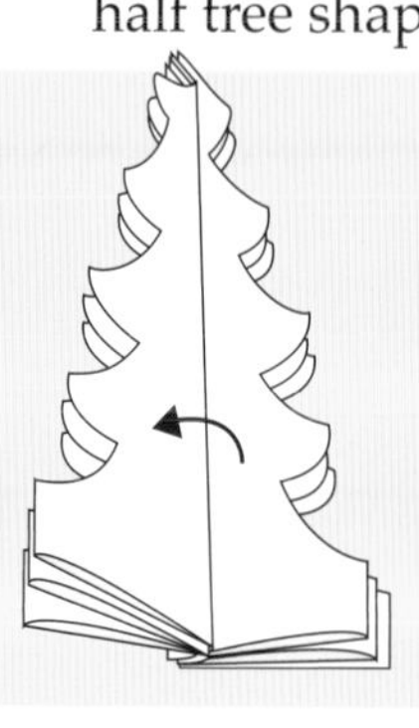

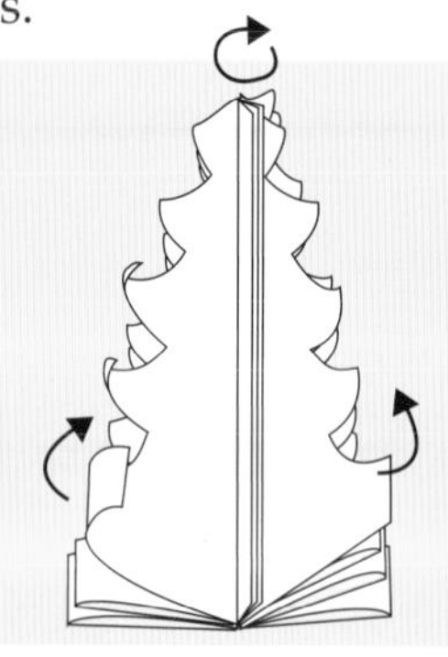

5 Lay one tree shape on a flat surface. Spread glue generously along straight side. Lay a second shape on top. Line up edges and press in place.

6 Spread glue along jagged side of top tree shape, as shown. *Do not glue the bottom 6 in (15cm).* Place another sheet on top and press in place, as before.

7 Glue along straight side. Add a fourth sheet. Continue to add sheets, alternating the side that is glued until all sheets are used. It is important to start and finish with glue on a straight side.

8 Fold 3 of the layers back along the inside straight edge, as shown, to make a full flat tree.

9 Turn the entire tree over so that the 2 unglued jagged sides are on top.

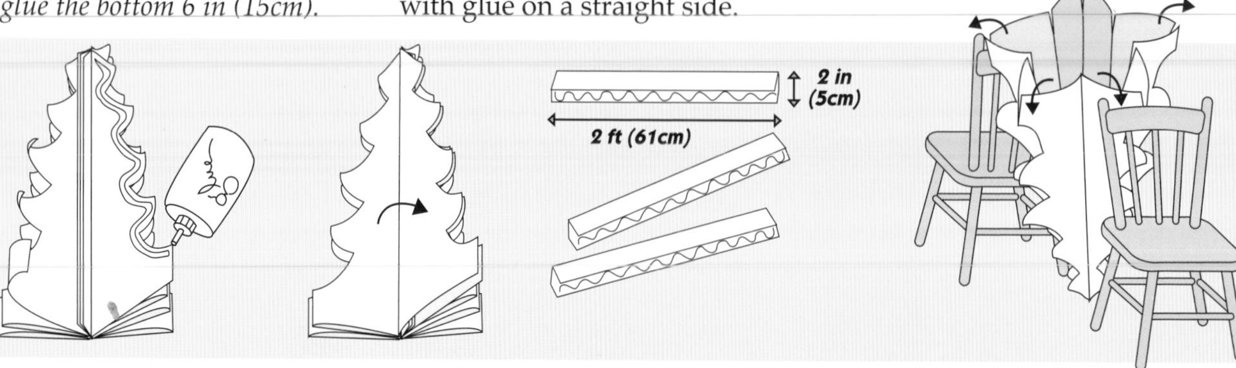

10 Spread glue along one jagged side. Fold other free jagged side over and onto the glue. Press in place. Allow glue to set.

11 Cut 5 pieces of cardboard, as shown. Set aside.

12 Turn paper tree upside down and open out. Support paper tree with chairs.

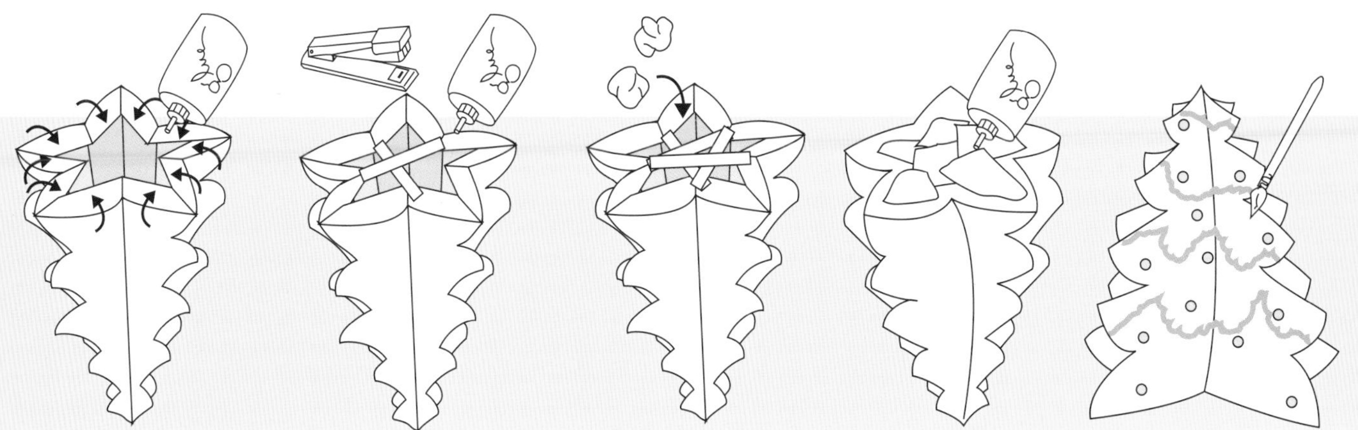

13 Fold over the unglued 6 in (15cm) bottom, overlapping at the peaks, as shown. Glue in place.

14 Glue and staple one end of a cardboard strip to the bottom of tree, as shown. Glue and staple other end of cardboard strip to an opposite fold. Glue and staple other strips to bottom of tree in the same way, to fix the folds of the tree in place.

15 Fill tree with crumpled newspaper. Stuff it firmly, but *do not stress glued seams.*

16 When full, close bottom of tree by laying several pieces of brown paper glued on one side over opening.

17 Turn tree right side up. Paint tree green with colored ornaments. Shellac. Decorate with paper projects, as desired. Fasten ornaments with straightened paper clips for hooks. (See photo, p57.)

Sponge Printed Gift Boxes

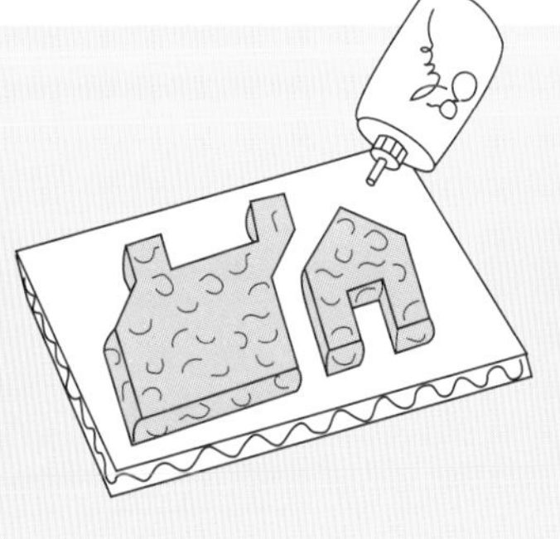

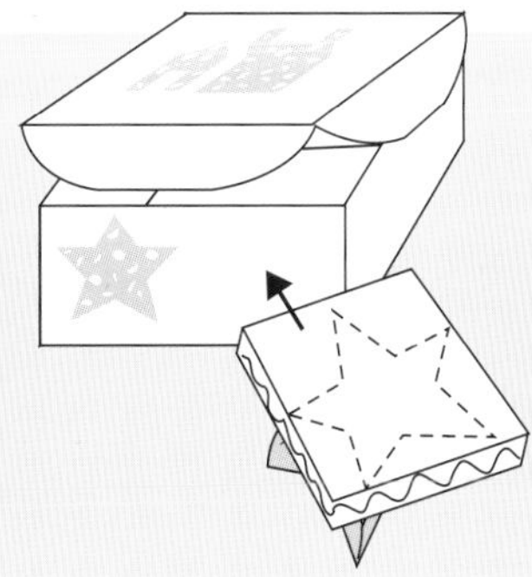

1 Purchase flat unmarked white cardboard boxes from a bakery. Assemble. Cut a sponge into decorative shapes, such as a heart, a tree, or a house.

2 Glue the cut-out sponge shapes onto small pieces of heavy cardboard.

3 Mix powdered paint fairly thin in the colors you choose.

4 Dip the pieces of sponge into the paint and press against the box. A light pressure will give a lacy effect, heavy pressure will give a more solid print.

Carrying Box

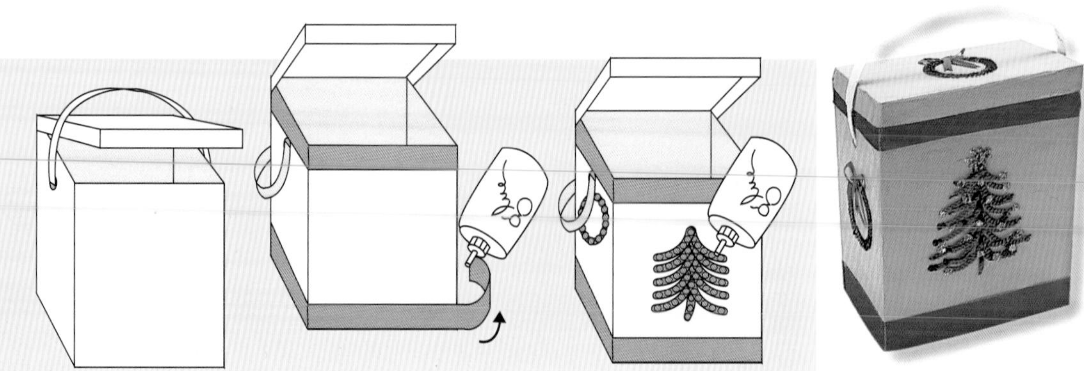

1 Use an empty cleaned laundry detergent box with a handle and a lid. Paint the outside of the box and the lid. Shellac.

2 Glue 1-in (2.5-cm) -wide ribbon around the top and bottom of the box, as shown.

3 Glue ribbon with sequins on front of box in the shape of a Christmas tree and on sides of box in the shape of a wreath. Use box for storage or for a gift.

Triangle Box

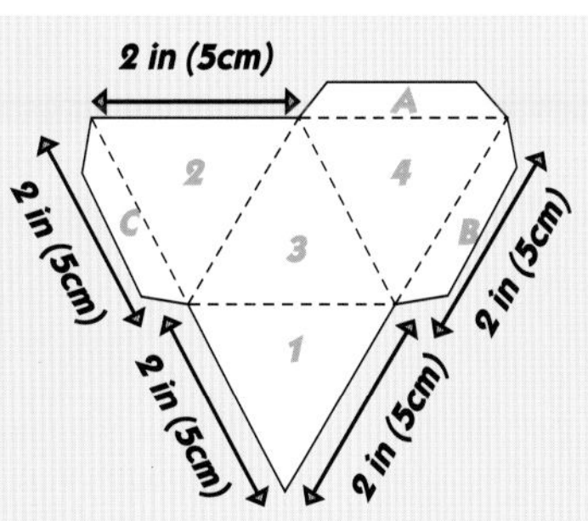

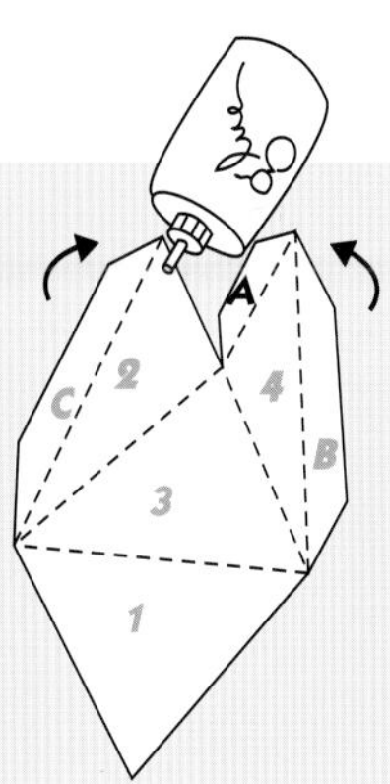

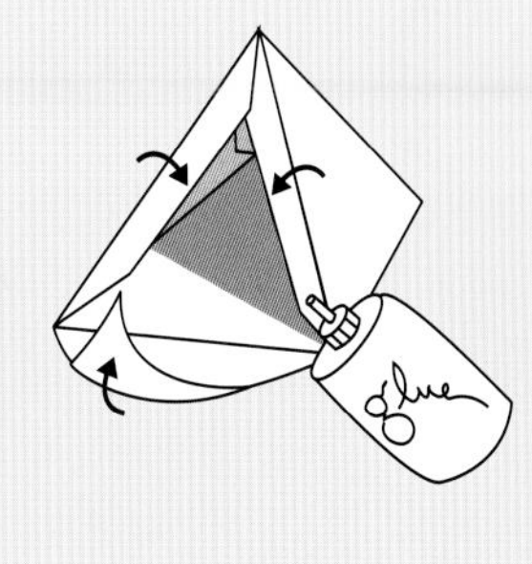

1 Draw pattern on colored construction paper. Cut out. Crease folds where indicated.

2 Place pattern on a flat surface. Bring triangles 2 and 4 up to meet in the center.

3 Tuck flap A inside triangle 2 and glue in place, as shown. Place gift inside the triangle.

4 Fold side 1 up and onto flaps C and B. Glue or tape closed. To decorate, cut 4 shapes out of gold paper to fit each side and glue in place. (See photo below.)

Pentagram Box

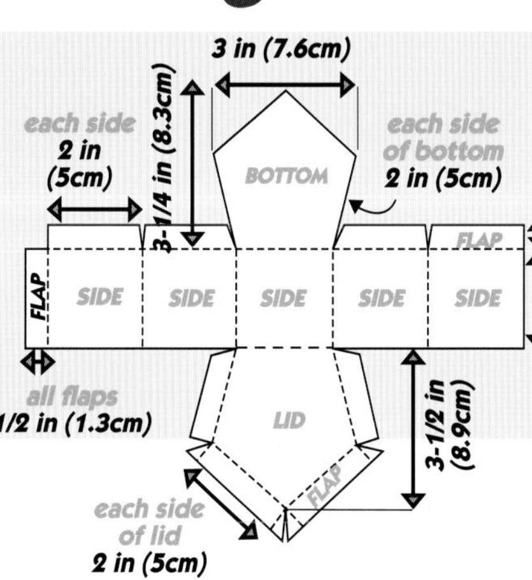

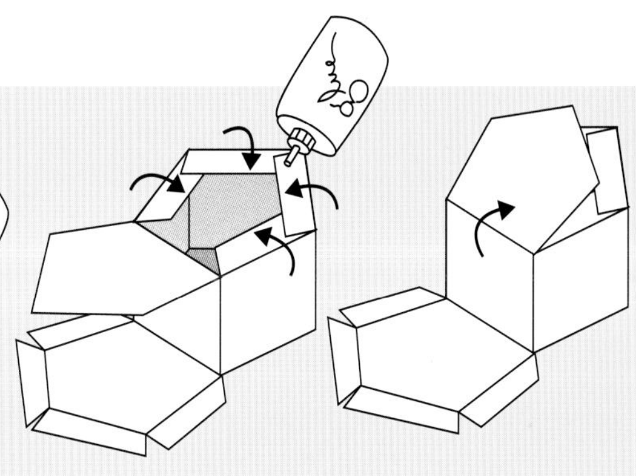

1 Draw pattern on colored construction paper and cut out. Crease folds where indicated.

2 Bring flap at one end of the row of SIDES to the opposite end of SIDES, forming a 5-sided shape. Glue flap on inside of this SIDE, as shown.

3 Fold all flaps around open side over the opening. Glue the side marked BOTTOM onto these flaps.

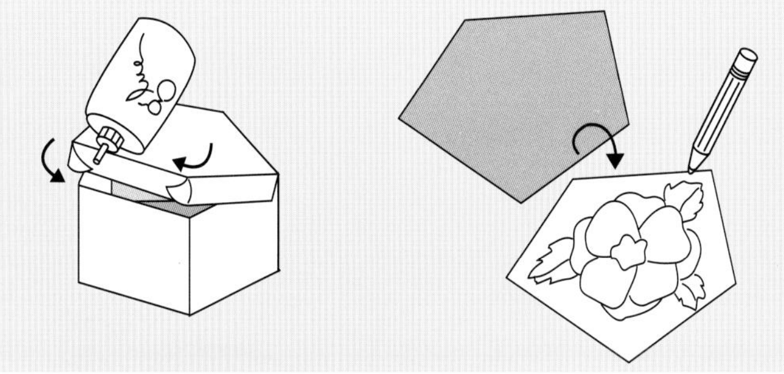

4 Turn box over. Fold over all flaps around the side marked LID. Overlap corners of these flaps and glue, as shown.

5 Cover sides with gold foil paper decorations.

6 **To make embossed foil rose,** cut gold foil paper to fit box lid, turn paper over, draw rose on back side of paper.

7 Turn over, and glue to box lid.

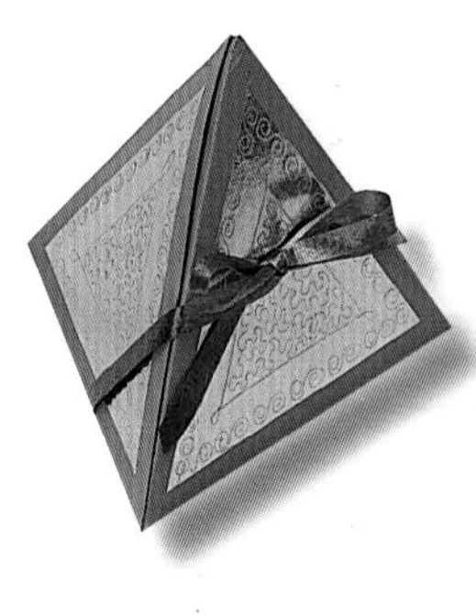

Book Box

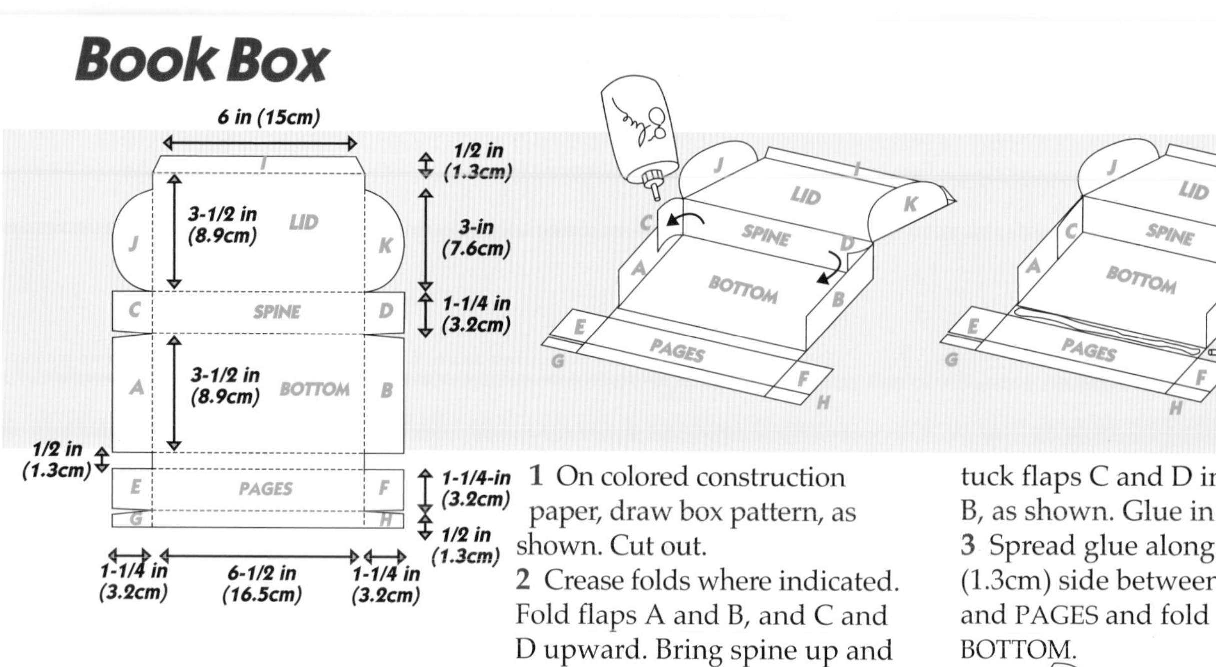

1 On colored construction paper, draw box pattern, as shown. Cut out.

2 Crease folds where indicated. Fold flaps A and B, and C and D upward. Bring spine up and tuck flaps C and D inside A and B, as shown. Glue in place.

3 Spread glue along the 1/2 in (1.3cm) side between BOTTOM and PAGES and fold back onto BOTTOM.

4 Tuck flaps E and F inside A and B and glue in place. PAGES section is now vertical, and A and B extends past PAGES.

5 Fold the last 1/2 in (1.3cm) side forward and tuck flaps G and H inside A and B, as shown. Glue in place.

6 Fold flap I back onto lid and glue in place.

7 To close lid, tuck flaps J and K inside the box and fold lid down.

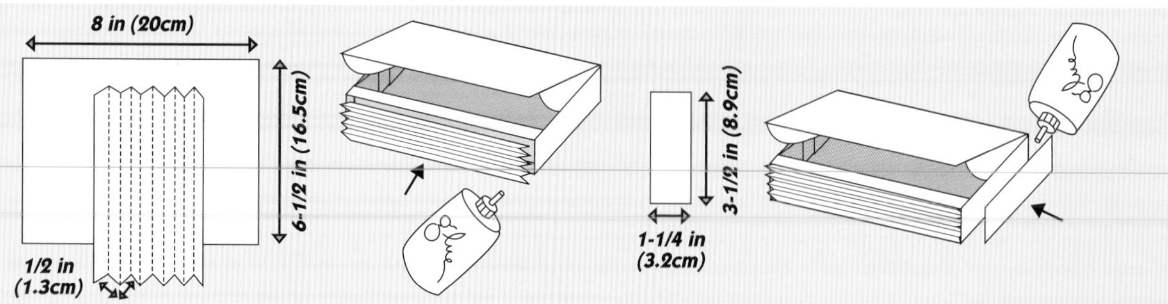

8 To make pages, cut a piece of gold paper, as shown. Crease in 1/2 in (1.3cm) folds starting from a short side.

9 Glue this pleated paper inside the space along the side of box marked PAGES.

10 Cut 2 pieces of gold paper, as indicated. Draw straight lines on the wrong side to represent pages. Glue one piece to each side.

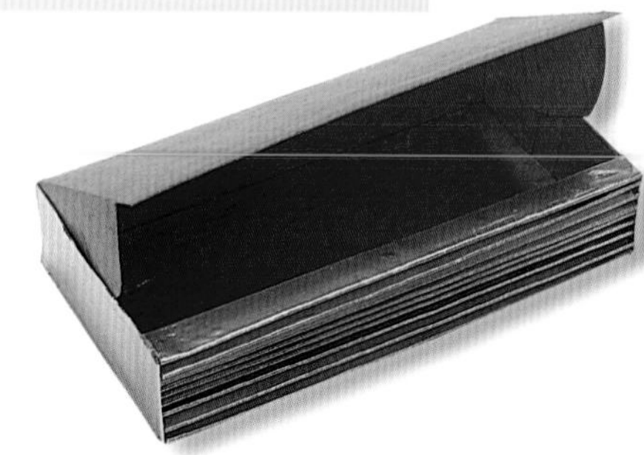

Mosaic Decoration Gift Box

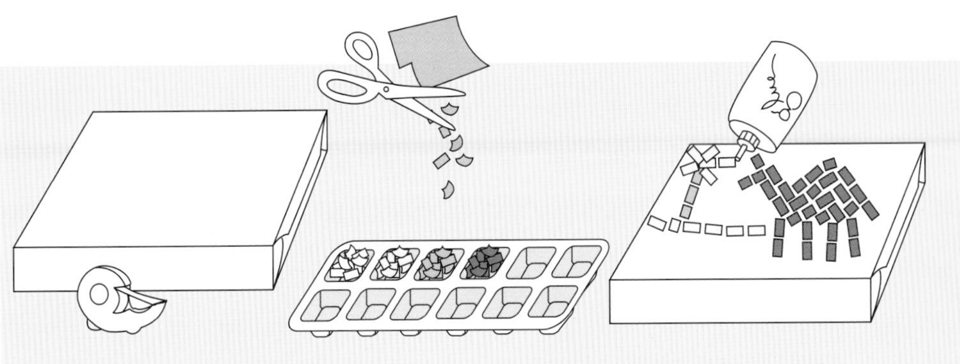

1 Wrap a gift box in brown paper. Choose a box that has a fairly large, flat top.
2 Cut scraps of different colored construction paper into pieces 1/4 in (.6cm) to 1/2 in (1.3cm) square. Keep colors separated in an egg carton box.
3 On the surface of the box, compose a picture or design using the squares of different colored paper. (Don't sneeze!) Glue the squares in place.
4 Make yellow construction paper bow (see below) and glue to side of box.

Wrapping Paper Bow for Gift Box

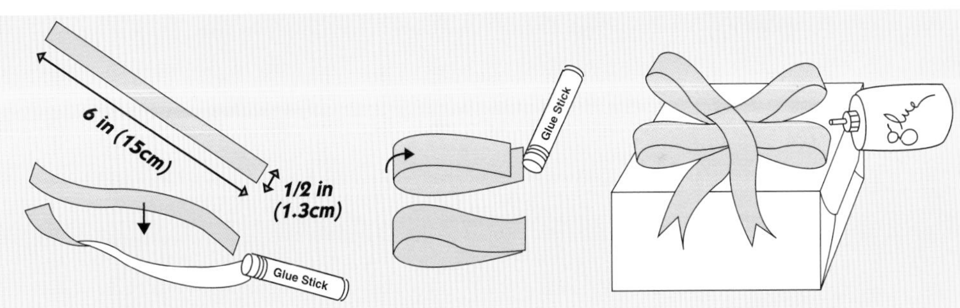

1 Cut strips of wrapping paper, as shown. If paper is printed on only one side, use a glue stick to glue 2 unprinted sides together.
2 Glue the 2 ends together to form a loop.
3 Glue loops onto the top of the package to form a bow.
4 Add more long strips to form ribbon ends.

Gift Bags

1 Purchase colored paper bags or collect clean used bags.
2 Draw shapes on colored construction paper.
3 Cut out and glue to one side of bag.

Window Decorations—Tree with Ornaments

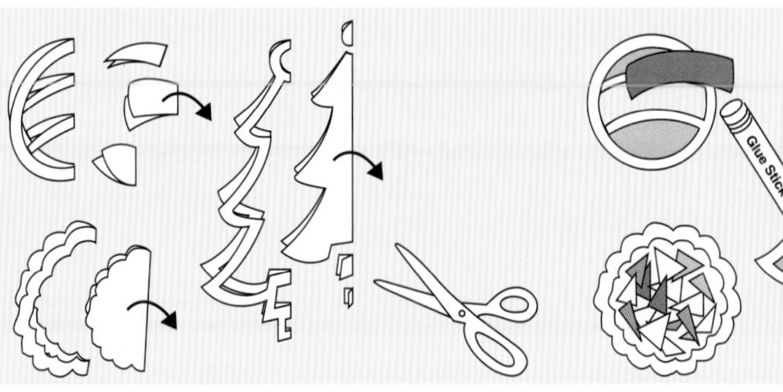

1 Draw ornament patterns, pp92 to 95, on brown paper. Cut out.
2 Fold shapes in half in order to cut out the inside of the shape, leaving a 1/4 in (.6cm) border.
3 Glue one side of border with glue stick and press tissue paper on brown paper.
4 Glue on a ribbon loop for hanging.
5 Transfer tree pattern, p94, to a large sheet of paper. Tape to the outside of the window.
6 Mix powdered poster paint with liquid dish soap. This mixture will stick to a window. Paint outlines of the pattern on the window with paint mixture. See photograph for color suggestions.
7 Use small pieces of tape to hang the ornaments in the tree spaces.
8 To clean the window, spray a mist of water over the paint to soften. Wipe off with a sponge. Protect floor with old sheet or newspaper.

Cookie Cutter Stencil

1 Mix powdered poster paint with liquid dish soap. This mixture will stick to a window.
2 Use cookie cutters as a stencil. Tape the cookie cutter to the glass and paint inside it.
3 Remove the cookie cutter.
4 To clean window, spray a mist of water over the paint to soften. Wipe off with a sponge. Protect floor with old sheet or newspaper.

Christmas Tree Centerpiece

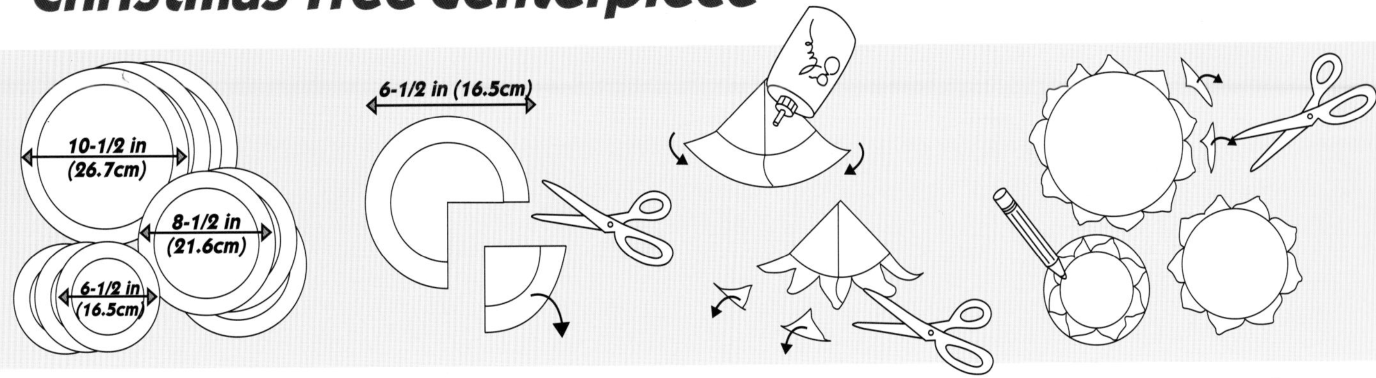

1 Use 3 of each of the paper plate sizes shown above.
2 Cut a pie shape from one of the smallest plates, removing a quarter of the plate, as shown.
3 Fold the plate into a cone and glue. Cut cone edge into points, as shown. Set aside.
4 Draw tree branches on each remaining plate, as shown. Cut out.
5 Turn all plates upside down.

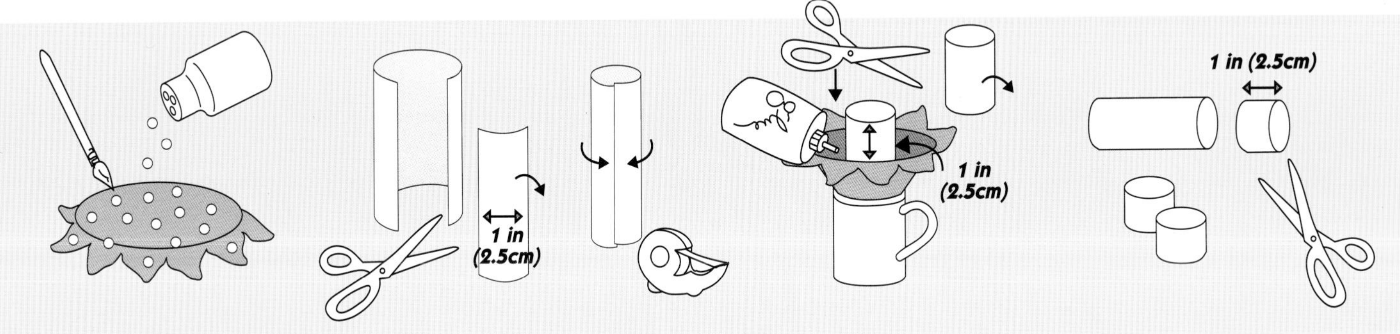

6 Paint green. While paint is still wet, shake tiny colored candies (used for cake and cookie decoration) over each plate. When paint is dry, shellac all plates and cone.
7 Cut a strip from a toilet tissue tube, as shown, to make a smaller tube. Tape tube together.
8 Set prepared cone upside down in a cup.
9 Glue tube inside cone. Trim end of tube so that it extends past the outside edge, as shown.
10 Cut rings from a cardboard tube, as indicated. Make 9 rings.

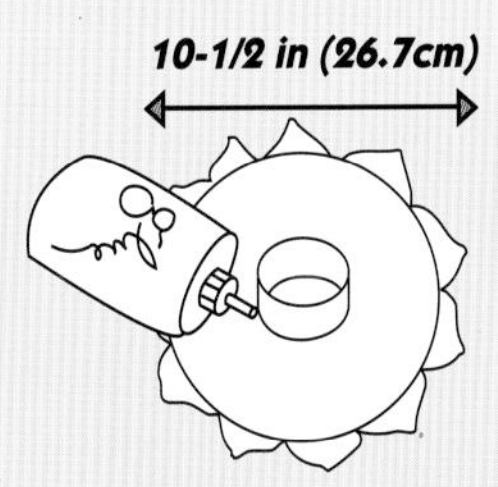

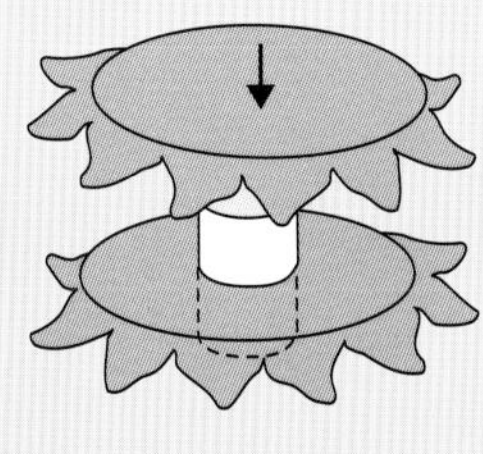

11 Glue one of these rings to the unpainted side of one of the largest paper plates. Glue it exactly in the center.
12 Turn this plate over (painted side up). Glue another cardboard ring on top, in the center. Dab glue on top of ring and place another large plate over the top, painted side up, as shown. Hold in place.
13 Continue to glue rings and plates to form tree, using large plates first then medium plates, and finally small plates. Glue prepared cone to top of tree.

Poinsettia Table Decoration

1 Draw petal shapes on 3—8 in (20cm) paper plates. Cut out, as shown.
2 Paint one plate green, and 2 plates red. Paint small yellow and white circles in center of one red plate. Shellac plates.
3 Glue the plain red plate on top of the green plate and the red plate with the circles on top of the plain red plate to form a poinsettia.

Christmas Tree Tray

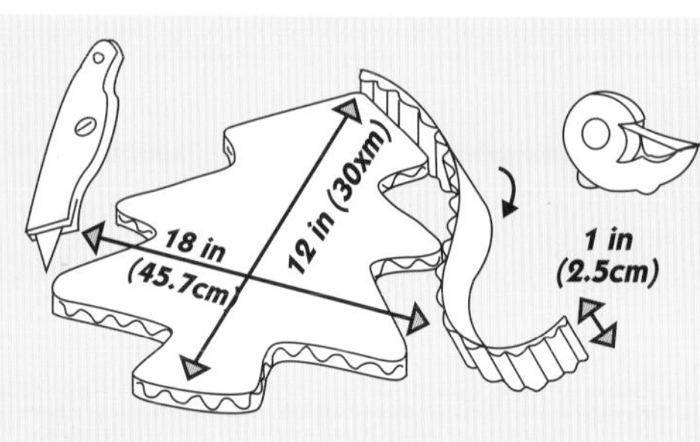

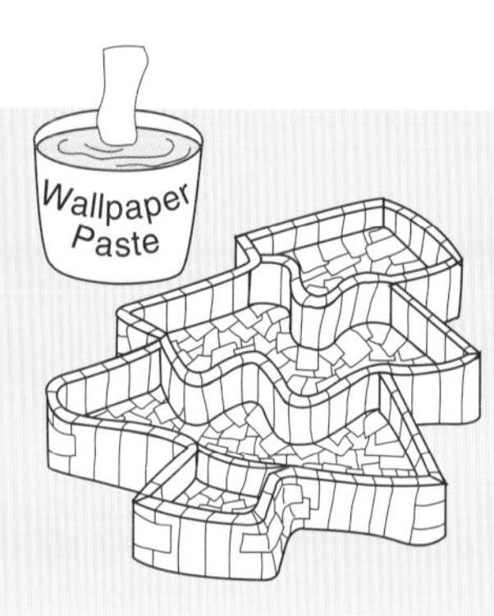

1 On a piece of heavy card-board, draw a tree shape, as shown, and cut out. From a piece of rippled cardboard, cut many strips across the ripples, as indicated.
2 Tape strips around tree shape cardboard base to make an edge, as shown. Tape 3 more strips across the tree in a branch shape, as shown, dividing the tray into sections. Trim strips to fit.
3 Cover entire tray with strips of newspaper dipped in wallpaper paste. When dry paint and shellac.

Christmas Ball Tray

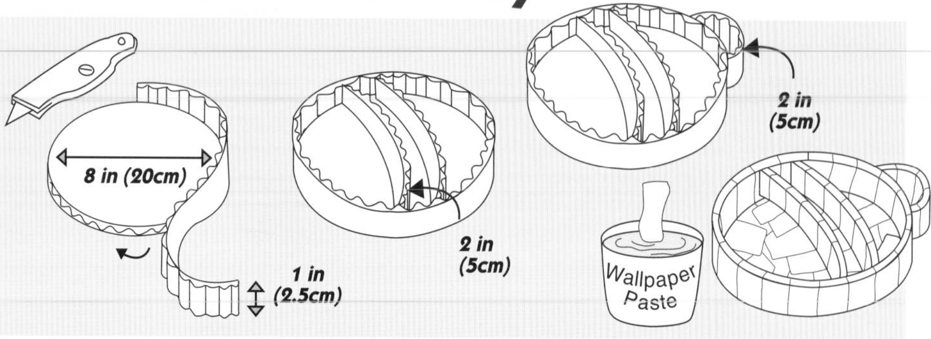

1 Draw a circle on heavy card-board, as shown. Cut out with knife. From a piece of rippled cardboard, cut strips of card-board across the ripples. Tape strips around ball to make an edge.
2 Tape 2 more strips across middle of ball, as shown.
3 Glue a strip across top of ball to form a loop.
4 Cover entire tray with strips of newspaper dipped in wallpaper paste. When dry, paint and shellac.

2-Tiered Heart Tray

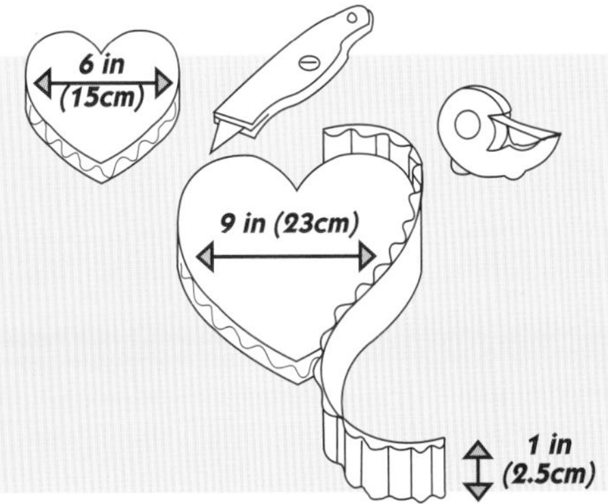

1 On heavy cardboard draw 2 hearts, as shown. Cut out with a knife.

2 Cut several strips of rippled cardboard across the ripples, as shown.

3 Tape strips around both hearts to make an edge. Trim strips to fit.

2-Tiered Heart Tray continued

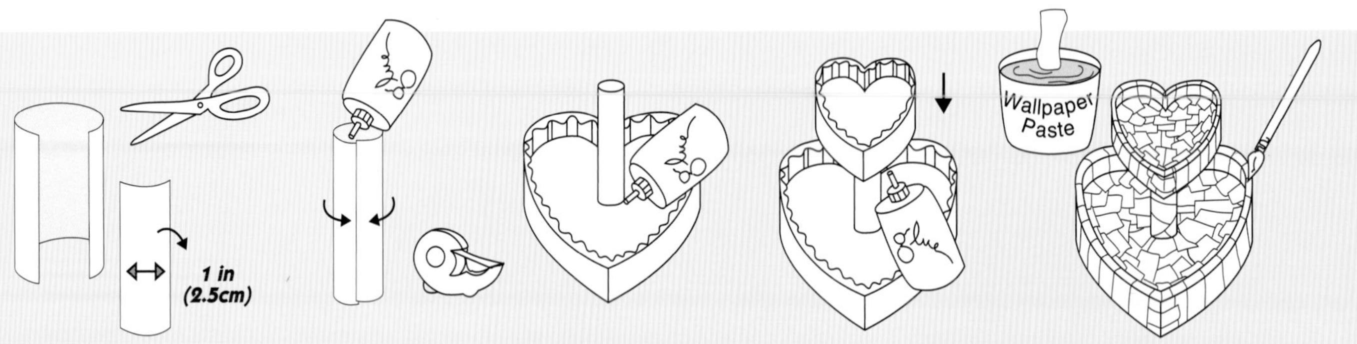

4 Cut a strip lengthwise from a toilet tissue tube, as shown. Discard strip.
5 Bring the 2 cut edges together and glue and tape to form a narrow tube.

6 Glue tube to center of large heart, as shown.
7 Center the small heart on top of the tube and glue in place.

8 Cover entire tray with strips of newspaper dipped in wallpaper paste. When dry, paint and shellac.

3-Tiered Round Tray

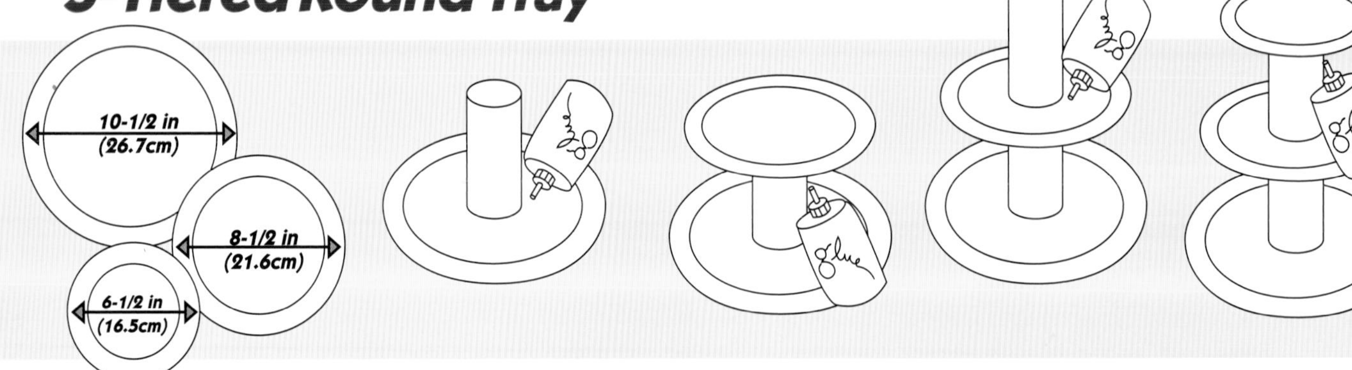

1 Use 3 paper plates, as shown.

2 Glue a toilet tissue tube upright in the center of largest paper plate.
3 Center middle-sized plate over tube and glue in place.

4 Glue another toilet tissue tube upright in the center of the top plate.
5 Center smallest plate over second tube and glue in place.

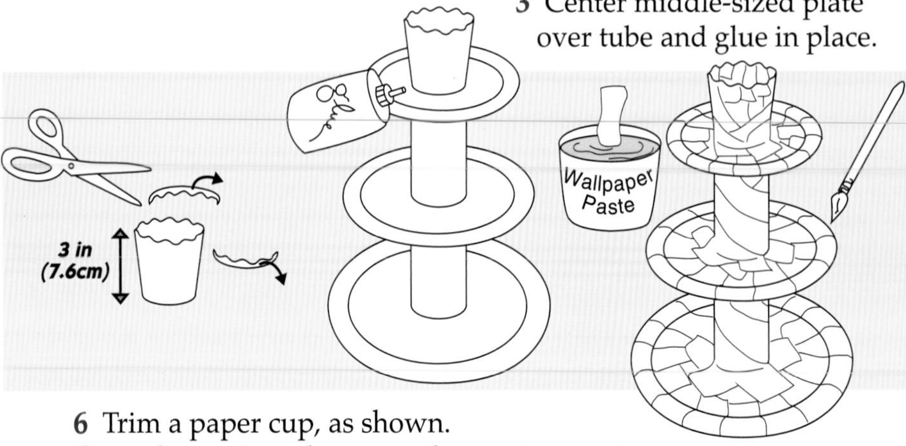

6 Trim a paper cup, as shown. Cut a decorative edge around the rim.
7 Glue cup to center of top plate.
8 Cover entire stand with 2 to 3 layers of newspaper strips dipped in wallpaper paste. When dry, paint and shellac.

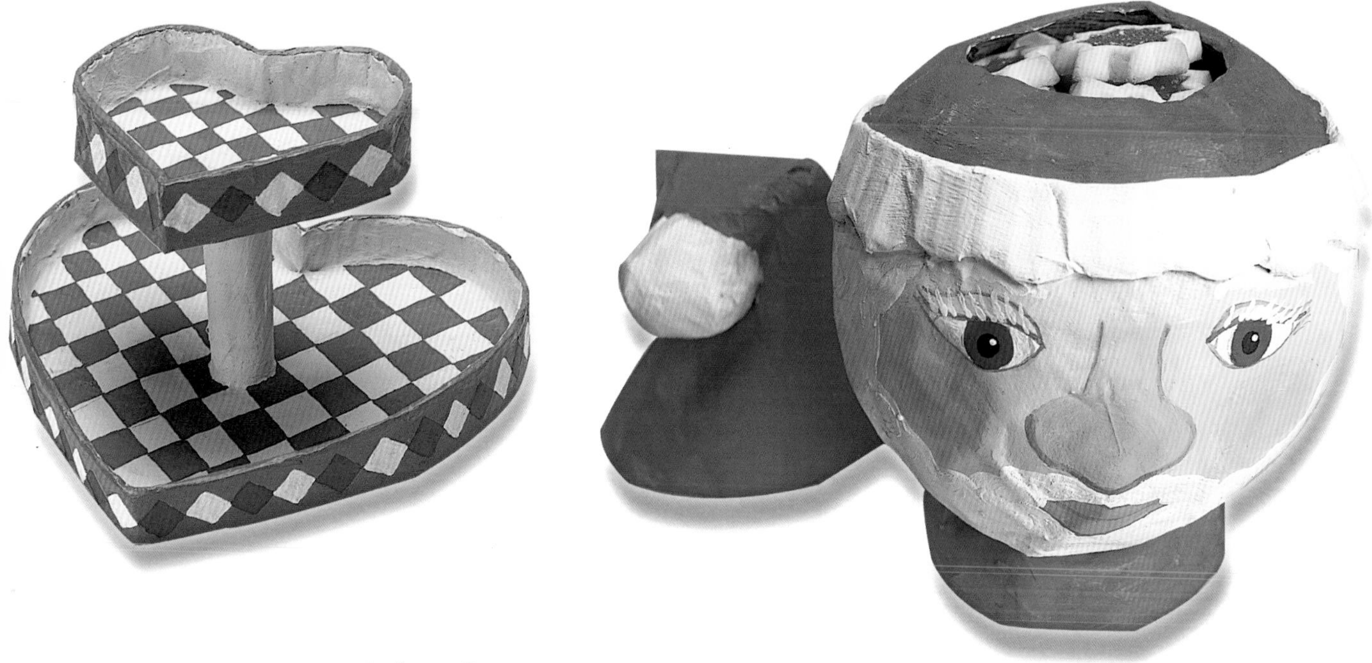

Santa Cookie Jar

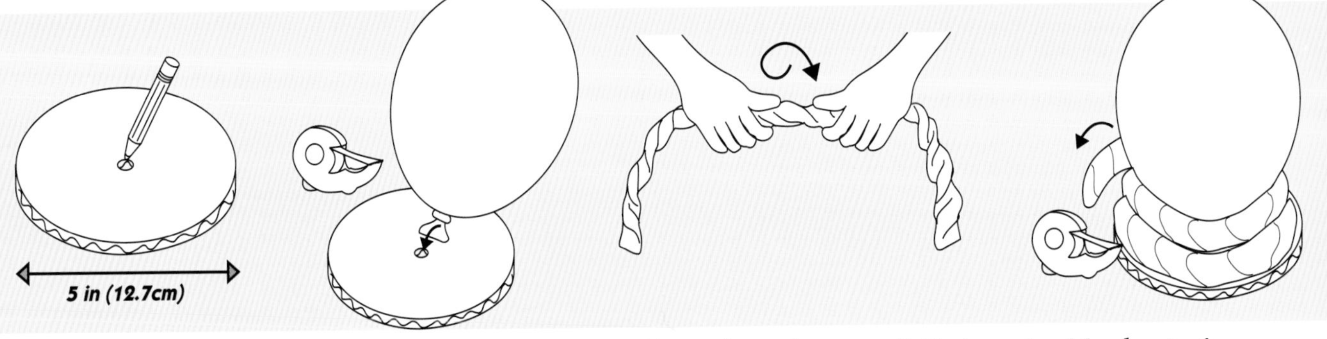

1 Cut a circle of heavy cardboard, as shown. Poke a hole in the center with a pencil.

2 Blow up a balloon, knot the opening. Poke knot through the hole. Tape in place under circle.

3 Twist a double sheet of newspaper into a long rope.
4 Wrap paper rope around base of balloon and tape in place.

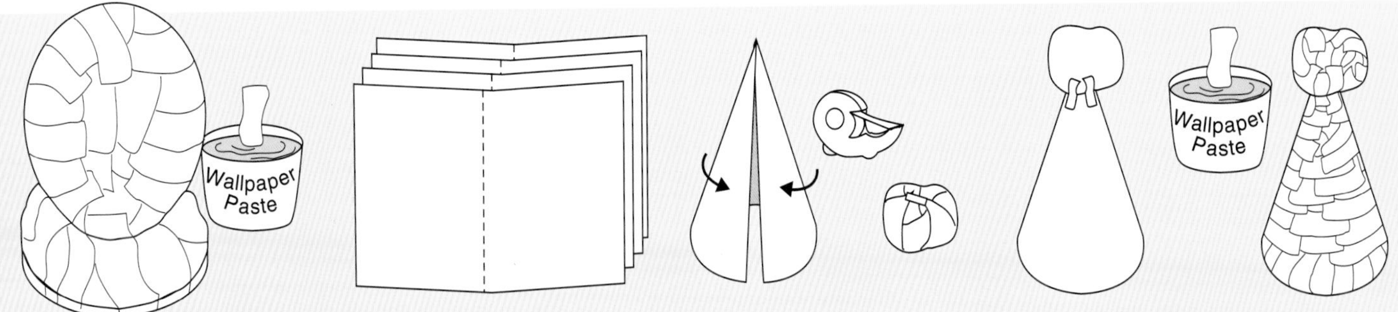

5 Cover balloon and base with 5 to 6 layers of strips of newspaper dipped in wallpaper paste.
6 Lay 4 double sheets of newspaper one on top of another.

7 Roll into a cone, making open end wide enough to fit over the balloon. Tape. This is the hat.
8 Crumple another double sheet of newspaper into a ball.

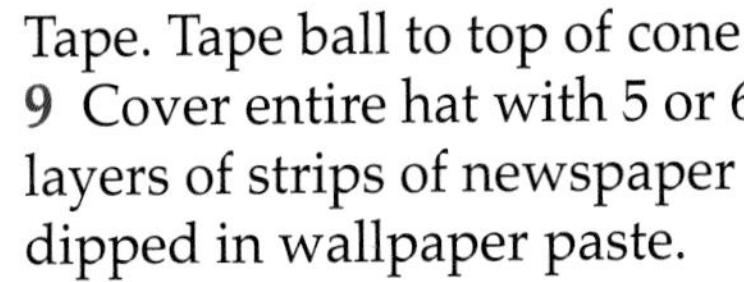

Tape. Tape ball to top of cone.
9 Cover entire hat with 5 or 6 layers of strips of newspaper dipped in wallpaper paste.

Santa Cookie Jar continued

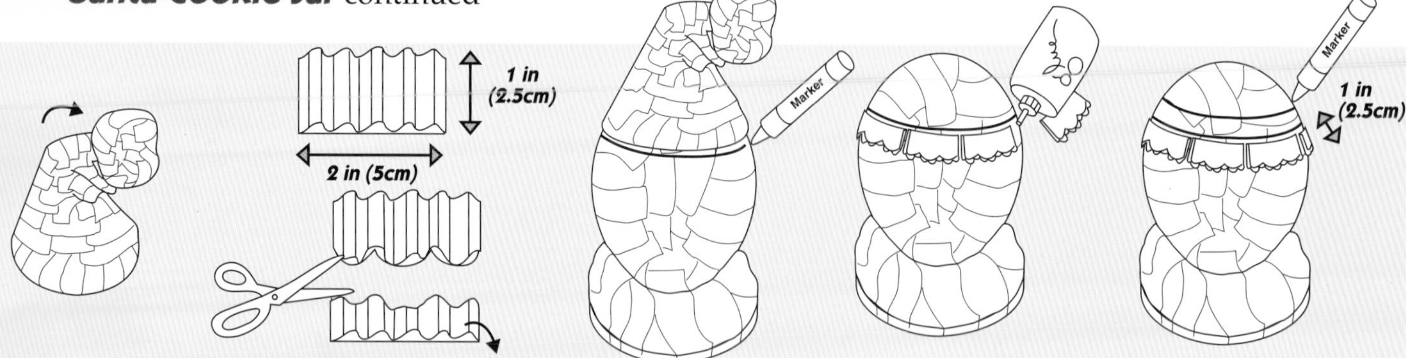

10 Bend top of hat over, as shown.
11 Cut pieces of rippled cardboard across the ripples, as shown. Scallop edge along one long side, as shown.
12 Place hat on top of head. Draw around hat on the head with a marker or pen that will mark wet paper.
13 Remove the hat. Glue scalloped pieces of cardboard directly below this line, all around head, as shown. Set hat and base aside to dry.
14 Draw a line around top of head shape above cardboard rim, as shown.

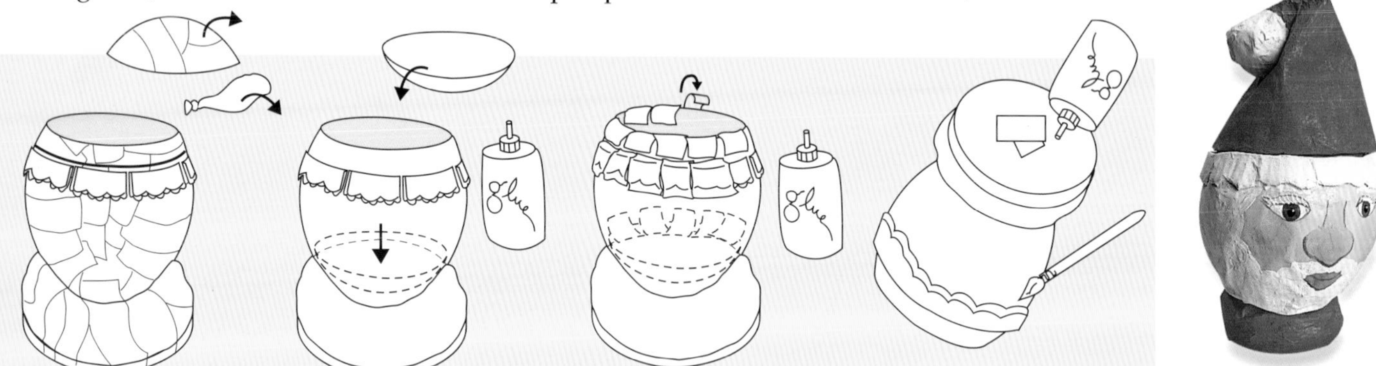

15 Cut out along line. Remove balloon.
16 Glue cut-out top inside for a bottom, as shown.
17 Cover seams in the bottom with strips of newspaper spread with glue. Cover edges of the opening and cardboard pieces around opening.
18 Turn head upside down and cover hole where balloon was poked through, with strips of newspaper spread with glue.
19 Paint a Santa face. When dry, shellac outside of jar. Put 2 coats of shellac on inside of jar.

Christmas Cake Surprise Centerpiece

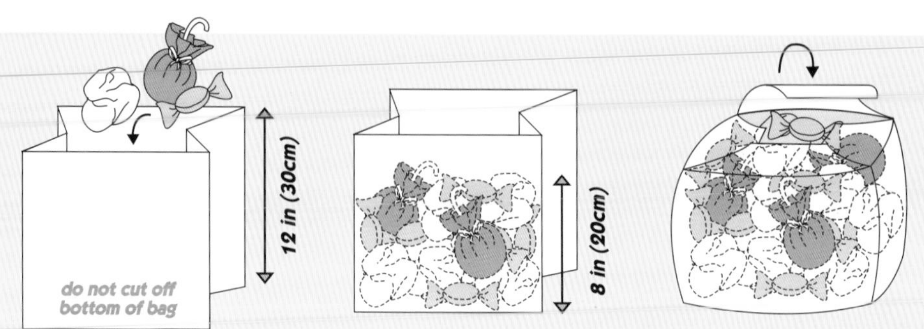

1 Cut a brown paper grocery bag, as shown. Stuff tightly with crumpled newspapers. Mix small gifts or wrapped candy in amongst newspaper.
2 Fill bag 8 in (20cm) deep.
3 Fold bag closed and glue all edges down.
4 Paint to resemble a fruitcake. Shellac. Children cut cake open to find the surprises.

For catstair garland, see p67, for star ornament, see p61.

Napkin Rings or Table Decorations

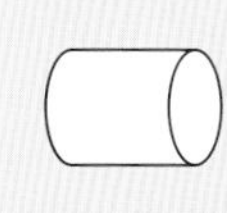
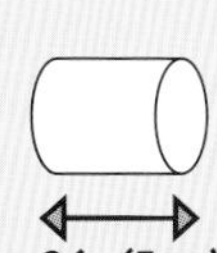
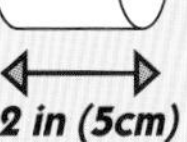
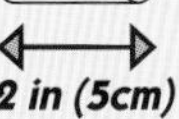

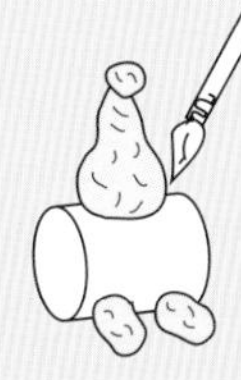

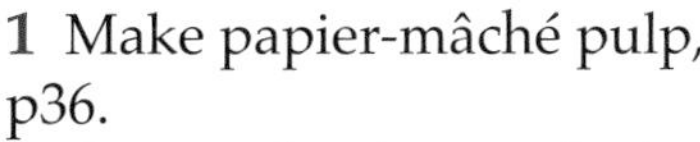

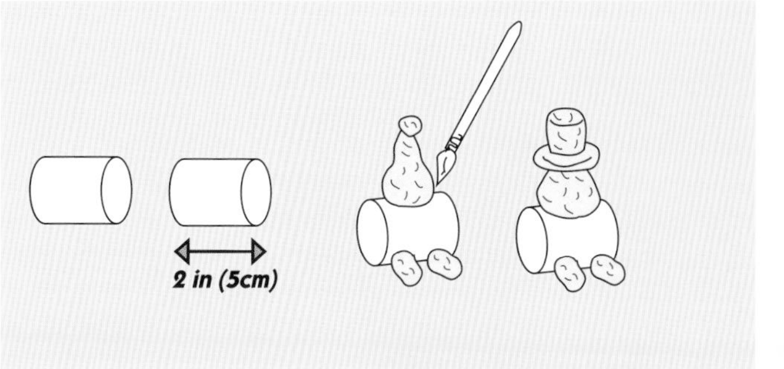

1 Make papier-mâché pulp, p36.
2 Cut a toilet tissue tube into 2 in (5cm) rings.
3 From pulp, form round ball heads and press on top of rings, as shown. Make feet from small balls of pulp and push against bottom of tube, as shown. Place in a warm dry place to harden. When dry, paint to make snowman or Santa. Shellac.

Tissue Paper Surprise Balls

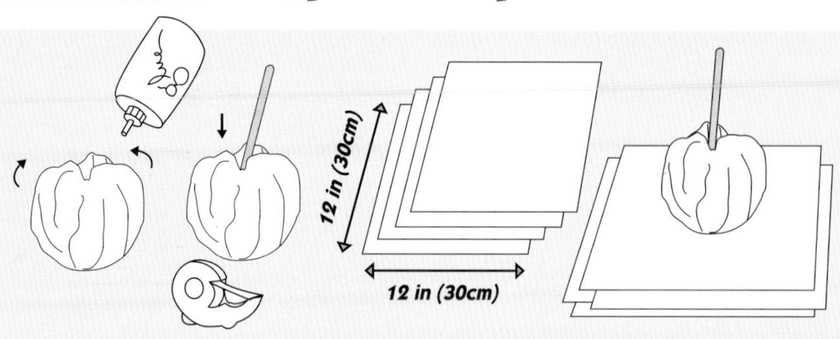

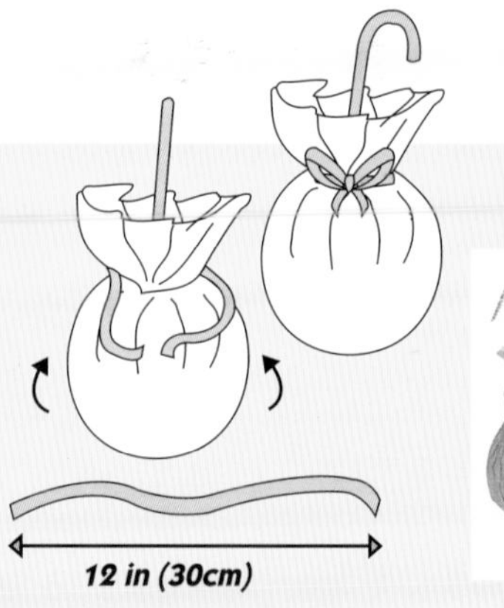

1 Crumple a double sheet of newspaper into a ball. Squeeze glue into a deep crease in the ball.
2 Place one end of a 6 in (15cm) chenille stem in the glue and squeeze crease closed. Tape in place to hold round shape.
3 Cut 4 pieces of colored tissue paper each 12 in (30cm) square.
4 Place them one on top of the other with newspaper ball on top, chenille stem sticking up, as shown.
5 Cut a piece of ribbon 12 in (30cm) long. Bring tissue up around ball gathering the extra tissue in ruffles around the chenille stem. Pinch tissue tightly, and tie in place with the ribbon.
6 Bend chenille stem in a hook for hanging.

Candle Holder

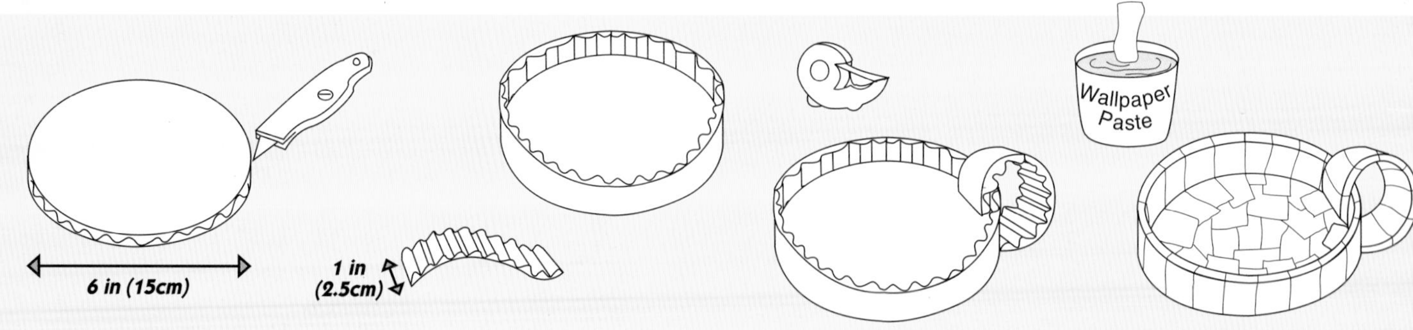

1 On heavy cardboard, draw a circle, as shown. Cut out with a knife.
2 Cut a few strips of rippled cardboard across the ripples, as shown.
3 Tape strip around circle to make a base.
4 Tape one end of strip to inside of base rim and tape other end of strip to the underside of candleholder base, as shown. This is the handle.
5 Cover entire holder with newspaper strips dipped in wallpaper paste.

6 Use a metal lid from a poster paint can, and a 3/4 in (2cm) copper cap available at any hardware store to hold the candle. Epoxy metal lid to center of base. This lid will catch dripping wax. Epoxy copper cap to center of lid. This holds candle. Paint entire candle holder gold.

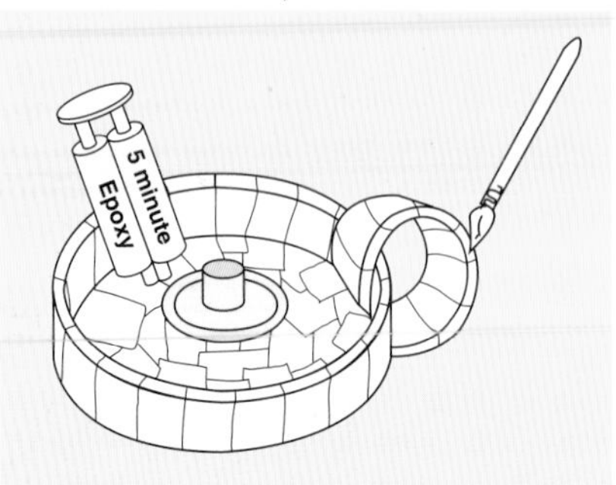

Light candle only when adults are present.

Sleigh Centerpiece

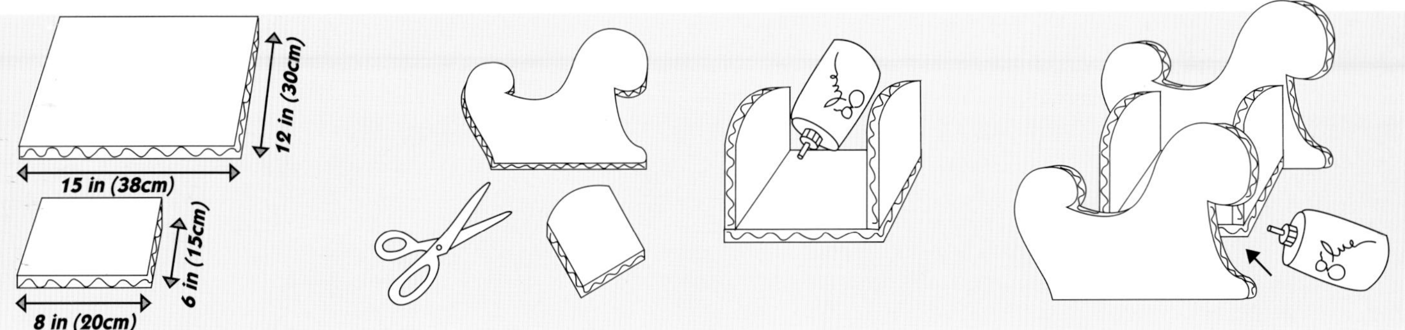

1 Trace sleigh pattern on heavy cardboard (p95) and cut out.

2 Glue front and back sections to the base, as shown.

3 Add sides and glue in place. Tape, if necessary.

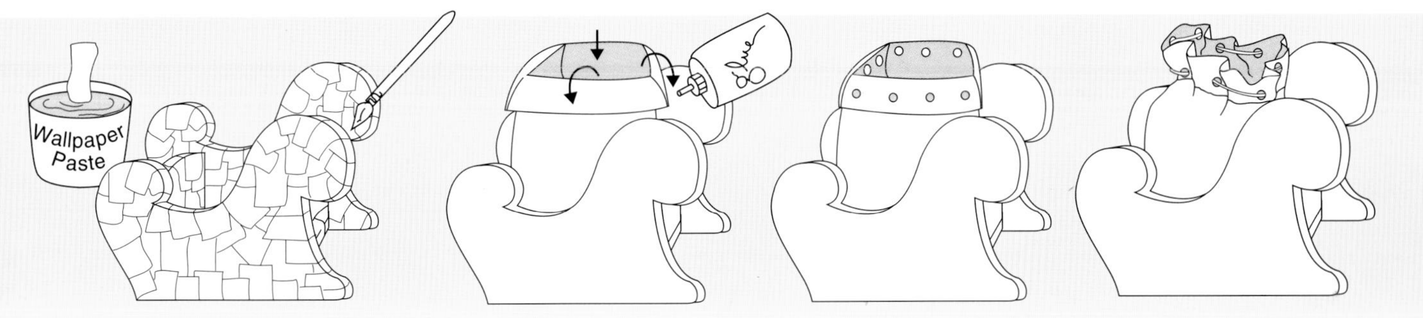

4 Cover entire sleigh with newspaper strips dipped in wallpaper paste. Allow to dry. Paint and shellac.

5 Fit a middle-sized brown paper bag inside sleigh. Fold top down to an appropriate height for Santa's bag and glue folds in place.

6 Punch holes 3 in (7.6cm) apart around top of bag.

7 Thread a string through the holes and partially close bag, as shown. Remove bag from sleigh and paint and shellac bag.

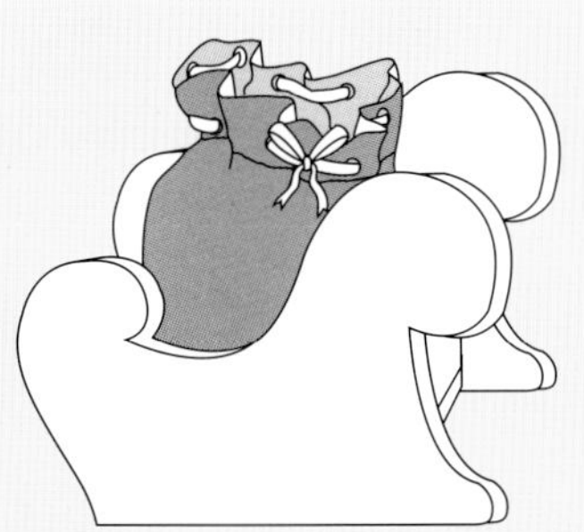

8 Remove string from bag, and replace with a ribbon.

9 Place bag in sleigh. Fill bag with small gifts. If you wish, attach one end of a long ribbon to each gift and tape other end to a place card at the table.

Teapot Stand

1 Draw wreath and bow teapot stand pattern on smooth cardboard, p93, as shown.
2 Cut out.
3 Cover with strips of newspaper dipped in wallpaper paste. Wrap newspaper strips around edges to cover the cut edges of the cardboard. When dry, paint and shellac.

Coasters

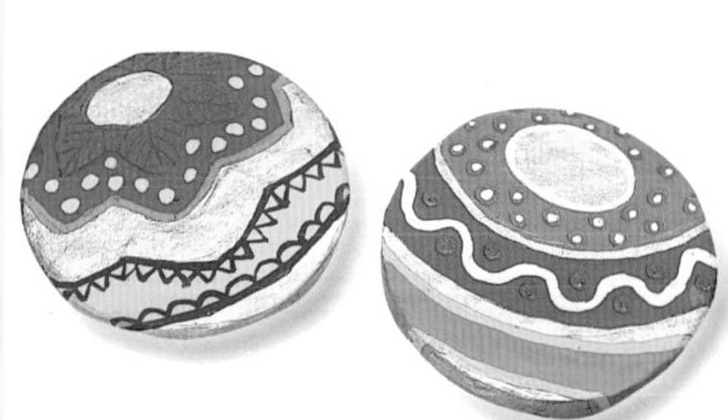

1 Draw circles on smooth cardboard by tracing around a middle-sized can.
2 Cut out.
3 Cover circles with strips of newspaper dipped in wallpaper paste. When dry paint and shellac, as shown.

Candelabra

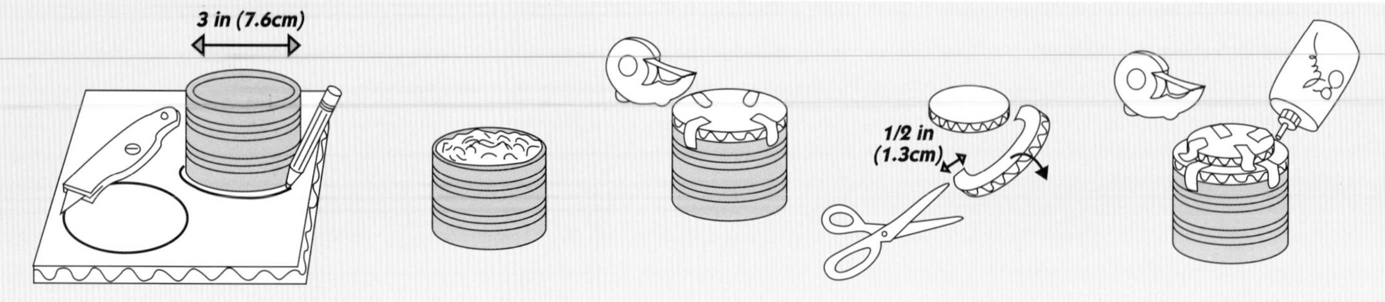

1 Trace around a middle-sized can on heavy cardboard twice, as shown. Cut out with a knife.
2 Fill can with sand or gravel to make a stable base.
3 Place one circle over can opening and tape in place.
4 Trim around the second cardboard circle, as shown.
5 Center circle on top of base and tape and glue in place.

6 Glue one toilet tissue tube upright to the center of the base.
7 Cut 2 curved notches from the top of this tube, as shown.
8 Lay a paper towel tube in these notches, center it, and tape in place.
9 Cut similar notches in one end of 3 other toilet tissue tubes.
10 Fit these tubes over the paper towel tube, as shown, one in the center and one on each end. Tape in place.

11 Cover entire structure with 2 or 3 layers of strips of newspaper dipped in wallpaper paste, covering open ends of tubes as well. When dry, paint and shellac.
For "antique" finish, paint entire candelabra medium green. Allow to dry. Cut a 1 in (2.5cm) piece of sponge, dip lightly in gold paint, and dab over green. Apply gold unevenly. Repeat sponge technique with black and white. Apply very sparingly. When dry, shellac.
12 Epoxy a metal lid to the top of each toilet tissue tube. Epoxy a 3/4 in (2cm) copper cap (available at any hardware store) to the center of each metal lid to hold candles. Paint the metal parts gold.
Light candles only when adults are present.

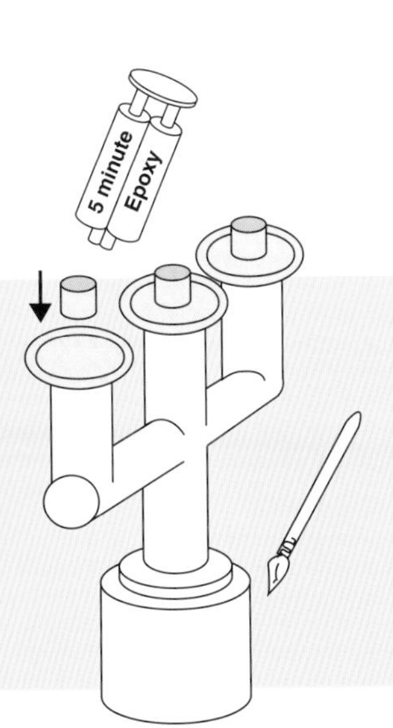

Christmas Ornament Pin

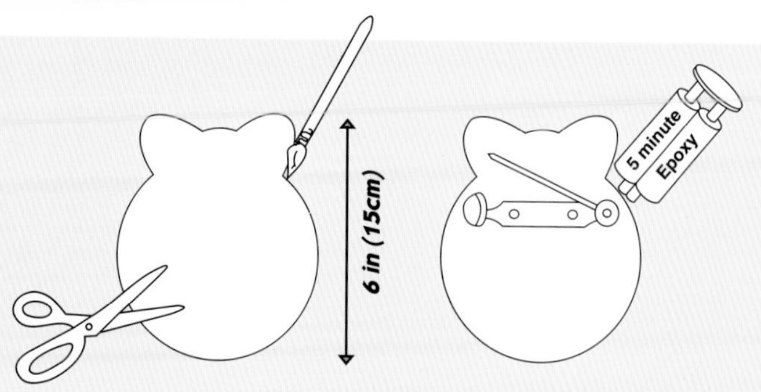

1 Draw ball shape with bow on wet papier-mâché slab (see fan brooch below). Cut out.
2 When dry, paint and decorate. Shellac.
3 Epoxy purchased bar pin to back of brooch.

Wire Necklace

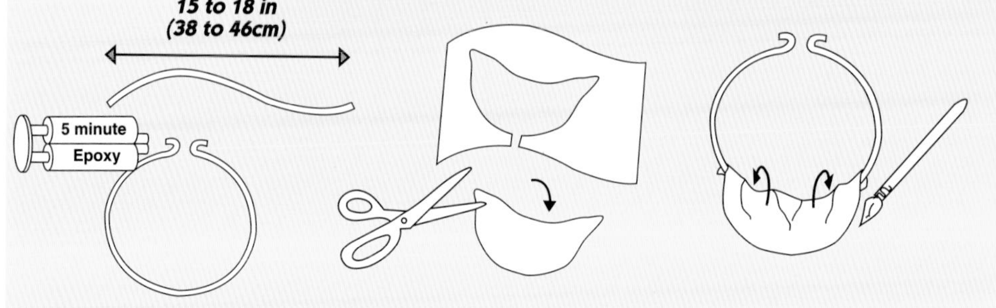

1 Cut a length of wire long enough to fit easily around the neck. Use copper wire or plastic coated wire. Bend in a circle and bend a hook in each end. Put a dab of epoxy on ends of wires to blunt them.
2 Cut pieces of wet papier-mâché slab (see fan brooch below).
3 Bend edges of paper around the wire. Set aside to dry. When dry, paint and shellac. To wear, hook ends of wire behind the neck.

Pleated Fan Brooch

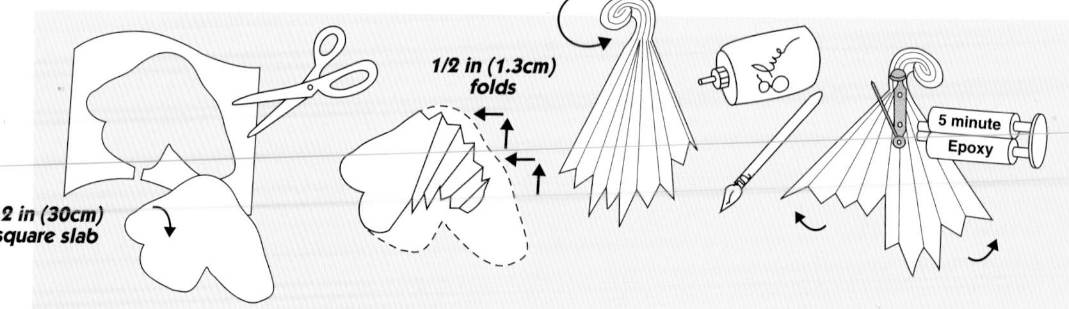

1 Make a papier-mâché slab, as shown. Lay a 12 in (30cm) square sheet of newspaper on a waterproof work surface. Spread with wallpaper paste. Lay another sheet the same size on top. Smooth into place. Repeat process to make a 5-layer slab.
2 From the wet paper slab, cut out a shape, as shown.
3 Pleat the wet paper shape in folds, as shown.
4 Curl one end, as shown, and glue in place. Open out the other end like a fan. Set aside to dry. When dry, paint and shellac.
5 Epoxy a purchased bar pin on the back of the paper.

Triangle Earrings

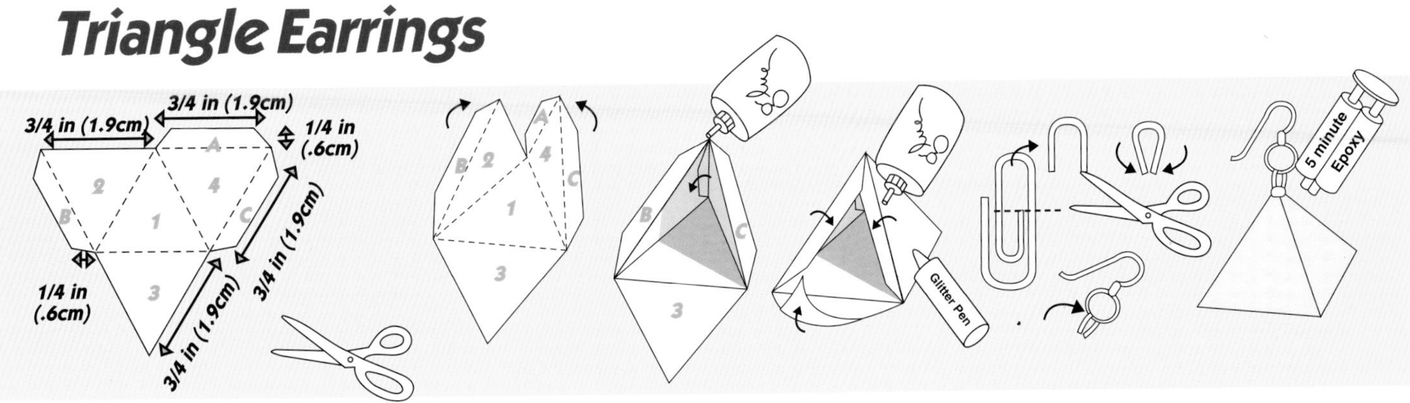

1 Draw pattern on colored construction paper. Cut out. Crease folds where indicated.
2 Place on a flat surface. Bring triangles 2 and 4 up to meet in the center.
3 Tuck flap A inside triangle 2 and glue in place, as shown.
4 Fold triangle 3 up and onto flaps C and B. Glue or tape closed. Decorate with glitter.
5 To make shepherd hook earrings, cut one end off a paper clip, as shown. Squeeze cut ends together. Thread this wire loop through ring of shepherd hook.
6 Epoxy cut ends of the loop to triangles.

Spiral Earrings

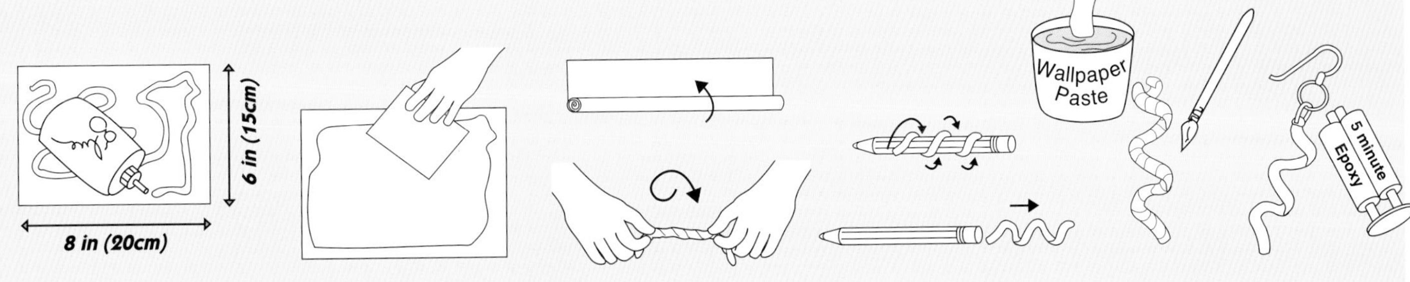

1 Cut a piece of newspaper, as shown. Drizzle with glue.
2 Spread glue to cover paper evenly.
3 Roll into a tight tube, as shown.
4 Twist tube into a thin rope.
5 To make a spiral, wrap rope around a pencil, as shown.
6 When dry, slide spiral off the pencil.
7 Cover spiral shape with small pieces of newspaper dipped in wallpaper paste. Allow to dry.
8 Paint and shellac.
9 Make shepherd hooks as in Triangle Earrings step 5, above. Epoxy ends of loop to top of the spiral.

Christmas Tree Earrings

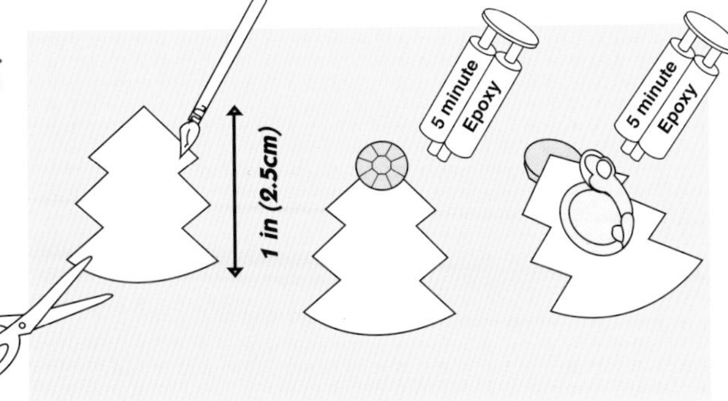

1 Cut out 2 identical tree shapes from wet papier-mâché slab (see fan brooch p86). When dry, paint and shellac both sides of shape.
2 Epoxy rhinestones to top of each tree and earring clips on the back of each tree.

Multi Picture Frame

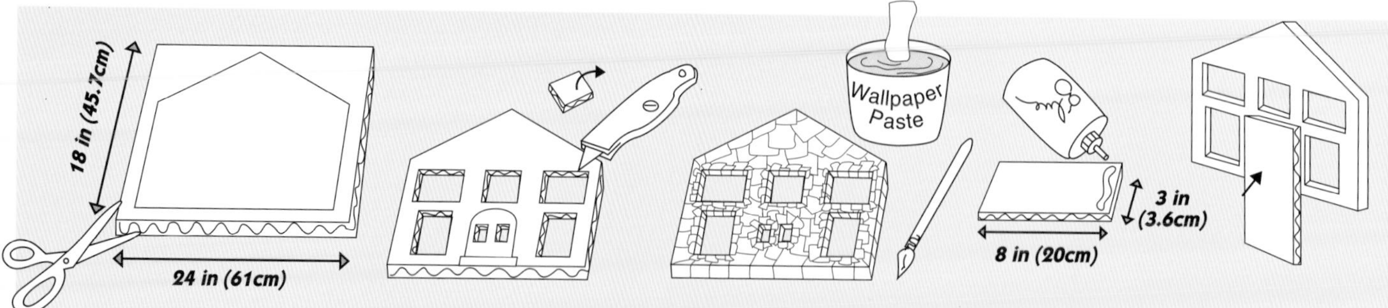

1 Draw a house shape on heavy cardboard, as shown. Cut out.

2 Draw windows slightly smaller than the pictures that will be used in the frame. Cut out with utility knife.

3 Cover entire cardboard house shape with pieces of newspaper dipped in wallpaper paste, wrapping pieces around all cut edges. Allow to dry. Paint and shellac.

4 Cut another piece of heavy cardboard, as shown, measuring across the ripples.

5 Spread glue across one end and attach to back of house.

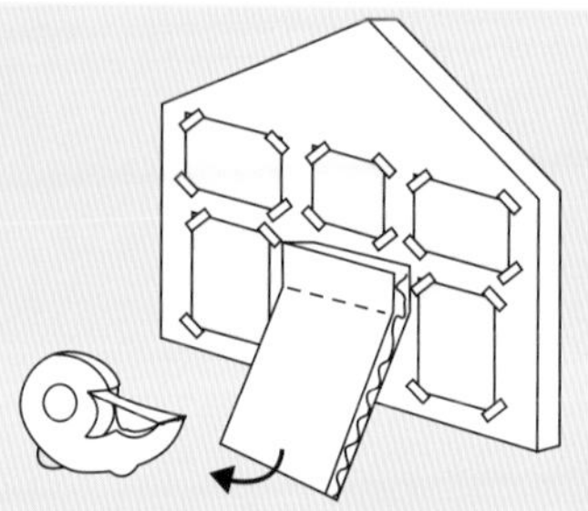

6 When glue is dry, bend unglued portion of strip backward. This is the stand. Tape pictures to the back of the house to show through the openings.

Single Picture Frame

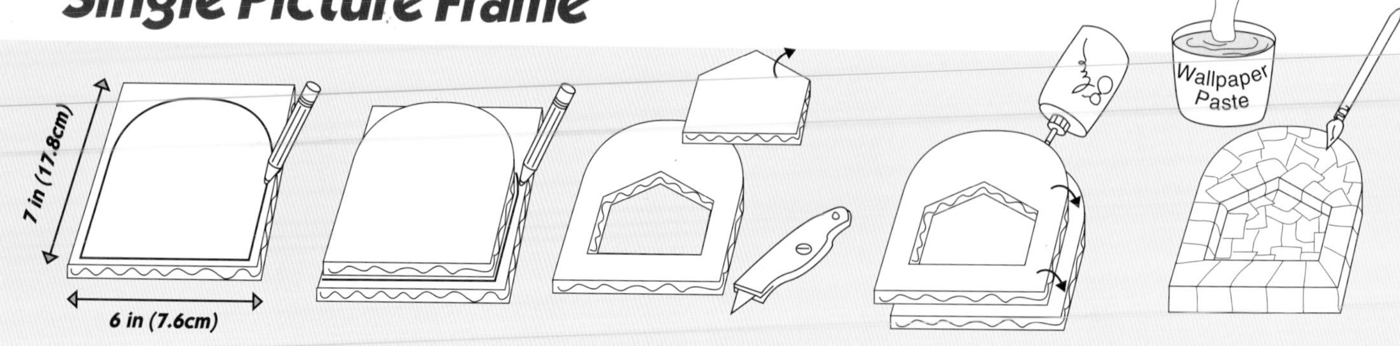

1 On heavy cardboard draw an arched shape, as shown.

2 Trace shape on cardboard and cut out an identical shape.

3 On one of the cardboard pieces draw a window, as shown. Cut out.

4 Glue the 2 arched shapes together, as shown.

5 Cover entire frame with pieces of newspaper dipped in wallpaper paste. Allow to dry.

Refrigerator Magnets

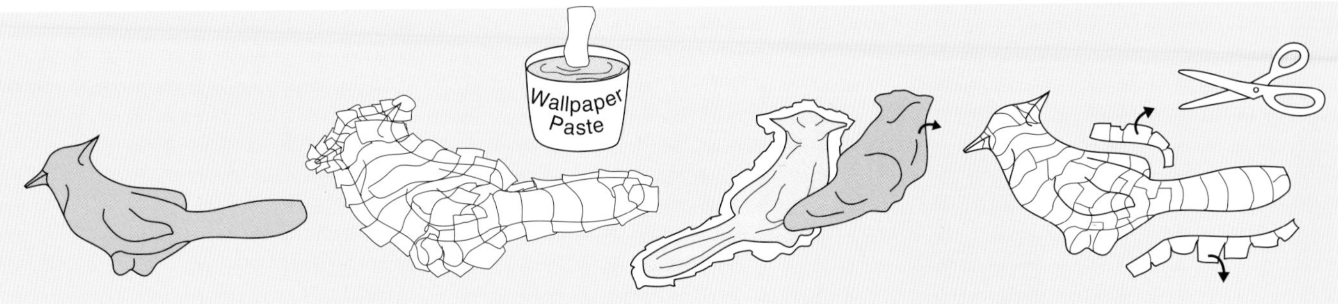

1 Form desired shape (this is a bluejay) out of plasticine. Make back of shape flat.

2 Cover top of plasticine with small pieces of newspaper dipped in wallpaper paste. Set aside to dry.

3 When dry, turn shape over, and pull plasticine out of back, leaving a hollow paper shape.
4 Trim edges of shape.

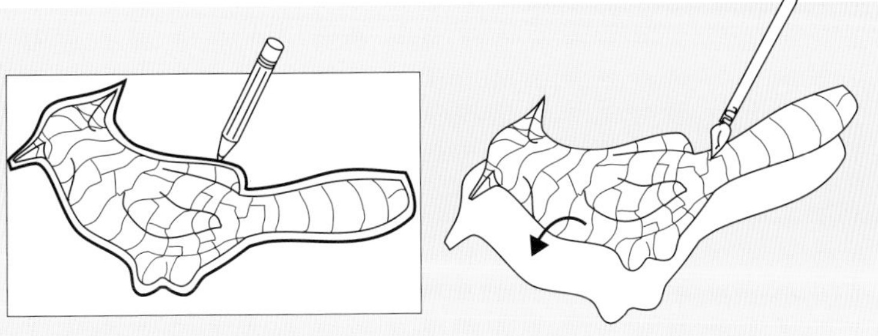

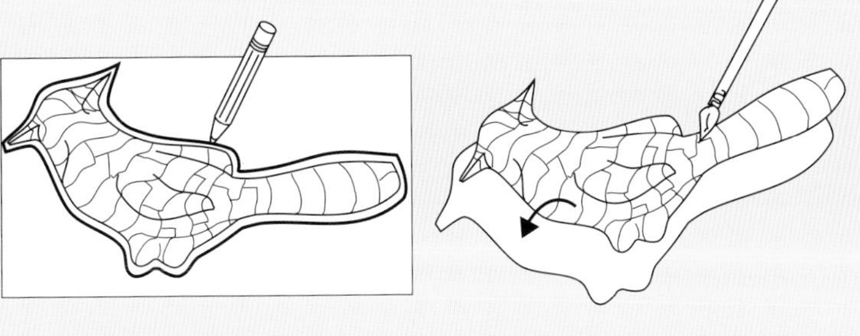

5 Set bluejay shape on thin cardboard and trace around it.
6 Cut out cardboard shape and glue it to the back of the bird shape. Paint and shellac.
7 Epoxy a piece of strip magnet (found in hardware or hobby stores) to back of shape and attach to refrigerator.

This technique is also great for making jewelry or hair clips (p31).

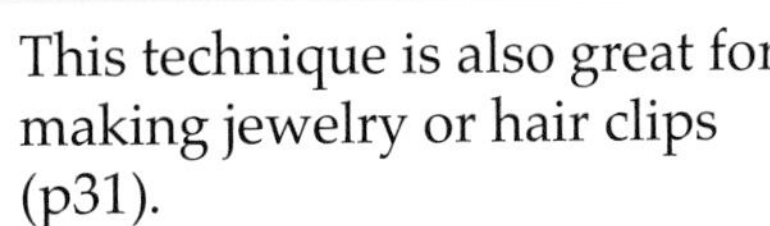

For Christmas stocking or pig refrigerator magnet shown in photo, make a papier-mâché slab (see fan brooch, p86), draw desired shape, cut out, paint, and epoxy strip magnet on back.

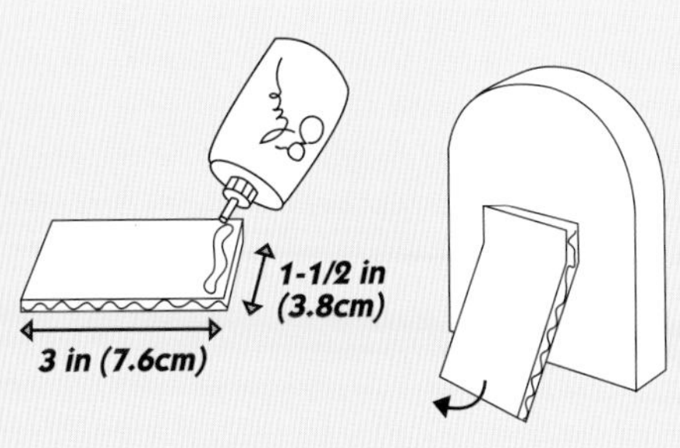

Paint an outline of a house around opening. Paint Santa and his reindeer on the roof. Allow to dry. Shellac. Tape picture in center of the frame.
6 To make a stand, cut out a piece of heavy cardboard, as shown, measuring across ripples. Spread glue across one end and attach to back of frame. When dry, bend unglued part downward.

Advent Calendar

1 Unfold a large cardboard box and lay flat. Draw a Christmas tree with a star, as shown. Cut out.
2 Draw 21 circles on the tree. Draw a star inside large star shape at top and draw the trunk divided into 2 squares. With a knife, cut out the circles, the star, and the 2 squares on the trunk, as shown.
3 Turn tree over. Cover all holes with scraps of cardboard and glue in place.

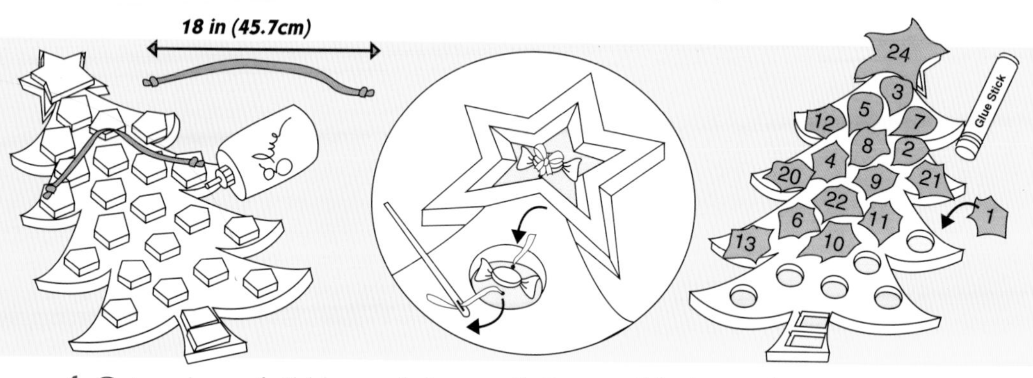

4 Cut a piece of ribbon and tie a knot in each end. Glue ribbon to back of tree to make a hanger.
5 Turn tree over. Paint branch area green. Paint inside the circles with bright colors to resemble decorations. Paint trunk brown. Shellac tree. If desired, tie candies inside each cut-out area. Thread a darning needle with ribbon or yarn. Poke needle through the recessed area to the back, then back out. Cut ribbon to leave 2 ends 4 in (10cm) long for tieing candies in place.
6 Cover all holes with pieces of green construction paper. Attach with dots of glue stick or other clear glue. Cover star and holes in trunk as well. Number all covers from 1 to 24. Make the star #24—the last one to be opened. Hang tree on the wall. Starting on December 1, child removes one cover every day, #1-24. The star is uncovered on Christmas Eve. If using the candy on the decorations, tie the ribbon in a bow after candy has been removed.

Door Wrap

1 Draw a pattern, as shown, using measurements taken from your door. Measure carefully for placement of hinges, doorknobs, and latch. Transfer pattern to a large sheet of brown paper. *You may have to glue several sheets together to make one large sheet.*

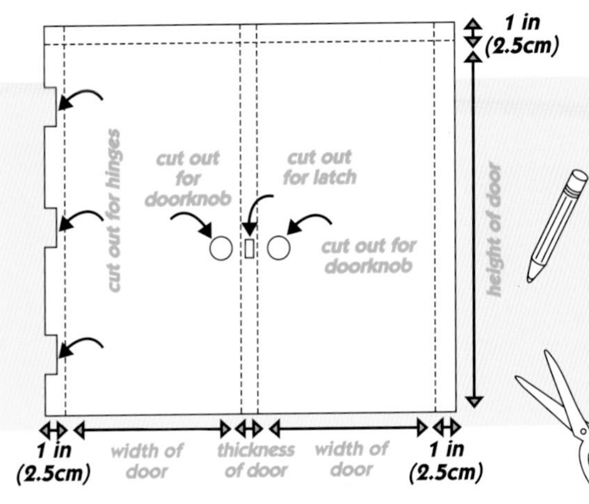

2 Cut out. Fold along all dotted lines.

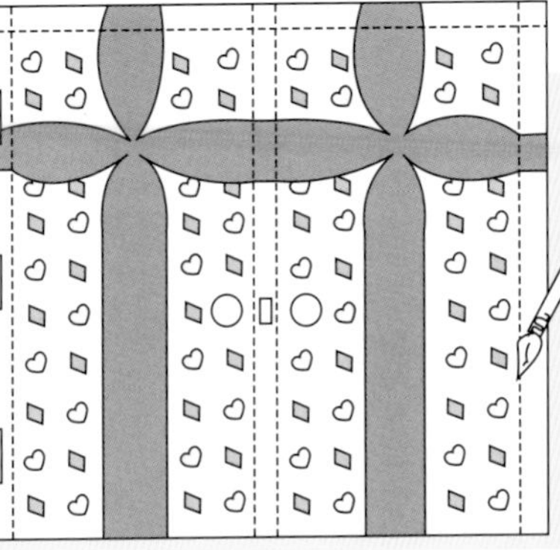

3 Lay the sheet flat on the floor. Paint to resemble both sides of a giftwrapped box, as shown. The pattern shown uses the sponge print technique (see p69).

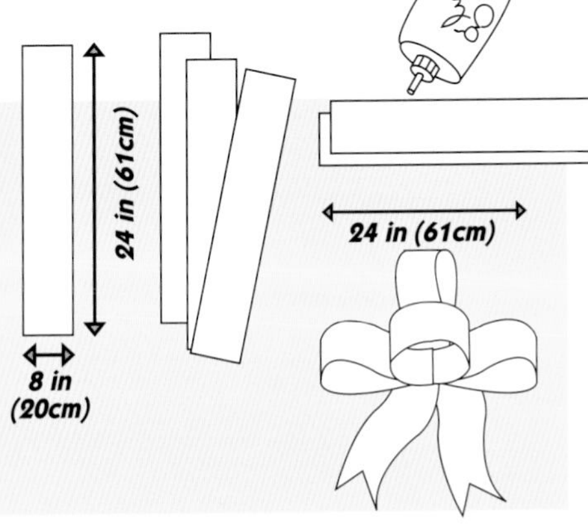

4 Cut 12 pieces of brown paper, as shown. Glue one piece on top of a second piece to make 6 double sheets.

5 Using these pieces make a large bow (see p66). Paint bow to match ribbon on the door.

6 Glue bow to paper wrap, as shown below.

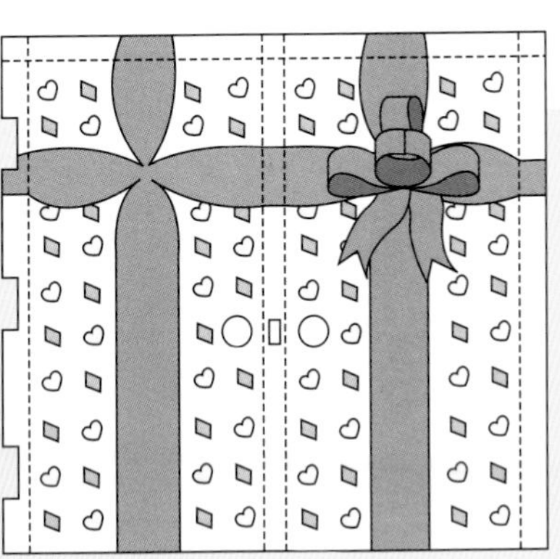

7 Wrap sheet around door. Start with edge of door. Slip latch on door through the hole cut for it in the center. Fold both sides around door. Slip doorknobs through holes cut out for them, as indicated on pattern. Fold the flaps over the top and around the hinge side. Secure with plenty of tape.

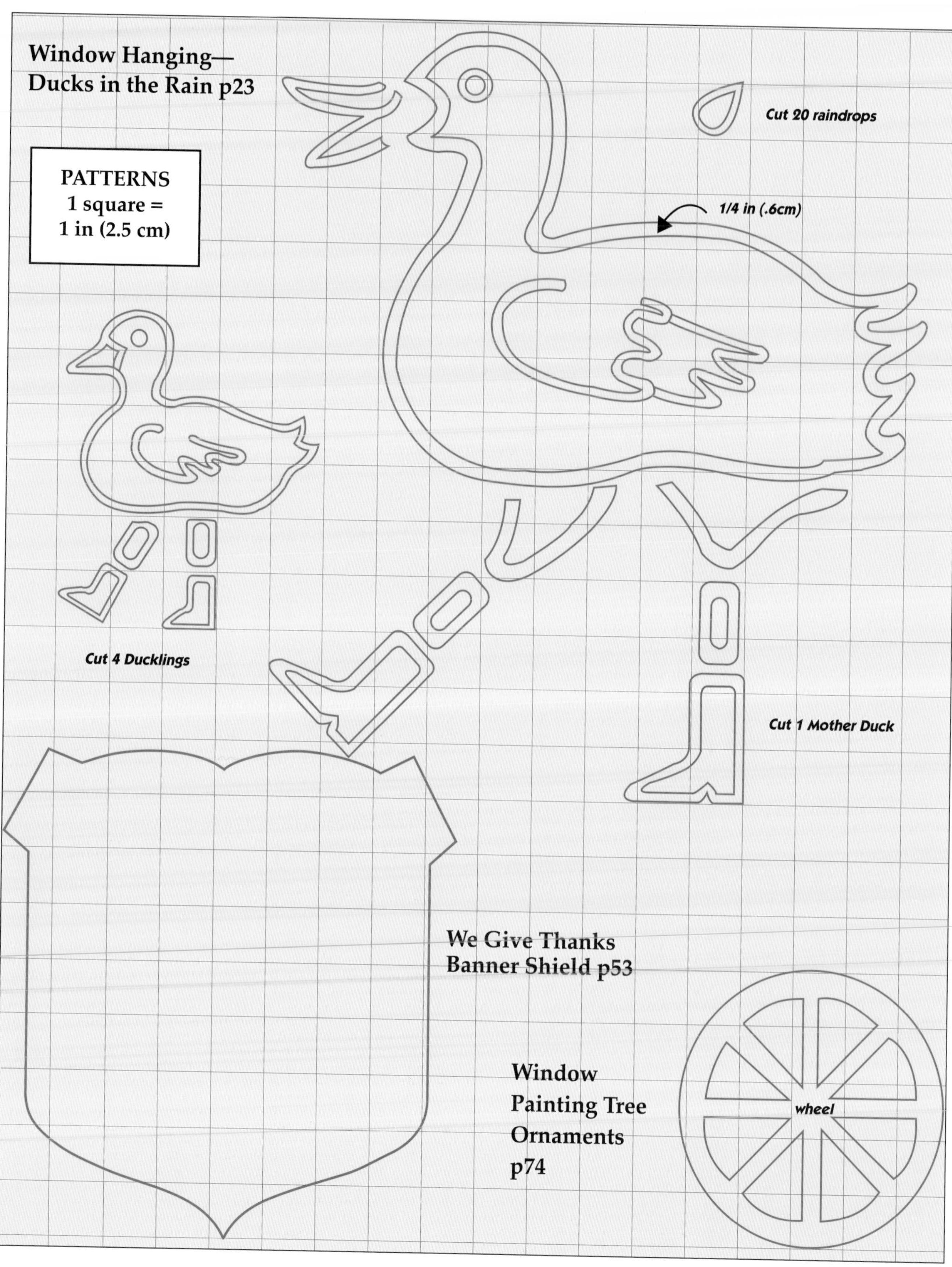
Window Hanging—
Ducks in the Rain p23
PATTERNS
1 square =
1 in (2.5 cm)
Cut 20 raindrops
1/4 in (.6cm)
Cut 4 Ducklings
Cut 1 Mother Duck
We Give Thanks
Banner Shield p53
Window
Painting Tree
Ornaments
p74
wheel

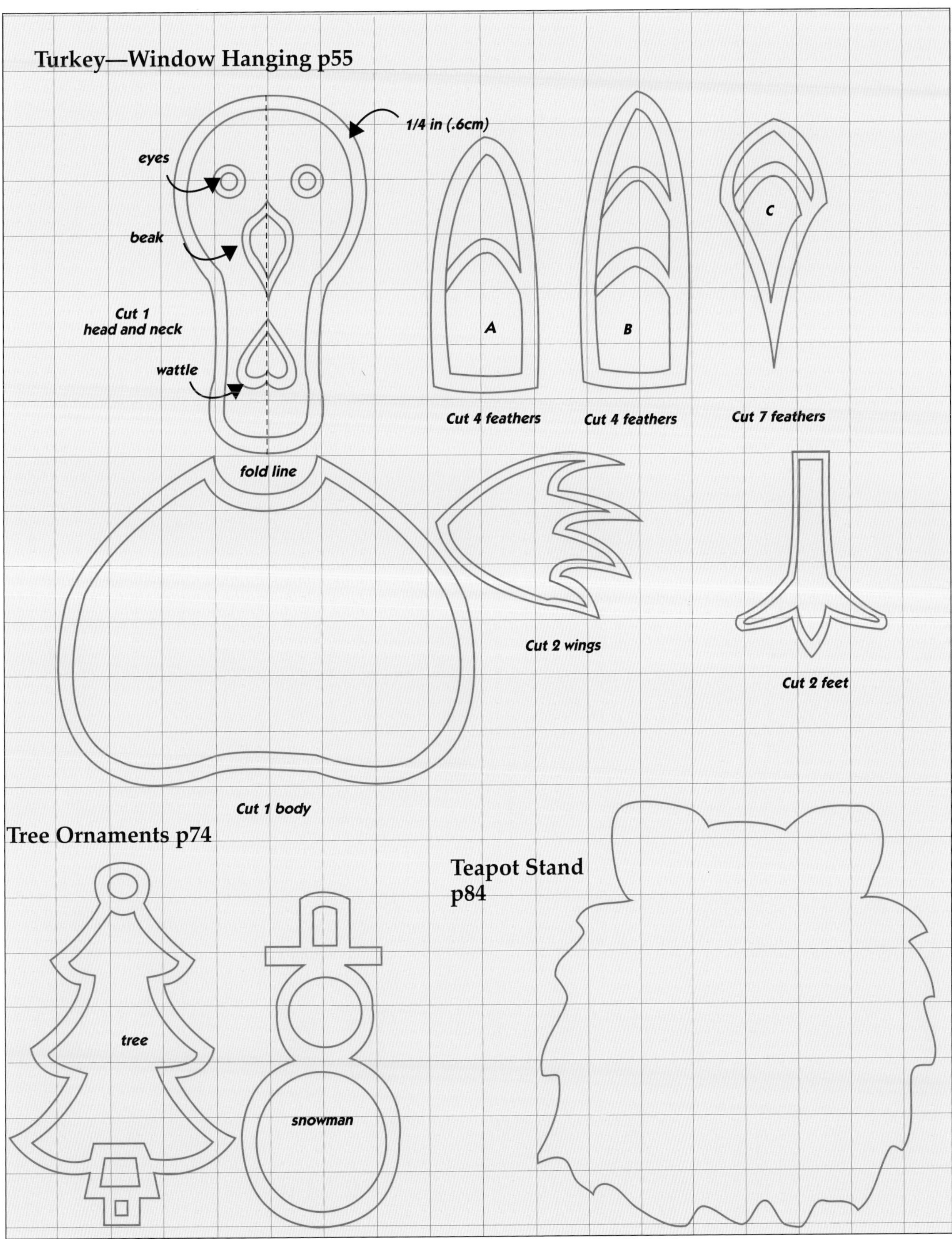
Turkey—Window Hanging p55
1/4 in (.6cm)
eyes
beak
Cut 1
head and neck
wattle
fold line
A
B
C
Cut 4 feathers
Cut 4 feathers
Cut 7 feathers
Cut 2 wings
Cut 2 feet
Cut 1 body
Tree Ornaments p74
tree
snowman
Teapot Stand
p84

Window Painting—Christmas Tree
p74
WINDOW
PATTERN
1 square =
3 in (7.6 cm)
flower
PATTERN
1 square =
1 in (2.5 cm)
Window Painting
Tree Ornaments
p74

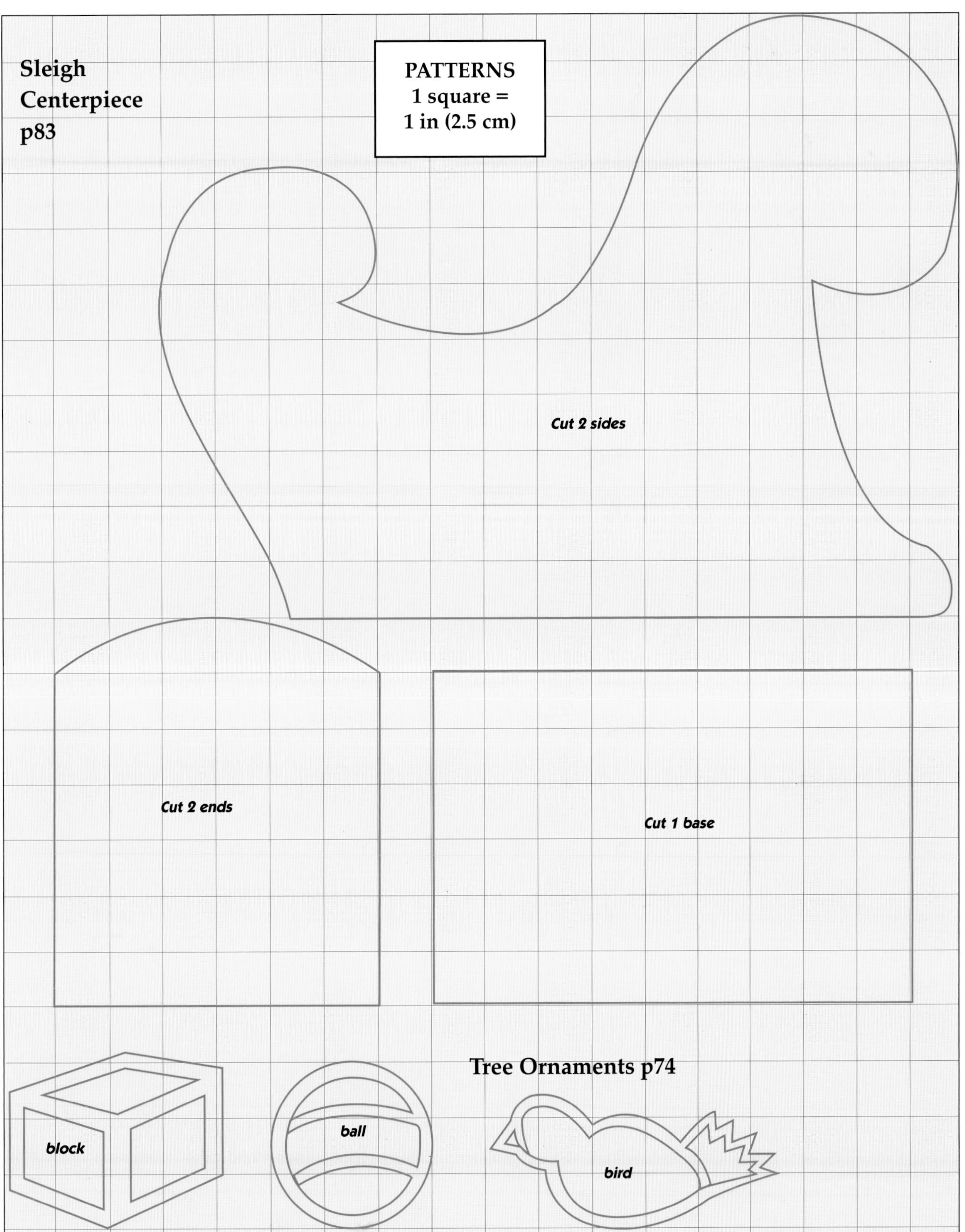
Sleigh
Centerpiece
p83
PATTERNS
1 square =
1 in (2.5 cm)
Cut 2 sides
Cut 2 ends
Cut 1 base
Tree Ornaments p74
block
ball
bird

Index